OXFORD CONSTITUTIONAL THEORY

Series Editors:
Martin Loughlin, John P. McCormick, and Neil Walker

The Metaethics of Constitutional Adjudication

OXFORD CONSTITUTIONAL THEORY

Series Editors:
Martin Loughlin, John P. McCormick, and Neil Walker

Oxford Constitutional Theory has rapidly established itself as the primary point of reference for theoretical reflections on the growing interest in constitutions and constitutional law in domestic, regional, and global contexts. The majority of the works published in the series are monographs that advance new understandings of their subject. But the series aims to provide a forum for further innovation in the field by also including well-conceived edited collections that bring a variety of perspectives and disciplinary approaches to bear on specific themes in constitutional thought and by publishing English translations of leading monographs in constitutional theory that have originally been written in languages other than English.

ALSO AVAILABLE IN THE SERIES

Constitutional and Political Theory
Selected Writings
Ernst-Wolfgang Böckenförde
Edited by Mirjam Künkler and Tine Stein

Constitutionalism
Past, Present, and Future
Dieter Grimm

Europe's Functional Constitution
A Theory of Constitutionalism Beyond the State
Turkuler Isiksel

Post Sovereign Constitution Making
Learning and Legitimacy
Andrew Arato

Popular Sovereignty in Early Modern Constitutional Though
Daniel Lee

The Cultural Defense of Nations
A Liberal Theory of Majority Rights
Liav Orgad

The Cosmopolitan Constitution
Alexander Somek

The Structure of Pluralism
Victor M. Muniz-Fraticelli

Constitutional Courts and Deliberative Democracy
Conrado Hübner Mendes

Fault Lines of Globalization
Legal Order and the Politics of A-Legality
Hans Lindahl

The Cosmopolitan State
H Patrick Glenn

After Public Law
Edited by Cormac Mac Amhlaigh, Claudio Michelon, and Neil Walker

The Three Branches
A Comparative Model of Separation of Powers
Christoph Möllers

The Global Model of Constitutional Rights
Kai Möller

The Twilight of Constitutionalism?
Edited by Petra Dobner and Martin Loughlin

Beyond Constitutionalism
The Pluralist Structure of Postnational Law
Nico Krisch

The Metaethics of Constitutional Adjudication

Boško Tripković

OXFORD
UNIVERSITY PRESS

OXFORD
UNIVERSITY PRESS

Great Clarendon Street, Oxford, OX2 6DP,
United Kingdom

Oxford University Press is a department of the University of Oxford.
It furthers the University's objective of excellence in research, scholarship,
and education by publishing worldwide. Oxford is a registered trade mark of
Oxford University Press in the UK and in certain other countries

First Edition published in 2017

Impression: 1

Published in the United States of America by Oxford University Press
198 Madison Avenue, New York, NY 10016, United States of America

British Library Cataloguing in Publication Data
Data available

Library of Congress Control Number: 2017947332

ISBN 978–0–19–880808–4

Printed and bound by
CPI Group (UK) Ltd, Croydon, CR0 4YY

For my father

Acknowledgements

There are many people who have contributed to the making of this book, and to whom I owe deep gratitude.

The book is a revised version of the doctoral thesis I defended at the European University Institute. My supervisor, Dennis Patterson, has always been a source of immense professional and personal support, during the doctoral years and beyond. It was truly a privilege to benefit from his unparalleled erudition and intellect. But an even greater privilege was his company: I am eternally grateful for his empathy, optimism, and humor, and for the good times we had in Florence. I am also profoundly indebted to the members of my defence committee—Hans-W Micklitz, George Pavlakos, and Neil Walker—for their insight, engagement, and kindness. I have been incredibly fortunate to benefit from their intellectual vision, invaluable comments, and incessant support.

A number of people have read and commented on different parts of this book, and their questions, observations, and challenges have improved my work considerably. In particular, I would like to express my gratitude to Tom Adams, Sina Akbari, Maciej Borowicz, Gavin Byrne, Daniel Correa, Jacobien van Dorp, Martyn Egan, Tiago de Freitas, Alexis Galán, Stephen Gardbaum, Payam Ghalehdar, Rachel Singerman Gur, Ivana Isailović, François-Xavier Millet, Joaquin Millon, Hillary Nye, Arie Rosen, Nil Vijayalingam, Guilherme Vasconcelos Vilaça, Joseph HH Weiler, Emily Kidd White, Jan Zglinski, and two anonymous reviewers for Oxford University Press. Some of the arguments from the book—in different shapes and forms—have been presented to audiences in Birmingham, Berlin, Copenhagen, Edinburgh, Florence, and New York, and I am grateful to all those who took part for their time and their thoughts.

I am deeply thankful to Oxford Constitutional Theory series editors—Martin Loughlin, John P McCormick, and Neil Walker—for supporting the project and reviewing the manuscript. I would also like to thank Alex Flach, Elinor Shields, and Eve Ryle-Hodges at Oxford University Press for patient and professional editorial work and guidance, Nancy Rebecca for the efficient organization of the production process, and Nicola Prior for careful copy-editing.

At the foundation of this book is the love of my family. I thank my sister, Ana, for always being there for me, and for—together with her family, Marko, Luka, and Tara—making my life joyful. I thank my mother, Gordana, for caring about my dreams, and for our endless talks that have been a tremendous source of inspiration.

And I thank my wife and my son, Milena and Sava, for giving meaning to all of this: their love and companionship are behind each and every word of this book. My father, Milan, passed away before I started writing the book, but has been writing it with me. This book is a part of his legacy in this world, and I dedicate it to his memory.

Contents

Table of Cases

CONSTITUTIONAL COURT OF SOUTH AFRICA

COURT OF JUSTICE OF THE EUROPEAN UNION

EUROPEAN COURT OF HUMAN RIGHTS

FEDERAL CONSTITUTIONAL COURT OF GERMANY

SUPREME COURT OF CANADA

SUPREME COURT OF ISRAEL

SUPREME COURT OF THE UNITED STATES

1

Introduction

In one of Plato's dialogues, Socrates encounters a man named Euthyphro who is prosecuting his own father. Euthyphro's confidence in this matter is based on his knowledge of what is pious. Preparing for his own trial for impiety, Socrates asks Euthyphro—not without the usual irony—to teach him about piety: if Euthyphro indeed had knowledge of piety then he would be able to explain it. But Socrates challenges and refutes each account that Euthyphro offers. Euthyphro asserts that doing what he actually does is pious, and Socrates answers that this is only an example and not a definition; Euthyphro claims that piety is what pleases the gods, but Socrates points out that the gods disagree among themselves; Euthyphro defines what is pious as being loved by all the gods, but Socrates reminds him that piousness should be a property of acts that are pious and not an attribute conferred upon them by someone else. One by one, Euthyphro's attempts to specify piety fail. When Socrates makes the final plea to him to reveal his moral knowledge, Euthyphro refuses to further question his beliefs and leaves. The dialogue does not say how much *confidence* in his moral judgment has Euthyphro lost, but it does say that Socrates—not being enlightened by Euthyphro's moral knowledge—does not intend to renounce the speculations that will eventually cost him his life: in other words, he chooses not to disavow the philosophical *reflection* about the nature of moral judgment.[1]

Both the confidence with which we assert our moral knowledge and the reflection about its nature have endured over the centuries. They are part and parcel of the human condition: moral judgments are inescapable and so is contemplation about their origins. Metaethics—the branch of philosophy that deals with the metaphysical and epistemological foundations of moral thought and language—has thus developed with much sophistication and

[1] Plato, *The Collected Dialogues of Plato* (Edith Hamilton and Huntington Cairns (eds), 14th edn, Princeton University Press 1989) 185. Socrates reveals his intentions with a dose of humour: by saying that he would have abandoned his 'innovations' had Euthyphro revealed his moral knowledge to him.

detail. But the question behind Socrates' dialogue with Euthyphro remains crucial: should the confidence in our moral knowledge be undermined by philosophical reflection about its source?

The book explores this problem in the context of contemporary constitutional law. In the spirit of Socrates' dialogue with Euthyphro, it aims to *challenge and explain the metaethical foundations of value-based arguments in constitutional adjudication*. The main driving force behind this project is an empirical observation that there is much confusion and uncertainty about the nature of value in comparative constitutional adjudication. As the book will aspire to demonstrate, constitutional courts use divergent argumentative patterns that rely on different underlying conceptions of value. Not all of these conceptions are plausible. The book thus identifies different types of value-based arguments in comparative judicial practice, explores the plausibility of their assumptions about the nature of value, and develops a theory that reconstructs their metaethical foundations.

While few people would deny that courts make value judgments, anyone who has ever read a single opinion of a constitutional court knows that they look nothing like the dialogue between Socrates and Euthyphro. Courts sometimes do admit that they are making moral judgments, but they rarely reflect on the source of moral value behind their judgment. Yet, the book aims to demonstrate that they feel the allure of both Euthyphro and Socrates.

The first temptation is Euthyphro's: to avoid these questions. Most people live their lives without caring about the source of value or metaethics. But judges might be in a specific position. They are moved to ponder the nature of value because of the constant public attention their authority receives. Under the circumstances of moral disagreement and value pluralism—and when they are unable to resort to sources of legitimacy that would remove the choice from their hands—constitutional courts face metaethical questions. How do they know what true values are and by which authority they impose them on others? The inescapability of ethical choices, which comes with the judicial role and incomplete determinacy of law, makes these questions pressing in constitutional law. Constitutional courts do not always have an option to claim that they are only applying the law and—as eventually Euthyphro did—leave the conversation about the nature of value.

Hence, courts cannot find comfort in disregarding this issue: Socrates' challenge is pressing. But they also rarely engage with it openly. Their positions on this matter remain implicit, and can be discerned from the premises of their arguments and from the language they use. These implicit assumptions reveal the ambiguities about the source of value. As the book will try to show, the manner in which judges make moral judgments confirms the suspicion that they are aware of some of the questions posed by Socrates, even if this awareness is only rudimentary. The first aim of the book is thus to bring to the fore the implicit commitments about the nature of value that follow from judicial value-based arguments. The second aim is to subject these commitments to philosophical scrutiny and initiate a Socratic dialogue about them.

The book thus takes an unusual approach to value-based arguments in constitutional adjudication: a more common strategy is to avoid metaethical issues.[2] On the one hand, we may think that constitutional adjudication has nothing to do with metaethics because, for example, value-based reasoning generally ought to be avoided. But—even if this were desirable—it is doubtful that any such strategy could be successful: it is impossible to reduce judicial discretion completely and any plausible theory of adjudication needs to accept that. On the other hand, taking the first-order judicial disagreement about values to the level of metaethics seems to invite an even greater—and perhaps more esoteric—uncertainty; for instance, one might believe that constitutional adjudication needs workable solutions and not grandiose theories. But such solutions still must face Socrates, and avoiding metaethical questions cannot silence his challenge. This route would only deprive us of a satisfying explanation and thus augment the discomfort arising from the inability to specify where these moral solutions come from.

The book aims to show that the fruits of such metaethical inquiry—if it is successful—could be rewarding. Most debates about constitutional adjudication belong to the domain of normative or applied ethics: they ponder what we ought to do in the institutional context of contemporary constitutional systems. However, if we remain at the level of normative ethics we do not have a complete account of our ethical experience. We stay at the level of Euthyphro and not Socrates. If we inquired about the metaethical foundations of judicial value-based arguments we would not only see some of the old problems of constitutional adjudication in a new light, and possibly resolve them, but we might also reach a non-question-begging justification of our values. Our philosophical spade would reach bedrock, and we would have a mechanism by which we could assess and refine our arguments. We could stay in the conversation with Socrates, and we would not leave without an answer as Euthyphro.

To further clarify the project, I should say why *constitutional adjudication* is important in this context, which *value-based arguments* will be analysed, why study their *metaethical foundations*, and what does it mean to *challenge and explain* them? Let me address these questions and in so doing explain the structure of the book. The book deals with *constitutional adjudication*: the

[2] For some reasons why this would be preferable see Jeremy Waldron, *Law and Disagreement* (Clarendon Press 1999) ch 8 and Cass R Sunstein, *One Case at a Time: Judicial Minimalism on the Supreme Court* (Harvard University Press 1999).

institutional situation in which a judicial body has a power to review actions of other branches of government on the basis of fundamental rights and freedoms.[3] I have already mentioned that the project is driven by an empirical phenomenon that appears in comparative constitutional practice. A significant part of the book—and a recurring thread running through all of its chapters—aspires to support and explore this empirical proposition. But there are other reasons why the question about the nature of value could be particularly intense and visible in constitutional law.

The first is the specific combination of concerns about the democratic legitimacy of courts to perform constitutional review and the indeterminate moral language used in constitutions. Both concerns about legitimacy and the use of moral language are present in other areas of law, and the difference is only in degree and not in kind; however, these elements are particularly strong in constitutional adjudication. This puts the value-based judgments of constitutional courts in the focus of attention, makes judges more anxious about Socrates' challenge, and consequently forces them to articulate their views on the matter. The second is the common view that constitutions are closer to the normative experience of the people than the rest of the law. People tend to think that law is normative: they abide by it most of the time and they also correct others by pointing out that their actions are illegal. But there is the idea that constitutions achieve this in a more direct, unmediated way. Constitutions are general, stable, and visible enough to become more ingrained in our contingent moral commitments; it could be then that we follow constitutions because we think what they say is right, and not primarily because we think that it is right to obey the law. Constitutional practice itself is sometimes seen as the embodiment of value or as a value-generating process: in other words, as the source of value that Euthyphro was unable to specify. These ideas may well be misguided, but—as we shall see—they play an important role in the way courts use value arguments.

The second issue I need to explain is: which *value-based judicial arguments* are examined? The book deals only with the arguments that go beyond existing law and that aim to offer solutions to unregulated—or inadequately regulated—moral problems. Locating the point at which courts move from law-applying to law-making is the holy grail of legal theory: much intellectual effort has been invested in this question and there is not even agreement that

[3] This broad understanding incorporates a range of institutional frameworks, including some that are outside of the nation-state setting. Disagreements about the meaning of the 'constitution' or 'constitutionalism' abound and much ink has been spilled in attempts to elucidate these concepts; they are often motivated by a normative conception of how we ought to live together in—or beyond—our current political communities. The book uses a concept that hopefully tracks the conventional understanding and is at the same time not extravagant in this normative sense. But most importantly, the concept allows the book to explore all the important metaethical dimensions of constitutional value-based judgments: the focus is on the phenomenon and not on the normative baggage of the term used to denote it.

such a point exists.[4] I do not harbour the illusion that the book can resolve this problem. But—since it is a preliminary question to delineate value-based arguments as the object of the study—the first part of Chapter 2 outlines the concept of an *ethical argument*[5] as an important interface between law and morality, and as the point in which judicial visions about the nature of value come to the fore. The book as a whole adds layers of complexity to this initial outline, in the hope that it will contribute to a better grasp of the paradigmatic features of ethical arguments and their variety. The important point is that such arguments—or more precisely argumentative patterns—aim to evaluate morally, but take quite a different form from ordinary moral arguments. The book suggests that methods of moral evaluation over time become entrenched in legal practice in the form of ethical arguments, and that they in turn embed a particular vision of moral value.

The fundamental metaethical issue that the book tries to solve are the divergent foundations of moral value behind judicial ethical arguments. The book identifies and analyses the three most prominent ethical arguments understood as ideal-types: the argument from constitutional identity (examined in Chapter 2), the argument from common sentiment (Chapter 3), and the argument from universal reason (Chapter 4). The central tension—and the main puzzle that motivates the project—arises along the two dimensions that threaten a coherent picture of values. Not surprisingly, these are the dimensions that match the most important metaethical dilemmas: on the one hand, there is a tension between the local and universal understanding of values, and on the other, between the place of emotions and reason in a credible conception of value. At one pole there is the argument from common sentiment that ties moral value to the emotive reactions of a particular community, and at the other there is the argument from universal reason that understands the universally human faculty of reason as the source of value. In between there is the argument from constitutional identity, which refers to the contingent traditions of a community as they evolve under the

[4] See Ronald Dworkin, *Law's Empire* (Belknap Press 1986) and *Justice for Hedgehogs* (Belknap Press of Harvard University Press 2011).

[5] In choosing the word 'ethical', and not 'moral' arguments, I follow the convention established in Philip Bobbitt, *Constitutional Fate: Theory of the Constitution* (Oxford University Press 1982) and *Constitutional Interpretation* (Blackwell 1991). Moreover, I use the words 'ethical' and 'moral' interchangeably. Sometimes a difference is made between ethical and moral, either because the former refers to how we ought to treat ourselves and the latter how we ought to treat others, *or* because the latter is considered to be a distorted version of the former in post-Enlightenment ethical thinking. For the first understanding of the distinction see Jürgen Habermas, *Between Facts and Norms: Contributions to a Discourse Theory of Law and Democracy* (MIT Press 1996) 95–99, and for the second Bernard Williams, *Ethics and the Limits of Philosophy* (2nd edn, Routledge 2006). These distinctions do not capture anything of relevance for my project. I thus choose the terminology that is more attuned to the common way these words are used: interchangeably. Arguably, the term 'ethical' better captures the spirit of the project, which aims to integrate metaethics and normative ethics more closely.

constitution, and which—in its different instantiations—contains elements of both of these rival poles: universal-reasonable and local-emotional.

These different types of ethical arguments are often understood to exclude each other, not least because of their iterative use in law: as we shall see, much of the time courts or individual judges opt for one type of ethical argument and reject the other. But in so doing, they resemble Euthyphro and do not justify their views. The analysis in Chapters 2 to 4 aims to bring Socrates' spirit into the discussion and distinguish implausible from plausible elements in each type of ethical argument. The picture that emerges from this analysis shows that all of these arguments—from identity, sentiment, and reason—are dissatisfying as self-standing sources of value, and that there are profound connections between them. This sense of dissatisfaction can only be overcome through a deep vindication of ethical arguments with an adequate conception of value. The main goal of the book is thus to articulate a plausible *constitutional ethics*: to offer a theory of ethical arguments in constitutional adjudication that would be supported by a sound understanding of value.

This opens the study of constitutional ethics to an objection: why should the legal practice of ethical arguments matter? Why not simply replace them with ordinary moral arguments? If ordinary moral reasoning is apt to reveal moral answers then it is puzzling why we should be concerned with ethical arguments in constitutional reasoning. In other words, if there is a specific conception of morality *in* law, it can present nothing more than the contingent and uninteresting views of judges about morality.[6] One answer to this is pragmatic: if there is a way to tweak the existing arguments to make them plausible this is a more fruitful strategy than an attempt at a complete overhaul of the practice. But apart from pragmatic concerns there are also more substantive reasons.

The existing ethical arguments did not arise in a vacuum, but often grew out of the awareness that courts make moral judgments in the name of others, and that the appropriate decision ought to take into account different perspectives. We could see ethical arguments as deceitful devices that serve as a cover for the imposition of ideological preferences, and we would probably be right to an extent, but we could also—more sympathetically—see them as genuine attempts to arrive at the best possible moral judgment

[6] This is, however, a controversial claim. Recall that in one of the challenges Socrates asks Euthyphro if piousness is the inherent property of pious actions or something ascribed to such actions by gods. One of the most basic and yet most important metaethical questions is whether goodness is an inherent property of moral actions, or something ascribed to such actions by us. Legal theory often takes for granted the distinction between 'positive' and 'critical' morality (see more in HLA Hart, *Law, Liberty and Morality* (Oxford University Press 1962) 17–24). But there is something perplexing about drawing too sharp a line between what we *believe* is moral and what actually *is* moral. At the very least, this relationship needs to be explained: we cannot simply disregard the issue by dogmatic fiat.

under the circumstances of disagreement and concerns about the institutional position of the court. One of the aims of the book is to understand constitutional ethics as a reconstruction of the moral point of view through the lens of a court. A court may be unsure both about the relevance of different metaethical elements that are in the background of its judgment—such as emotions and reason—but also about its own role as an agent that puts these pieces together. Most of the time the differences between ordinary moral arguments and judicial ethical arguments are a consequence of these kinds of concerns, which ought not to be neglected in a theory of constitutional ethics.

The final reason for focusing on the existing argumentative patterns is that the most prominent theories of moral reading of constitution may not resonate well with those who are uncertain about the existence of timeless and universal moral values and about the judicial ability to cognize them.[7] As I will argue, our contingent moral experiences must figure prominently in any moral judgment. This gives constitutional ethics—which consists of patterns of reasoning that occur in the course of deciding how to live together—a constitutive role in answering moral questions in contemporary constitutional systems. As a consequence, contingent constitutional ethics cannot be simply disregarded, but demands careful treatment; while it might give way to our deeper ethical convictions, it cannot be simply refuted on the basis of an assumption that there might be a better procedure out there for resolving moral dilemmas. Whereas it would be inaccurate to describe this project as a moral reading of constitution for moral skeptics, it certainly is a moral reading that is more cautious about presupposing mind-independently true moral answers, and even more cautious about developing a theory of constitutional interpretation from that metaethical premise.

This is the point at which the third issue I need to clarify becomes important: why study the *metaethical foundations* of ethical arguments in constitutional reasoning? It is certainly not impossible—as Euthyphro—to exercise moral judgment without being aware of the background conception of value. However, such conception is often implicit in our moral judgment, or becomes explicit through a Socratic contestation of our moral attitudes.

[7] Ronald Dworkin did more than anyone else to motivate the moral approach to constitutional interpretation (see for example Dworkin, *Law's Empire* (n 4) ch 10, and Dworkin, *Freedom's Law: The Moral Reading of the American Constitution* (Harvard University Press 1996) 1–38). The most appealing part of his theory is that moral reading—in some cases we may add *pace* Dworkin—does not really have an alternative: there will always be cases unregulated by previous decisions, or regulated in unsatisfactory ways, and any judicial choice in such cases will entail a moral choice. But Dworkin's theory rests on a robust version of moral realism: a belief that there are mind-independent, universal and timeless moral answers. Dworkin was always very quick to dispel any skeptical worry about the existence of moral truths as confused (see for example Dworkin, *Law's Empire* (n 4) 76–85 and Dworkin, *Justice for Hedgehogs* (n 4) chs 2–5). However, such worries persist and—as I will show—they persist for a good reason.

The judicial idea of value is visible in the explicit endorsement of a certain metaethical position, or—for example—in the choice of materials that are considered relevant for a moral judgment. In the legal context, this idea of value often becomes entrenched in interpretive conventions and through the use of the same arguments in subsequent cases.

Such conceptions of value can be mistaken. Hence—whereas the standard question asks whether the judges got *moral answers* wrong—the book asks instead if the judges got the *morality itself* wrong. As I explain in more detail later, any ethical judgment is susceptible to Socrates' challenge: if we claim that our judgment is apposite we must also be able to explain in virtue of what it is apposite. The other possibility is to be as dogmatic as Euthyphro. But this neither is nor should be an option for constitutional judges. They decide some of the most important issues in our polities: we should want our judges to get what they ought to do right, and we should want this not to be a coincidence but to arise from an understanding of what makes things right. To achieve this, judges would need to be aware of the source of value they rely on. As I will attempt to demonstrate, many of the actual judicial disagreements show that they lack a clear enough conception of value, and—perhaps more importantly—the tools to understand what such disagreements are about.

The basic premise is that if judges do make moral judgments we should want them to make good moral judgments. But how is the conception of good moral judgment connected to the nature of value? Good moral judgment is an evaluative notion itself and it might—regardless of the nature of value—be a function of the most apposite ethical theory, argument or emotion. It could be that a good moral judgment is utilitarian or deontological, but that they are both equally compatible with a particular metaethical standpoint. However, the metaethical question is both *pressing* and *prior*. It is pressing because actual ethical arguments from constitutional practice demonstrate divergent conceptions of value which need to be sorted out: is value local or universal, emotion or reason-based? It is prior because we have no way of knowing whether a particular fragment of normative ethics is correct if we do not say in virtue of what it is correct. The bottom line is: we want courts to make good judgments and good judgment is a function of moral value; to the extent that a judgment relies on a wrong conception of value it is probably misguided.[8]

There are, of course, many competing explanations of ethical arguments. Some of these explanations do not presuppose that ethical arguments implicate metaethical questions: they aim to offer a normative account—based on

[8] I say 'probably' for it may not be misguided as a matter of coincidence (eg one may accidentally discover a new chemical element while doing alchemy).

a substantive moral principle—of why the courts should or should not use a particular ethical argument. I will deal with these arguments in relevant chapters, but a few general points about the relevance of metaethics are in order. Compared to a purely normative explanation, an account that problematizes this issue on the level of metaethics might be more successful for several reasons.

First, the metaethical explanation accounts better for the weight that different arguments acquire in constitutional practice. Because of their reiterative use in law, certain types of ethical arguments tend to consume moral decisions of a court completely. Ethical arguments start to eliminate all other moral concerns, including competing normative principles and—in particular—other potential sources of value: over time, they begin to exclude other sources of value to the extent that amounts to a specific metaethical position. It is certainly not the case that judges always explicitly and consciously adopt a particular metaethical view, but in practice, because of the weight ascribed to some arguments they become equivalent to a position about the nature of value.

Second, most ethical arguments cannot be explained without resort to metaethics. Partly this is connected to the previous point: if a court is making a moral judgment which does not depend on a substantive moral value but on a specific source of value, then—to the extent that this source excludes other possible sources and substantive moral values—it becomes an exclusive ground of moral judgment and this raises metaethical questions. But it is still a separate point, because metaethical concerns are often directly implicated by constitutional arguments. As we shall see, ethical arguments rely on metaethical concepts—such as rationality or subjectivity—which cannot be understood with the tools provided for by normative ethics.

Third, the metaethical explanation of ethical arguments is more complete in two different senses. On the one hand, as I will aim to demonstrate, the metaethical explanation is able to account for all ethical arguments, illuminate the interaction between them, and show how they relate to each other. While a purely normative explanation may be able to account for some instances of ethical arguments, the metaethical explanation is able to connect all the pieces of the puzzle into one coherent narrative. On the other hand, a theory that does address metaethical issues better accounts for the entirety of our ethical experience. There is a sense in which mere normative explanations do not go far enough. If we take Socrates' question seriously, we have a reason to prefer an account that offers answers to both normative and metaethical questions.

This brings us to the final preliminary question that I need to explain: what does it mean to *challenge* and *explain* the metaethical foundations of ethical arguments in constitutional law? The book not only aims to expose their metaethical assumptions, but also to reconstruct them around a credible understanding of the nature of value. The central intuition behind this project is that morality cannot be very different from what we actually do when we take the moral point of view. And to explicate the moral point of view, we must start from the perspective of an ordinary and competent moral agent. Throughout the book I argue for an ethical theory that makes no sharp distinction between critical and popular, or philosopher's and folk morality. What we seek to explain is a social and human phenomenon. Moral philosophy cannot disregard the elements of moral talk or intuitions on which ordinary people rely. These intuitions need to be addressed—vindicated or shown wrong—by using the tools of ordinary moral practice. While philosophers spend more time and resources in figuring out hard moral questions, the mechanism by which they arrive at conclusions are not very distant from how we go about these issues.

Philosophy is a humanistic discipline, and ethics in particular is about our self-understanding.[9] In the same way WVO Quine thought that '[t]he scientist is indistinguishable from the common man in his sense of evidence, except that scientist is more careful',[10] so the moral philosopher is indistinguishable from an ordinary moral agent except that she might be more studious. Her 'sense of evidence' is the same: she relies on common ways of making ethical judgments, and is convinced of moral conclusions in much the same way ordinary people are convinced. But the object of inquiry of ethics, unlike science, is not the world out there; its method is introspection, and it would fail miserably if it were not able to relate on a deep level to our self-understanding.

To be sure, just like science, moral philosophy can reach beyond what we may figure out on our own.[11] But even if it reaches beyond our common intuitions, moral theory will do so by employing the same mechanisms, or it will fail as a project in self-understanding. Ethical theory must render us, ordinary people, able to make sound moral judgments starting from our own evaluative frameworks. We may fail to notice more subtle points, fully detach from our habits of the heart, or liberate ourselves from prejudice. Philosophy can help us to overcome this, but it must remain true to the ways

[9] Bernard Williams, 'Philosophy as a Humanistic Discipline' (2000) 75 Philosophy 477, 493.

[10] WVO Quine, 'The Scope and Language of Science' in WVO Quine, *The Ways of Paradox and Other Essays* (Harvard University Press 1976) 233.

[11] Rawls famously compared the sense we have for native language with our moral sense, and the rules of grammar with moral rules: '[t]he aim [of linguistics] is to characterize the ability to recognize well-formed sentences by formulating clearly expressed principles which make the same discriminations as the native speaker. This undertaking is known to require theoretical constructions that far outrun the ad hoc precepts of our explicit grammatical knowledge. A similar situation presumably holds in moral theory'. John Rawls, *A Theory of Justice* (rev edn, Belknap Press 1999) 41, footnotes omitted.

we are as humans, and—in particular—locally situated humans. While this position will be in the background of the analysis, I will defend it in full detail in Chapter 5. I wish to proceed more carefully and—instead of trying to mould different positions and judicial arguments into my theory from the beginning—give them space of their own and let them feed into this theory.

Chapter 5 is hence the metaethical epicentre of the book, and aims to offer an understanding of the nature of value and express the dialectic between Euthyphro and Socrates in more abstract and analytic terms. It analyses the relationship between the two perspectives that we as humans are able to occupy—practical and theoretical—and explains how they affect each other. The book does this with notions of *confidence* and *reflection*: the objective is to illuminate the source of practical confidence in our values after the Socratic challenge, but also to clarify the consequences of Socratic reflection for pre-reflective moral attitudes.

In Chapter 6, the book applies the conception of value based on confidence and reflection to ethical arguments in constitutional adjudication. To complete the explanation of the metaethical foundations of ethical arguments in constitutional reasoning, the book translates the notions of confidence and reflection to the specific institutional context of constitutional adjudication. This chapter goes back to previously identified types of ethical arguments and shows how they are vindicated and transformed once we have a better grasp of the nature of value, and how they can be integrated into a coherent constitutional ethics. The book then investigates to what extent this account of constitutional ethics could be a useful framework for thinking about some quintessential constitutional dilemmas. The explanation of the metaethical foundations of ethical arguments in constitutional reasoning thus takes the following pattern: first, the book exposes the metaethical inadequacy of some common ethical arguments; second, it offers a conception of value that could remedy these inadequacies; and third, it shows how ethical arguments can be refashioned around such a conception of value.

Finally, any explanation must specify its methodology. The book combines philosophical inquiry with analysis of comparative constitutional law. It builds on comparative constitutional case law and identifies the central features of ethical arguments in different jurisdictions. But the empirical analysis does not attempt to offer a causal explanation of the factors that contribute to the use of these arguments; instead, it seeks to illuminate similar patterns of reasoning in different jurisdictions and capture the nuances that are relevant for the philosophical analysis. The guiding idea behind the case selection is always the same: to illustrate general trends in constitutional reasoning, clarify important distinctions, and provide the foundation for philosophical investigation. The fact that the book insists on an empirical grounding for its claims should not obscure the fact that its primary objective is philosophical.

This raises the question of the ambition of the conclusions in terms of their universal validity. As will become clear, such ambitions are modest: the aim is not to discover universal truths, but to contribute to the understanding of the world we inhabit. The book hence studies constitutional systems that accept certain basic liberal democratic principles. The empirical claim of the book is not that these particular ethical arguments exist in all constitutional systems, but that they are to a significant extent representative of many important liberal democratic constitutional systems. The hope is that the book will show the pervasive character of such arguments, and that its findings will resonate with some of the intuitions or concerns about the nature of value in constitutional reasoning. In other words, while the empirical findings are not universal, they should be relevant enough to justify the philosophical inquiry.

2

Constitutional Identity

2.1 INTRODUCTION

This chapter examines the argument from constitutional identity as one of the central ways in which ethical considerations permeate constitutional reasoning. The argument from constitutional identity locates the source of value in a set of deep and self-identifying evaluative commitments that develop in a society in virtue of the fact that it has a constitution. The purpose of this chapter is to explore the implicit metaethical assumptions behind this argument and assess its ability to serve as a self-standing form of moral evaluation in judicial reasoning.

The argument from constitutional identity bears a strong connection with existing constitutional practices. It associates the grounds of judicial moral judgment with evaluative attitudes that arise in a community governed by a constitution. For this reason, it may appear that law determines both its form and content. However, the argument from constitutional identity shares common traits with other types of ethical arguments: it is but one of legally accepted ways of moral evaluation. The normative force of constitutional identity is best explained with a reference to its plausibility as a basis of moral judgment.

The chapter first explains the notion of ethical argument, and situates the argument from constitutional identity in the wider framework of constitutional ethics. Because of its connections with constitutional practice, the argument from constitutional identity has often been considered as the only (legitimate) form of ethical argument. But—as I will explain—all ethical arguments are embedded in existing conventions of constitutional interpretation. At the same time, they identify a specific source of value as the foundation of court's moral judgment. The argument from constitutional identity is no different in this respect. It proceeds from a conception of value that is attached to a host of evaluative commitments that arise within a constitutional framework.

The chapter then explains the conception of value that is at the foundation of the argument from constitutional identity. Drawing on comparative constitutional law, it demonstrates that there are two dimensions of constitutional identity: general and particular. The former relies on the notion that constitutions as such entail evaluative commitments that are generally applicable in any constitutional system of government. The latter relies on specific values discernible from the layers of moral judgments that have been made in local constitutional practices.

The final part of the chapter investigates the plausibility of the vision of moral value that is presupposed by the argument from constitutional identity. It challenges the notion that constitutional identity can serve as an independent foundation of judicial moral judgment. Particular constitutional identity suggests that moral values are mind-dependent and that they exist in virtue of social practices of a given community; however, it is then neither clear what generates the normativity of the descriptive social and psychological facts that constitute particular constitutional identity nor why we should give priority to evaluative attitudes attached to constitutional identity as opposed to current moral sentiments. General constitutional identity implies that certain constitutional values may be universally shared and are perhaps even mind-independent; however, it is neither clear what makes them universal, nor how such values can be revealed without reliance on the argument from universal reason. The argument from constitutional identity both extends into other types of ethical arguments—from common sentiment and universal reason—and incorporates in itself the tension between the emotive-local and reasonable-universal dimension of moral value. The chapter concludes that constitutional identity cannot be an exclusive basis of constitutional ethics.

2.2 THE IDEA OF CONSTITUTIONAL ETHICS

This book elucidates and reconstructs the philosophical foundations of ethical arguments used in constitutional reasoning. This raises several preliminary questions. First, what are the ethical arguments used in constitutional reasoning? Second, why are their philosophical foundations specifically unclear or in need of reconstruction? Third, what is the suitable perspective to elucidate and reconstruct their philosophical foundations? This section seeks to answer these questions and position the argument from constitutional identity in relation to other forms of ethical arguments.

Posing a question about ethical arguments in constitutional reasoning already suggests that there is something specific about them worth investigating; otherwise, we would analyse ethical arguments as such, or—once the specific context of constitutional reasoning is added to the general study of ethics—we would explore a set of ethical concerns that apply to judicial reasoning. This would imply classical questions about moral duties, principles, or character traits that are apposite in contemporary constitutional systems. But this is not what I am aiming at. While these questions look at law from the standpoint of ethics, there is an equally interesting and pressing question that asks how ethics appears from the standpoint of law. The focus is on the actual ways in which constitutional courts incorporate ethical concerns in their legal reasoning. One of the central claims of the book is that law as a contingent social practice entrenches certain patterns of reasoning that in turn embed particular visions of moral values. These patterns of reasoning—ethical arguments—differ significantly from arguments that we find in ordinary moral discourse. The question is what morality looks like when seen through the lens of constitutional reasoning, and not only the other way round.

Let me clarify what I mean by ethical arguments with some examples. In his opinion in *Furman v Georgia*, Justice Marshall of the US Supreme Court held that capital punishment violates the Eighth Amendment 'because it is morally unacceptable to the people of the United States at this time in their history', but that 'this is not to suggest that with respect to this test of unconstitutionality people are required to act rationally', and that the test is 'totally dependent on the predictable subjective, emotional reactions of informed citizens'.[1] Another example is a remark the Supreme Court of Canada made in *Multani v Commission scolaire Marguerite-Bourgeoys*, claiming that the prohibition of wearing a Sikh religious dagger in school 'does not take into account Canadian values based on multiculturalism' and neglects the fact that '[r]eligious tolerance is a very important value of Canadian society'.[2] The German Federal Constitutional Court declared in *Lüth* that the constitution establishes the 'objective order of values' and that—when the courts interpret 'general' clauses containing ethical concepts—'they must start from the order of values adopted by the society in its constitution at that stage of its cultural and spiritual development'.[3] Similarly, Justice Sachs of the Constitutional Court of South Africa reflected on—as he put it—'the source of values' in *S v Makwanyane* and argued that the function of the court is to 'articulate the fundamental sense of justice and right shared by the whole nation as expressed in the text of the Constitution'.[4] Finally, Sachs also offered a different and more universalistic conception of values in *Minister of Home Affairs v Fourie* when he argued that '[a]s the conditions of humanity alter and as ideas of justice and equity evolve, so do concepts of rights take on new texture and meaning'

[1] *Furman v Georgia* 408 US 238 (1972) 360—62 (Marshall).

[2] *Multani v Commission scolaire Marguerite-Bourgeoys* [2006] 1 SCR 256 paras 71 and 76 (McLachlin).

[3] *Lüth* (1958) 7 BVerfGE 198 para B.II.1. See also eg *Abortion Decision I* (1975) 39 BVerfGE 1 para C.I.3.

[4] *S v Makwanyane and Another* 1995 (3) SA 391 para 362 (Sachs).

and thus that 'the horizon of rights is as limitless as the hopes and expectations of humanity'.[5] Aiming at a related understanding of values, Justice Kennedy remarked in *Roper v Simmons* that the court ought to 'acknowledge the overwhelming weight of international opinion against the juvenile death penalty'.[6]

Although these excerpts do not do justice to actual opinions and positions, they support two conclusions: first, all these arguments are ethical in the sense that they aim to contribute to an appropriate evaluative judgment; and second, even though we may have an intuitive sense of the nature and place of these arguments which suffices to group them together, they appear to be so heterogeneous that it may seem that the only proper way to distinguish between them is by a negative definition and in relation to the more usual legal arguments. Particularly perplexing are the ways in which these arguments locate the source of moral value. Is it people's moral attitudes at a particular moment that matter? Is there an order of values that is inherent to a properly interpreted constitution? Or can the only genuine lead be discerned from universal moral principles? Notwithstanding their differences, all these arguments offer a vision of the nature of values that are brought to resolve constitutional dilemmas. The question hence becomes: what are the metaethical foundations of values that are implicit in these arguments?

The examples allow us to identify at least three distinct answers to this question. We can group ethical arguments into three ideal types on the basis of their understanding of the source of value. The German Constitutional Court in *Lüth* and Justice Sachs in *Makwanyane* refer to common evaluative commitments of the society as articulated in the constitution to justify their moral claim. According to this type of ethical argument, the value stems from the specific constitutional tradition. Call this *the argument from constitutional identity*. Another version of ethical argument is based on the prevailing moral intuitions of citizens in the constitutional order. The examples of this approach are Justice Marshall's opinion in *Furman* and the Canadian Constitutional Court's remark in *Multani*. Call this the *argument from common sentiment*. Finally, Justice Sachs in *Fourie* relies on a conception of moral value that exists by virtue of our humanity, and is thus applicable to all human beings and transcends national or communal borders. This type of argument typically refers to foreign law to find support for moral judgments, as demonstrated by Justice Kennedy's opinion from *Roper*. Call this *the argument from universal reason*. Given that ethical arguments in constitutional reasoning have divergent foundations, it is impracticable to define them in advance; the hope is that the book as a whole will offer a better idea about their nature and role in

[5] *Minister of Home Affairs and Another v Fourie and Another* 2006 (1) SA 524 para 102 (Sachs).

[6] *Roper v Simmons* 543 US 551 (2005) 578.

constitutional reasoning. Let me nonetheless go through a set of preliminary intuitions that can help us understand the concept of ethical argument. All these intuitions are interconnected, and in the neighbourhood of the main attribute of ethical arguments: their orientation towards morally justified solutions to constitutional dilemmas.

First, ethical arguments depend more on their *persuasiveness* than on authority. Each constitutional argument detects a source of law: an object to be interpreted, such as a constitution, statute, precedent, etc. These sources of law have prima facie authority; to even count as sources of law they must be considered binding. If we wish to act within legal practice, we need to consult them, and only then can we develop them further, make new law, or refuse to be bound by them. In other words, we cannot disregard them without first checking. In contrast, the arguments we use to interpret these sources may draw their appeal from the authority of the source or from their ability to lead to better moral answers. For example, textual, historical, doctrinal—and other arguments which are not ethical—for the most part draw their force from the authority of the source of law. This is not to say that this authority need not be justified on moral grounds, but only that the issue of justification is considered settled or at least constant when such arguments are used. Conversely, ethical arguments mostly depend on their persuasiveness and ability to lead one to discern moral values that ought to apply to a particular problem. They do not derive their appeal from the source of law directly and should thus be justified as a reliable source of moral knowledge.

This distinction is simplified and can only be true as a matter of degree.[7] On the one hand, original intentions or particular precedents could be followed because of the belief that they are more likely to get the moral answers right. This view may not be common in modern legal systems, as the justification of the authority of legal sources is usually divorced from moral truth and attached to a conception of legitimacy, but it cannot be fully excluded either.[8] On the other hand, the normative appeal of ethical arguments may lessen as the time passes, but the canons of interpretation may remain and obtain authority of their own. Ethical arguments can thus become more or less entrenched and acquire a binding character, but at least initially they depend

[7] Consider eg the following argument from Justice Scalia's dissent in *McCreary*: 'Those who wrote the Constitution believed that morality was essential to the well-being of society and that encouragement of religion was the best way to foster morality' (*McCreary County v ACLU of Kentucky* 545 US 844 (2005) 887 (Scalia)). Although it carries an ethical message, this argument is not ethical in the sense used here. What justifies this argument is a theory about the authority of constitution-framers, and not the sense that framers have a better insight into moral answers.

[8] See Arie Rosen, 'Two Logics of Authority in Modern Law' (2014) 64 University of Toronto Law Journal 669.

on their persuasiveness and on the idea that they will point to morally appropriate solutions. Therefore, calling an argument 'ethical' is a function of the degree to which such argument aims at a morally apposite answer, and not at the meaning of the authoritative directive. Ethical arguments interfere with our reasons for action more because of their proximity to moral values, and less because of their proximity to (legitimate) authority.

Second, ethical arguments are characteristically used to interpret constitutional clauses which contain *ethical concepts*. Constitutions—like other legal materials—encompass moral language. The examples include predicates such as 'cruel and unusual', 'equal', 'discriminatory', 'just', or 'fair', and concepts such as 'dignity' or 'liberty'. These are usually thick ethical concepts, which at least partially depend on an evaluative judgment.[9] For example, by uttering that someone is 'just', 'fair', or 'cruel', we can, at the same time, both describe and evaluate that person or her actions. The fact that ethical arguments interpret ethical concepts does not make them entirely different from other types of constitutional arguments. Within the legal practice of constitutional reasoning, ethical concepts are often applied using arguments that draw their force from an authority. That is why the difference between the two types of arguments is more nuanced and context-dependent: we use ethical arguments almost exclusively to interpret ethical concepts from the constitution, while we use other types of arguments across the board. But the legal character of ethical arguments also makes them different from ordinary arguments in moral discourse that we use to explicate the very same ethical concepts outside of constitutional reasoning. The application of ethical concepts in law is different from ordinary ethical application, for the descriptive part (say, describing something as 'cruel') over time acquires layers of legal meaning that push back against the force of evaluative judgment. The evaluative judgment in constitutional reasoning thus frequently depends on arguments that are different from both legal arguments and the ethical arguments used in moral discourse. One way to capture the specific character of ethical arguments in constitutional reasoning is to say that they are legal in their form—they are legally accepted ways of argumentation—but they aspire to evaluate morally.

Third, ethical arguments are more often than not oriented towards *innovative interpretation* rather than towards conserving interpretation. This makes them different from other constitutional arguments in two senses. On the one hand, the sources to which ethical arguments point are more prone to change. Original intentions, textual meaning, and doctrine are more fixed than—for example—the current moral feelings of citizens or foreign law. The distinction is not clear-cut: doctrines or rules of language can change,

[9] Bernard Williams, *Ethics and the Limits of Philosophy* (2nd edn, Routledge 2006) 140–42.

while moral opinions and foreign law can be stable. So—on the other hand—the distinction focuses on the intentions of judges that use these arguments rather than on a conceptual difference between the stability of the sources behind them: ethical arguments are typically connected with the idea that existing law is unsatisfactory and needs to be changed or specified. For example, foreign law never assists the courts in confirming a clear precedent; rather, it is used to support a moral judgment that proceeds from the idea that existing law is inadequate or indeterminate. Ethical arguments are almost exclusively directed towards innovation and the development of law, while other arguments predominantly preserve (but may also change) the existing state of affairs.

Fourth, ethical arguments will sometimes be *characterized as such by judges* themselves. Sometimes they even explicitly engage in the question of what morality is. This is predominantly a consequence of the moral language used in constitutions, but is still a separate point because judges openly recognize that they need to have a concept of morality to resolve the constitutional issue before them. Often, this is almost inescapable. For example, when a concept such as 'morals' is used as one of justifications for limiting fundamental rights, the court that first decides on this issue has to define morality.[10] In so doing—while it can still rely on non-ethical arguments, such as the intentions and purposes of the framers—the court typically opts for an understanding of morality by using a particular type of ethical argument, and this choice in turn constrains future alternatives.

Fifth, ethical arguments will sometimes rely on *sources that are not necessarily a product of institutional activity* in their legal system in order to interpret the constitution. While this element needs to be specified further, the point is simple enough if previously mentioned elements are taken into account. The sources in question can range from public polls to foreign law. This distinguishes ethical arguments from persuasive sources of interpretation, which are a consequence of institutional activity or people acting in an official capacity within the system, such as dicta from previous cases or preparatory works in the legislature. However, if taken in isolation, this element is both too narrow and too broad. It is too narrow, for example, because it disregards relying on moral opinions of juries and legislatures as an ethical argument, and it is too broad because it includes considerations that may not always aim at reaching moral solutions, such as academic articles. But the sources at the basis of ethical arguments are more fluid and underspecified, even when they are a product of institutional activity; for example, instead of pointing to a specific decision of a previous court, they rather refer to

[10] See eg European Convention for the Protection of Human Rights and Fundamental Freedoms (ECHR) arts 6(1), 8(2), 9(2), 10(2), and 11(2).

the 'spirit' of a previous practice or prevailing 'trends'. Moreover, the use of these sources is an ethical argument only if the court considers them a reliable indication of a morally appropriate judgment.

Ethical arguments could thus tentatively be described as arguments that are: at least partially explained by the belief in their moral attractiveness (regardless of whether that belief is justified); present when ethical concepts in constitutions are interpreted; aimed at innovation rather than conservation; openly embraced as ethical by courts; or dependent on sources which are not a consequence of a particular decision of an institution in the domestic legal system. They derive their appeal from their moral soundness, whereas other arguments may be taken into account regardless of their moral status. To be accepted, ethical arguments have to obtain a legal form that is customary in the given constitutional system and—at the same time—be considered a reliable way of gaining moral knowledge or reaching a morally sound judgment. Over time, canons of interpretation themselves acquire the prima facie authority that characterizes sources of law, while remaining in conversation with moral considerations. As a consequence, the legal character of ethical arguments may entrench them as particular ways of understanding morality.

The criteria for identifying ethical arguments include a fair amount of persuasive sources that we bring to bear on the interpretation of legal materials. However, I shall focus on three particular types of ethical arguments mentioned in the beginning: argument from constitutional identity, common sentiment, and universal reason. This is because they are the most prominent ethical arguments in practice, the idea that they are connected to moral judgment is still strong, and this connection is at the same time in need of elucidation.

The conglomerate of ethical arguments conventionally entrenched in a constitutional system forms the structure that I shall call *constitutional ethics*. Constitutional ethics presents a number of legally accepted ways in which ethical considerations enter constitutional reasoning. The idea of constitutional ethics thus relies on the notion that constitutional interpretation consists in the use of modalities of arguments pertinent to a specific constitutional culture. Moral arguments must take legal form to be successful in constitutional litigation. This presupposes not only that law is not subverted to moral reasoning but also that morality employed through ethical arguments is different from ordinary moral reasoning. The key is then to explain how morality becomes legalized in constitutional practice.

The idea of constitutional ethics presupposes a distinction between law and morality, for otherwise the intuitions about ethical arguments cannot escape being circular: ethical arguments must in some sense be different from all other arguments that are 'legal'. But there is something vexed about the possibility of differentiating between law and morality *within* legal reasoning. If ethical arguments are legal, how can they be moral at the same time if the difference between law and morality is assumed? On the one hand, the law determines the ways in which morality enters judicial reasoning; on the other, it affects the kind of morality that enters judicial reasoning. To explain ethical arguments, we need an understanding of both the interaction between morality *and* law, and the nature of morality *in* law.

Let me then start with a modest observation: morality that appears in constitutional case law differs from ordinary moral reasoning. Legal reasoning is affected by morality, but legal reasoning in turn affects the kind of morality we find in law. This is rather uncontroversial: it is natural for a discourse to adjust to the ways in which moral issues are authoritatively resolved. Changing the landscape of moral theory, GEM Anscombe argued that much of moral language had been misguided because it relied on a divine authority that was absent in modern circumstances.[11] She characterized this flawed morality as 'law conceptions of ethics':

> [b]etween Aristotle and us came Christianity, with its law conception of ethics . . . In consequence of the dominance of Christianity for many centuries, the concepts of being bound, permitted, or excused became deeply embedded in our language and thought.[12]

Christian ethics may not be the dominant model of ethical thinking today, but we still have—as it were—a 'law conception of ethics'. The new paradigm is constitutional ethics. All significant moral debates are profoundly influenced by the ways the supreme judicial bodies reason about them. Abortion, euthanasia, torture, hate speech, capital punishment: philosophical and political discourses about these issues are, if not hijacked by legal reasons, then at least significantly affected by them.

Any attempt to influence judicial decision-making must abduct the grammar of legal argumentation to be successful. Take for example 'The Philosophers' Brief', written by six leading political philosophers about the assisted suicide cases pending before the US Supreme Court.[13] The substantive part of their Brief states in its opening:

> These cases do not invite or require the Court to make moral, ethical, or religious judgments about how people should approach or confront their death or about when it is ethically appropriate to hasten one's own death or to ask others for help in doing so. On the contrary, they ask the Court to recognize that individuals have a constitutionally protected interest in making those

[11] GEM Anscombe, 'Modern Moral Philosophy' (1958) 33 Philosophy 1. [12] ibid 4–5.

[13] Ronald Dworkin and others, 'Assisted Suicide: The Philosophers' Brief' The New York Review of Books (27 March 1997) http://www.nybooks.com/articles/archives/1997/mar/27/assisted-suicide-the-philosophers-brief/ (last accessed 16 July 2014).

grave judgments for themselves, free from the imposition of any religious or philosophical orthodoxy by court or legislature.[14]

Contrary to what one would expect from a perspective taken by Ronald Dworkin on behalf of other authors in the introduction—'I am unaware of any other occasion on which a group has intervened in Supreme Court litigation *solely as general moral philosophers*'[15]—the philosophers begin their Brief with the explicit renouncement of what could actually be the domain of their mastery. That was not just lip service to the Court. The general tenor of the Brief is legal and doctrinal. The main conclusion of the philosophers is that a decision that would run against their Brief would be 'flatly in conflict with the spirit and letter of the Court's past decisions'.[16] This is not to say that the moral position has not been defended; however, this has been done using constitutional and not philosophical or moral grammar.

This is not surprising: success in passing a policy depends on engaging in those types of arguments that have a chance to succeed. Had the Philosophers' Brief been written as a philosophical treatise it would have been bound to fail. Culturally embedded ways of legal argumentation together with the pressure on courts to appear as law-applying and not law-making institutions makes them less sensitive to pure moral arguments and less prone to use them in their reasoning. Going back to Anscombe's argument, we can see that contemporary moral discourse is—for better or worse—influenced by legal types of arguments. We still have 'the law conception of ethics', although a different one: the divine will of today is constitutional reasoning.[17] The point I wish to make with this metaphor is that it is a mistake to think of morality as something that exists apart from legal reasoning and that at times finds its way to judicial decisions while retaining its distinctive character, unaffected by the whole process. Instead, the morality used in constitutional cases is by and large constructed by constitutional reasoning. It is not the case that morality is just 'abducted' by law. Law also makes it quite different.

Let me use a classic example to illustrate this. The 8th Amendment to the US Constitution proscribes 'cruel and unusual' punishment. The clause contains an ethical concept ('cruel'). It further refers to 'unusual' punishment, which may serve to specify what is 'cruel' (assuming that prevailing penal practices will not be cruel), or it could be a self-standing ethical concern (not to punish in unusual and broadly speaking unexpected ways). The constitution thus invites moral judgment and suggests—on one reading at least—that the court ought to look for clues about the appropriateness of

[14] ibid. [15] ibid fn 2 (emphasis added). [16] ibid.

[17] This much has been clear to most social theorists. See eg Emile Durkheim, *Durkheim and the Law* (Steven Lukes and Andrew Scull eds, St Martin's Press 1983) ch 2.

punishment in penal practices. But it is not clear which and whose practices are relevant: contemporary practices, or those prevailing at the time of the adoption of the constitution; American, or global? There is thus some leeway for the court's moral judgment.

The US Supreme Court developed a test in *Tropp v Dulles*, according to which the meaning of the phrase 'cruel and unusual' is to be derived from 'the evolving standards of decency that mark the progress of a maturing society'.[18] This test has further restrained the kind of ethical arguments that might be put forward. Notice how many assumptions about morality this simple test makes: moral knowledge is expressed in contingent social practices (in their 'standards of decency'); apposite moral answers can change over time with the development of social standards; the evolution of morality is always for the better (the reference to 'progress' of a 'maturing' society); the progress of morality is potentially ever-growing (there is no certain point in which we can tell that we have achieved moral truths). This interpretation narrows down the kinds of ethical arguments that the court employs in its reasoning as it excludes the possibility to argue from a different perspective about morality; for example, one that would fix moral knowledge with a reference to the wisdom of the constitution framers or teachings of moral philosophers. It also leaves the space open to connect the idea of morally appropriate punishment to both local or global trends: as we shall see, one interpretation of the test is that moral answers ought to be found in the positions of domestic legislatures or juries, and the other that these positions need to be corrected on the basis of foreign legal practices.[19]

Now we come to the main point: law limits the kinds of arguments that can be brought to interpret an ethical concept to a set of concerns that have no or very little purchase in ordinary moral discourse. Consider how this question would be answered if there were no constitution or doctrine. Would anyone in ordinary moral discourse rely on what courts in other countries do? Do we look at legislative trends to determine whether something is cruel? Almost certainly not: we would consider such arguments as confused. Thus, the layers of legal decisions restrict the understanding of morality and bring an altogether different set of concerns and arguments to bear on moral judgment. Instead of arguing—for example—whether cruel punishment violates one's dignity, brings the greatest happiness for the greatest number, or corrupts character, we look at trends in foreign or domestic legislation.

Observe the level at which the difference between ethical arguments in constitutional reasoning and pure moral arguments arises: because ethical arguments focus on certain contingent facts as proxies for moral knowledge

[18] *Trop v Dulles* 356 US 86 (1958) 100–101.

[19] See the discussion of US death penalty cases in ch 3.

they are compatible with many different substantive moral positions as long as they are expressed in these facts. The restriction thus occurs at the level of metaethics. Interpretive conventions answer questions such as: in virtue of what are moral judgments true; how do we know what is morally good; is moral value universally human or contingent upon different cultures; is the foundation of moral judgment emotive or reason-based? Because of entrenched patterns of ethical arguments these questions are sometimes answered by the constitutional culture which predates the choice of a particular judge.

While ethical arguments in constitutional reasoning do take on a different shape from ordinary moral arguments, it is hard to pin them down with sufficient precision. At least two reasons make ethical arguments hard to distinguish from other types of arguments. First, just like the Brief written by Ronald Dworkin and others, discussed above, they frequently start from another argument based on precedent, history, or possible readings of constitutional text. In fact, at least one of them—the argument from constitutional identity, discussed later in this chapter—considers constitutional framework as a whole to be a source of value. In the case of the 8th Amendment, the judgment about morally appropriate punishment proceeds from the text itself and from the previous precedent that determined the approach to its interpretation. By so doing ethical arguments tacitly accept the authority of the rule-maker, which makes them appear completely legally constrained. Second, through this process moral principles do become 'legalized' as they transform into doctrines. This process is obvious when notions that invite moral reading—such as 'reasonable'—are being specified in legal practice. For example, 'reasonable damages' might in ordinary language imply different things, but in law they would usually be set in accordance with what has been the practice in similar cases before. This is also true of ethical arguments in constitutional reasoning; a previous precedent may already answer whether—for example—capital punishment for rape is cruel and unusual.[20] But more importantly, while the moral soundness of these arguments does play a role in their attractiveness and persuasive force, over time they obtain a legal form to be followed in order to reach a substantive moral judgment.

How can we explain this mix between law and morality? It seems to invite the conclusion that we cannot draw a sufficiently sharp line between the two domains, even though it is deeply engrained in our vocabulary. It is typical to move from the thought about intricate connections between the two modes of reasoning to a conceptualization of law as completely subordinate to ethical concerns.[21] This is the conclusion I want to resist. As we have seen from

[20] See eg *Coker v Georgia* 433 US 584 (1977) and *Kennedy v Louisiana* 554 US 407 (2008).

[21] See eg Ronald Dworkin, *Justice for Hedgehogs* (Belknap Press of Harvard University Press 2011) 405.

the examples of ethical arguments—and as the book will attempt to show in full detail—the law has a significant constraining force over morality. In fact, judicial efforts to develop or specify the law in a morally appropriate way often do not even resemble typical moral arguments. We may intuitively describe their arguments as ethical or moral, but we never use such arguments in ordinary moral talk.

The rules determining the acceptability of a particular argument are embedded in conventions of interpretation in a given constitutional culture. Law is an argumentative practice, and ethical arguments that are used in law are constrained by the rules of that practice.[22] Judges are frequently criticized for not applying law but 'doing politics' or legislating their 'ideological preferences'. To remain within the practice of law—often understood as the only legitimate position for judges to take—they apply legal forms of arguments. For example, Philip Bobbitt gives an account of the accepted modalities of constitutional argument in the American context as follows:

> [h]istorical (relying on the intentions of the framers and ratifiers of the Constitution); textual (looking to the meaning of the words of the Constitution alone, as they would be interpreted by the average contemporary 'man on the street'); structural (inferring rules from the relationships that the Constitution mandates from the structure it sets up); doctrinal (applying rules generated by precedent); ethical (deriving rules from those moral commitments of the American ethos that are reflected in the Constitution); and prudential (seeking to balance the costs and benefits of a particular rule).[23]

The philosophical lesson goes beyond the specific point about the American constitutional system: each constitutional culture has its own grammar. Ethical arguments are part of this grammar. The most intuitive way to make sense of ethical arguments is to say that judges act legally when they use them because they have a legal warrant to do so, which is entrenched in constitutional argumentative practice; however, their aim is to evaluate morally.

2.3 ELEMENTS OF THE ARGUMENT FROM CONSTITUTIONAL IDENTITY

A plausible intuition that ethical arguments are legally constrained has led some to believe that law also determines their content. A clear example of this is the argument from constitutional identity. As understood here, constitutional identity denotes a range of evaluative concerns that contingently

[22] Dennis M Patterson, *Law and Truth* (Oxford University Press 1996).

[23] Philip Bobbitt, *Constitutional Interpretation* (Blackwell 1991) 12–13. The concept of ethical argument that I develop differs from Bobbitt's both to account for a wider range of phenomena in comparative practice and to underline the intrinsic connection between ethical arguments and moral value.

develop in a society but—crucially—by virtue of the fact that such a society has (its own and sometimes quite specific) constitution.[24] Even though it is attached to the constitution, the argument from constitutional identity is ethical, as its force does not derive from specific intentions behind authoritative directives or from the textual meaning of ethical concepts in the constitution, but from a range of deep moral commitments that arise in a community that is governed by the constitution; these commitments become a part of identity of a constitutionally established community and the way in which people recognize themselves as being a part of it.[25]

The most sophisticated accounts of ethical arguments in constitutional reasoning—which recognize their legal entrenchment and the metaethical problems this brings about—often identify the entire constitutional ethics with the argument from constitutional identity. This is because they are concerned not only with an accurate representation of the ways in which values penetrate constitutional reasoning, but also with justifying the judicial review of legislation. The argument from constitutional identity seems like a candidate to carry this double burden, for it appears legally constrained and thus leaves the impression of judicial law-applying and not law-making. In such views, the argument from constitutional identity legitimizes constitutional review since it refers to the values that are already 'in' the constitution and are precise enough to reduce judicial discretion. But focusing on the argument from constitutional identity is neither descriptively accurate (as there are other types of ethical arguments) nor does it solve the problem of judicial discretion (as it often does not give much content to underspecified and contested ethical concepts from the constitution). It is worthwhile looking at some of the existing accounts in more depth to illustrate the kind of metaethical analysis that is needed for an adequate account of constitutional ethics.

For example, Philip Bobbitt defined ethical arguments in the following way:

> By ethical argument I mean constitutional argument whose force relies on characterization of American institutions and the role within them of the American people. It is the character, or *ethos*, of the American polity that is advanced in ethical argument as the source from which particular decisions derive.[26]

[24] For some recent treatments of the issue of constitutional identity see Michel Rosenfeld, *The Identity of the Constitutional Subject: Selfhood, Citizenship, Culture, and Community* (Routledge 2010) and Gary J Jacobsohn, *Constitutional Identity* (Harvard University Press 2010).

[25] Of course, this is not to suggest that the constitution and constitutional identity do not themselves arise from general moral commitments or identity of a community. The process is typically dynamic and the separation between the two can never be precise.

[26] Philip Bobbitt, *Constitutional Fate: Theory of the Constitution* (Oxford University Press 1982) 94.

Bobbitt thus identifies ethical arguments with the argument from constitutional identity, which becomes the main source of evaluative judgments in constitutional adjudication. He is also quick to avoid possible confusions between ethical arguments in constitutional reasoning and general moral arguments:

> As I shall use the term, ethical arguments are not *moral* arguments. Ethical constitutional arguments do not claim that a particular solution is right or wrong in any sense larger than that the solution comports with the sort of people we are and the means we have chosen to solve political and customary constitutional problems.[27]

The reason to reject the use of general moral arguments in constitutional law is their suspect metaethical foundation that would bring uncertainty to constitutional reasoning.[28] For Bobbitt, divorcing ethical arguments from general moral reasons and tying them to constitutional ethos is

> a way of compensating for the principal shortcoming of ethical argument, that is, its lack of nonethical referent . . . If so, then we may be able to identify a class of ethical arguments that originate in a specifically *constitutional* ethos and hence avoid the difficulties of ethical and moral arguments generally.[29]

By narrowly defining ethical arguments from constitutional ethos he wishes 'to use the resolving power of constitutional argument and avoid introducing a competition of moral conventions'.[30] Clearly, Bobbitt's concern is the lack of mechanisms to resolve moral disagreements and scepticism about the proposition that moral truth can be the function of correspondence between moral statements and some kind of objective reality. But if this is the case, his argument may be confused: first, Bobbitt is advancing a moral argument based on our inability to advance moral arguments; second, if the only reason for preferring the argument from constitutional identity is the stability through agreement, the argument is not morally attractive, for there are more important moral concerns than stability and more effective ways to achieve it; third, while the argument from constitutional identity might be slightly more determinate than general moral arguments, it comes nowhere near resolving Bobbitt's worries about the disagreements and uncertainties that plague our moral universe. While Bobbitt is correct to recognize legal

[27] ibid 94–95. There are other authors that use concepts similar to ethical arguments. Richard Fallon, for example, describes 'value arguments' as those that refer to the 'moral or political significance of facts or about the normative desirability of outcomes'. Richard H Fallon, 'A Constructivist Coherence Theory of Constitutional Interpretation' (1987) 100 Harvard Law Review 1189, 1205. Fallon correctly notices that 'value arguments' do not only refer to values but also construe analytical processes through which these values are cognized or point to the sources of these values. ibid 1204–1209. See also Richard H Fallon, *Implementing the Constitution* (Harvard University Press 2001) 46–52.

[28] See Bobbitt, *Constitutional Fate: Theory of the Constitution* (n 26) 139.

[29] ibid 140–41; see also 172–75.

[30] ibid 150.

constraints to moral arguments and their unstable metaethical foundations, his concern with the legitimacy of judicial review, and the view that it could only be attained if courts remain within the practice of legal reasoning, leads him astray. The question is, however, what explains the value of constitutional identity? To the extent to which constitutional identity is the only source of value that grounds judicial moral judgment, it is of paramount importance to elucidate its metaethical foundations.

Other accounts of the value of constitutional identity also identify metaethical problems arising from the fact that the courts—when they rely on this type of argument—locate the source of value in the evaluative attitudes of a community that is governed by a constitution. An example is Wil Waluchow's theory of 'constitutional morality'.[31] Waluchow recognizes legal limitations to judicial moral arguments, wishes to offer a moral reading of the constitution that is divorced from the baggage of robust moral realism, and at the same time aspires to provide a legitimation for the judicial review of legislation; again, these multiple goals leave the theory both descriptively inaccurate and normatively unstable. Waluchow differentiates 'constitutional morality' from both 'Platonic' or 'Kantian' morality, which is 'universal, valid, rationally justified, or maybe even "objectively true"',[32] and from 'conventional or positive morality rooted not in the fabric of universe, but in the variable beliefs and convictions of a particular community'.[33] He thus defines constitutional morality as 'the set of moral norms and considered judgments properly attributable to the community as a whole as representing its true commitments, but with the following additional property: they are in some way tied to its constitutional law and practices'.[34] Waluchow's conception of 'constitutional morality' thus overlaps with what I have referred to as 'constitutional identity'.

Waluchow differentiates between two sets of relevant motives that play a role in our ordinary moral reasoning—'true moral commitments' and 'moral opinions'—which can come into conflict. True moral commitments are more stable, deep, and significant moral principles which we accept, while moral opinions are prone to change and readjustment. Waluchow then identifies the true moral commitments with constitutional morality as a social fact of overlapping consensus about the most important moral principles.[35] In his interpretation, we aim for a 'reflective equilibrium' where our 'true commitments' trump our opinions, and so constitutional morality

[31] See Wilfrid J Waluchow, *A Common Law Theory of Judicial Review: The Living Tree* (Cambridge University Press 2007) and Wilfrid J Waluchow, 'Constitutional Morality and the Bills of Rights' in Grant Huscroft (ed), *Expounding the Constitution: Essays in Constitutional Theory* (Cambridge University Press 2008).

[32] Waluchow, 'Constitutional Morality and the Bills of Rights' (n 31) 65.

[33] ibid.

[34] Waluchow, *A Common Law Theory of Judicial Review: The Living Tree* (n 31) 227.

[35] ibid 220–22.

containing such principles and commitments precludes our (wrong) opinions.[36] His aim is to show that the fact that courts review our moral opinions expressed in legislatures is simply bringing them in line with the more fundamental principles from the constitution that we already accept.

While the distinction between principles and opinions is intuitive and uncontroversial, it might be too crude. We may indeed be misled in our moral opinions because they conflict with the principles we also accept; however, it is important to notice that the same argument works both ways: we can reconsider our moral principles or 'true moral commitments' in cases when they collide with our opinions. But—more importantly—general moral principles (eg respect for equality) are prone to different interpretations and their content is determined by a host of moral opinions which we find pertinent to certain kinds of moral problems. The principles of constitutional morality—as social facts—cannot be far away from our contingent moral opinions about their application. If the meaning of general principles is at least partly constituted by our own attitudes about their application, then constitutional morality does not have enough bite to be strongly counter-majoritarian and justify judicial review. And the dispute about the legitimacy of judicial review is precisely about whose understanding of these principles should be controlling.

A consequence of Waluchow's account of constitutional morality is that it may collide with two other 'moralities' he identifies: 'popular' and 'ideal'. Waluchow agrees: 'One could ... explain ... much of the early-twentieth-century South African law as presupposing racist moral norms and beliefs. Such norms and beliefs were part of that community's (deplorable) "constitutional morality" '.[37] Because it is a social fact that exists in the practices of officials, it is impossible that all those involved in this practice are mistaken about the substance of constitutional morality. This might prove to be morally hazardous: for example, if the 'reflective equilibrium' exercise shows that the community is committed to racial segregation and if moral opinions of people also demonstrate the same, how can judges overcome this only by looking to these two sources of moral authority? Waluchow's answer is to depart from such practices on the basis of objective normative reasons and thus to break ties with constitutional morality as a social fact. When we run out of reasons that point to incoherent social practice, we must turn to 'ideal' morality: 'It is also important to remember ... that questions concerning legality—even those requiring appeal to community's moral standards—must never be confused with, or supplant in our thinking, our ability to challenge accepted norms from the moral point of view'.[38] But if the moral point of view is something different from constitutional morality, then what

[36] ibid 224–30. [37] ibid. [38] ibid 237 n 25.

is the normative force of the latter? Why not simply apply ideal morality if constitutional morality is a normatively inert social fact? Finally, if there is an ideal morality, what is its connection with parochial and contingent opinions that constitute constitutional morality?

In his attempt to justify judicial review of legislation that can void popular will, Waluchow detaches the conception of constitutional morality from several commonly criticized positions. Personal moral opinions of judges are unacceptable as they are not 'philosopher kings'. Popular moral opinions of citizenry are known to be prejudiced and as such are disregarded. Ideal morality based on objective reasons is controversial. Waluchow thinks he offers a way out of this problem but his theory fails to strike a plausible middle way. Because Waluchow wants to justify judicial review he misses important types of ethical arguments in constitutional reasoning, such as the argument from common sentiment and universal reason. For the same reason he leaves his conception of constitutional morality on shaky metaethical grounds: if there is agreement on moral principles, constitutional morality has no critical bite; if there is no agreement, or we think that the agreement is wrong, we need to resort to 'ideal' morality, so again constitutional morality has no critical bite. Constitutional morality is redundant.

Is there a lesson to be learned? Because they start from the problem of the legitimacy of judicial review, Bobbitt and Waluchow fail to engage successfully with the metaethical foundations of ethical arguments and account for the full complexity of constitutional ethics. They are at pains to show that when employing ethical argument courts stay within the practice of law; for this reason, they miss other types of ethical arguments that emerge in constitutional reasoning, such as arguments from prevailing moral opinions (the argument from common sentiment) or foreign law (the argument from universal reason). Moreover, because they see the argument from constitutional identity as constituted by social facts that obtain in a constitutional system, they make it appear weak in relation to 'ideal' morality. If there is 'ideal' morality, they need to explain the normative foundations of such social facts. What we need is a theory of constitutional ethics that can remedy these inadequacies.

However, Bobbitt and Waluchow raise two important issues about the argument from constitutional identity. First, they both appreciate the legal character of this argument, but they also recognize its ethical dimension. The argument from constitutional identity is one of legally accepted ways of moral evaluation; at the same time, references to constitutional identity are best understood as efforts to reach morally adequate decisions. Second, both Bobbitt and Waluchow correctly point out that the use of argument from constitutional identity raises metaethical questions. This form of argument perceives the constitutional framework as a source of value, which is detached from current moral opinions of the members of a constitutional community, but at the same time does not claim to provide universal, mind-independent, and timeless answers to moral problems. As Waluchow argues, constitutional identity is different from 'conventional' or 'popular' morality, but it does not amount to 'ideal' or 'Platonic' morality. It is thus important to clarify the distinction between public moral opinions and constitutional identity, and explain how constitutional identity gains normative traction if it does not reveal normative truths about constitutional dilemmas.

These questions demand taking a closer look at the metaethical foundations of constitutional identity. The argument from constitutional identity has two distinct but connected dimensions. We can tentatively distinguish between general and particular constitutional identity. While general constitutional identity follows from the reasons for having a constitution as such, particular constitutional identity follows from the gist of the specific constitution. General constitutional identity thus relies on the *value of constitution* (that is, the value of having a constitution), and particular constitutional identity on *constitutional value* (the value from the constitution). Let me explain.

General constitutional identity derives its force from the fact of having an entrenched and written constitution containing the basic moral commitments of the community. It is relatively independent from the substance of any of these commitments in particular; instead, it is based on the moral authority of constitutions stated in abstract. Bobbitt provides a succinct definition: 'What is needed in judge's chambers is the same reasoning from the constitutional ethos that produced the first Bill of Rights'.[39] Such reasoning is equally applicable to any constitutional system that contains a bill of rights and shares the basic commitment to government limited by law. However, this kind of reasoning is more constrained than ordinary moral reasoning: it is curbed by the idea of the purpose of a constitution. It is also limited in its reach as it is indeterminate and does not offer clear answers to moral problems.

Particular constitutional identity arises from the concrete constitutional spirit or tradition, and refers to the specific constitutional experience of the community in question. It proceeds from the historical heritage of a society that is ruled by a constitution. Particular constitutional identity itself may favor more universalistic values such as dignity, equality, and liberty, support more parochial understandings of these values, or even celebrate specificities of the particular community.[40] All these perspectives fall into the category of particular constitutional identity, for they locate the source of value in the

[39] Bobbitt, *Constitutional Fate: Theory of the Constitution* (n 26) 150.

[40] Often the orientation of the particular constitutional identity will be visible from the constitutional text or its preamble. For some examples see Gary J Jacobsohn, 'Constitutional Values and Principles' in Michel Rosenfeld and Andras Sajo (eds), *The Oxford Handbook of Comparative Constitutional Law* (Oxford University Press 2012) 778–79.

specific spirit of the constitution and its interpretation over time in a multitude of practices. Among other things, particular constitutional identity explains why constitutional rights differ between jurisdictions, and why any universal mechanism of moral reasoning tells us little about the outcomes of legal cases, even under the circumstances of strong indeterminacy.

To understand the distinction between particular and general constitutional identity, it is apposite to analyse the patterns of judicial reasoning in comparative constitutional law. The focus is on cases that represent distinct constitutional cultures but nonetheless exemplify similar approaches to the argument from constitutional identity: the United States, South Africa, and Germany. Differences between the selected systems are significant enough to enable some general insights into the role of constitutional identity in judicial reasoning. In determining the content of constitutional identity, the Supreme Court of the United States draws upon the rich and long constitutional history, the Constitutional Court of South Africa builds upon the novel and explicitly transformative ethos of its constitutional system, and the German Constitutional Court—being in the middle between these two opposites—develops its views from the perspective of well-established but still broadly reformative constitutional practices. All these constitutional systems have distinct traditions and consequently differ in the way they understand their own particular constitutional identity. At the same time, they exhibit similarities when it comes to general constitutional identity and the way in which they understand the value of constitutional governance.

2.3.1 United States

The two dimensions of constitutional identity depart from a similar premise. There is most often no explicit textual basis for the judgment of the court, and the court expounds a concept from the constitution which has a strong ethical dimension. This sets the stage for a judicial ethical judgment. The source of value that grounds such judgment is in some way connected with the fact that the community is governed by a constitution. The argument from particular constitutional identity locates the value in the spirit of a specific constitutional tradition, and the argument from general constitutional identity focuses on the value of constitutional government as such.

We can illustrate the role of particular constitutional identity with an example. For instance, what explains US jurisprudence in the affirmative action cases is not the reasoning from universal moral principles, but a specific history of segregation that makes the Supreme Court wary of any racially-based distinctions. The particular ethics of the American constitutional order preserves liberal values of merit and competition and a unitary vision of citizenship. However, this vision is not based on constitutional text or intentions of constitution-framers, nor is it—at least initially—supported with clear precedents. Instead, it is fixed by reference to a constitutional tradition that is marked by a specific understanding of equality.

The equal protection clause of the American Constitution prescribes that a state cannot 'deny to any person within its jurisdiction the equal protection of the laws'.[41] It has long been recognized that interpretation of this clause demands a moral judgment and purposive approach to interpretation. In the first judgment that interpreted the 14th Amendment, the court proclaimed that 'in any fair and just construction of any section or phrase of these [Reconstruction] amendments, it is necessary to look to the purpose which we have said was the pervading spirit of them all, the evil which they were designed to remedy'.[42] In judicial practice, this 'fair and just reconstruction' has often proceeded from a specific history of attempts to establish equal treatment of different segments of American society, and has been connected to the 'spirit' of a number of judicial decisions, legislative acts, and political judgments that have arisen around the 14th Amendment. The constitution is silent on affirmative action, and interpretations of the amendment in this context have typically relied on deep commitments inferred from layers of opinions that are best understood as constitutive parts of particular constitutional identity.

A prominent part of that identity has been the idea that the American constitution is 'colour-blind'. This notion first appeared in Justice Harlan's lone dissent in *Plessy v Ferguson*, where it served to counter racial segregation under the 'separate but equal' doctrine.[43] However—notwithstanding its initial purpose—it has over time become a part of the way in which the American constitutional community understands itself and consequently an important element of the judicial approach to racial discrimination. Once a vehicle of struggle against racial oppression, it has eventually made all racial distinctions suspect from the constitutional point of view. This has had immense consequences for the way in which the Supreme Court understands affirmative action.

An example of such colour-blind approach is Justice Powell's opinion in *Bakke*.[44] The question in this case was whether an affirmative action program that reserved some places for disadvantaged students—including racial minorities—was constitutional. Justice Powel recognized that the equal protection clause from the constitution was 'majestic in its sweep' and 'susceptible of varying interpretations'.[45] However, he found guidance in a particular constitutional history of American society. Justice Powell proceeded from

[41] 14th Amendment to the US Constitution, Section 1.

[42] *Slaughterhouse Cases* 83 US 36 (1873) 72.

[43] *Plessy v Ferguson* 163 US 537 (1896) 559 (Harlan).

[44] *Regents of the University of California v Bakke* 438 US 265 (1978).

[45] ibid 284 (Powell).

the idea that colour-blindness of the constitution had become an accepted way to resolve ethical dilemmas in the domain of equality, and he consequently argued that the notion of equality involves rights of persons and not of groups. The relevant perspective to support this conclusion was to be found in the specific evaluative commitments rooted in constitutional history: 'The clock of our liberties, however, cannot be turned back to 1868. It is far too late to argue that the guarantee of equal protection to all persons permits the recognition of special wards entitled to a degree of protection greater than that accorded others'.[46] As a consequence, Powell found that the government carried the burden of meeting the most stringent test when treating people differently on the basis of race: under the 'strict scrutiny' analysis the government must show that classifications based on race are 'narrowly tailored measures that further compelling governmental interests'.[47] On the grounds of this test, Justice Powell declared in *Bakke* that strict quota systems based on race were unconstitutional,[48] and this reading was later upheld in *Gratz v Bollinger* and *Grutter v Bollinger*.[49] The presumption was established that affirmative action is an aberration from the principle of equality, hence discriminatory unless the opposite is proven.[50]

The approach to affirmative action in the US is specific: it differs from other jurisdictions and international documents.[51] At the same time, it is embedded in the spirit of American constitutional practice rather than in any particular constitutional clause or precedent. There is nothing much in the text of the constitution or in doctrines (at least prior to *Gratz* and *Grutter*) that would compel such understanding of equality. To the contrary, there is still a debate on the bench whether the constitutional ethos of the American polity demands the opposite: a substantive notion of equality that would entail more leeway for affirmative action measures. Justice Breyer, dissenting in *Parents Involved in Community Schools v Seattle School District*, held that the particular constitutional ethos of the American constitution actually implies the constitutionality of affirmative action measures:

> In this Court's finest hour, *Brown v. Board of Education* challenged this history [of racial divisions] and helped to change it. For *Brown* held out a promise. It

[46] ibid 295 (Powell), references omitted.

[47] *Adarand Constructors Inc v Peña* 515 US 200, (1995) 227 (O'Connor).

[48] There is significant controversy about the reach of Powell J's conclusions in *Bakke*, as there was no controlling opinion in the case. See *Regents of the University of California v Bakke* (n 44).

[49] *Gratz v Bollinger* 539 US 244 (2003); *Grutter v Bollinger* 539 US 306 (2003).

[50] In the field of education, for instance, legitimate governmental interests for affirmative action include only past discrimination and diversity of educational context. See eg *Parents Involved in Community Schools v Seattle School District No 1* 551 US 701 (2007).

[51] See eg *Minister of Finance and Another v Van Heerden* 2004 (6) SA 121 or art 4 of the Convention on the Elimination of all Forms of Discrimination against Women of 1979.

was a promise embodied in three Amendments designed to make citizens of slaves. It was the promise of true racial equality—not as a matter of fine words on paper, but as a matter of everyday life in the Nation's cities and schools. It was about the nature of a democracy that must work for all Americans. It sought one law, one Nation, one people, not simply as a matter of legal principle but in terms of how we actually live.[52]

Even though the interpretation of particular constitutional identity is disputed, there is agreement that it does contain the answer. When Breyer and other justices ask 'what of the long history and moral vision that the Fourteenth Amendment itself embodies?',[53] they bring two distinct features of particular constitutional identity together—they see the ethical judgment of the court as being based on a unique and historically embedded constitutional experience. They do not find the solution in current moral opinions or universal morality: the 'moral vision' and source of value they refer to is the specific ethos of the American constitution.

This makes the response to the problem of racial segregation distinctively American. It took long enough for the Supreme Court to recognize formal equality in *Brown v the Board of Education*,[54] and it is perhaps this victory that the court is trying to preserve today by not liberalizing affirmative action. The notion of equality established in the Supreme Court case law has become—for better or worse—a part of the American constitutional identity. Although subject to different interpretations, such as the one pursued by Justice Breyer, it is still distinct from the identity of other constitutional systems.

But the argument from constitutional identity does not always rely on particular constitutional experiences of a constitutional community. In its other form, this argument may depart from local constitutional traditions and expand into a more universalistic approach that seeks to uncover certain principles that (ought to) apply under any constitutional framework. This approach is most visible when courts try to understand the value of having a constitution as such. An obvious example from the American constitutional tradition is *Marbury v Madison*,[55] the decision that established judicial review of legislation in the US, and that was consequently regarded as a historical foundation of the institution of judicial review in constitutional democracies. The case concerned the ability of the new president to overturn the judicial appointments of a previous president by not delivering already issued commissions. In the course of the case, the court had to resolve some fundamental constitutional questions about the limits of the

[52] *Parents Involved in Community Schools v Seattle School District No 1* (n 50) (Breyer). [53] ibid.

[54] *Brown v Board of Education of Topeka* 347 US 483 (1954). [55] *Marbury v Madison* 5 US 137 (1803).

executive power, the judicial role in policing the separation of powers principle, and—ultimately—the very purpose of the constitution.

The court first considered whether, if there is a violation of a right, the court ought to afford a remedy. The court took this question to entail a general inquiry about the basic principles of the rule of law and about the nature of constitutional government. It proceeded from the idea that the United States government is a 'government of laws, and not of men',[56] but it did not understand this question as a purely local one, to be resolved by virtue of the specific wording of constitutional provisions or intentions of constitution framers. Instead, this question was to be analysed in light of constitutional fundamentals that builds upon but also transcends the local constitutional experience. The court found that '[t]he very essence of civil liberty certainly consists in the right of every individual to claim the protection of the laws whenever he receives an injury'.[57] To determine this, the court did not look into precedents and domestic constitutional provisions, but took cue from constitutional practices of Great Britain and works of William Blackstone.[58]

Upon finding that every right must have a remedy in other constitutional systems, the court concluded that the government under the rule of law would 'cease to deserve this high appellation if laws furnish no remedy of a vested legal right'.[59] While the outlook of the court was not local, the matter was one of identity and self-perception: the court aimed to explain how a constitutional community ought to understand itself in light of its commitment to constitutional government. Justice Marshall, for example, did not want to allow that 'obloquy' be 'cast on jurisprudence of our country' by denying redress in case of rights violations.[60] The very nature of constitutional government—according to him—incorporated the idea of judicial protection of rights.

In the course of the case, the court also had to determine how it should treat an act of Congress that contradicts the Constitution. The American Constitution did not explicitly authorize judicial review of legislation. The court developed a completely new instrument of judicial review based on its reading of the central building blocks of constitutionalism. The starting idea is that the source of constitutional authority is to be found in the principle of self-government of the people who establish fundamental constitutional principles that—in their view—'most conduce to their own happiness'.[61] This principle is tied to a sense of identity and contingent attitudes that a constitution creates: Justice Marshall argued that if the court were not able to give effect to these constitutional principles it would betray the expectations of the people who view written constitutions with 'reverence'.[62] But much

[56] ibid 165. [57] ibid. [58] ibid 163–69. [59] ibid 165. [60] ibid. [61] ibid 178.
[62] ibid 180.

more prominently, the court's argument derived its force from the mere existence of a written constitution. While the court did also rely on textual arguments, hypothetical intentions of constitution-framers, and assumed attitudes of people that chose to be bound by the constitution,[63] the gist of court's analysis was based on its ideas about the kind of commitment that followed from having a written constitution in general.

In court's opinion, judicial review of legislation is a logical consequence of the fact that the constitution is entrenched and that its purpose is to limit the government. Justice Marshall asks: 'To what purpose are powers limited, and to what purpose is that limitation committed to writing; if these limits may, at any time, be passed by those intended to be restrained?'[64] His conclusions about judicial review are far-reaching and not limited to the American constitution. According to Justice Marshall, any written constitution would have such property:

> Those then who controvert the principle that the constitution is to be considered, in court, as a paramount law, are reduced to the necessity of maintaining that courts must close their eyes on the constitution, and see only the law. This doctrine would subvert the very foundation of *all written constitutions*.[65]

The reason for the judgment is not (only) the morality grounded in the specific American circumstances, but the moral purpose of constitutionalism. On the one hand, the court must hear individual cases, and on the other, it cannot disregard the constitution as the expression of the supreme will of the people. So if a piece of legislation is to be given legal force despite its incongruence with a constitution, 'then written constitutions are absurd attempts on the part of the people to limit a power in its own nature illimitable'.[66] And if the merit of Justice Marshall's argument is to be measured by its acceptance in other constitutional systems, then his reasoning is truly universal: today, there are no entrenched constitutions without some form of judicial review.[67]

But apart from being universal or general, the moral reasoning applied here is also constitutional. It is derived from the perspective of having a constitution and not from general moral reasons. To sustain the judicial review afresh without there being an entrenched constitution would require many more arguments. The form of argument from general constitutional identity is neither completely embedded in existing moral attitudes, nor does it follow from universal moral principles that perhaps ought to govern any form of political community.

[63] ibid 174–80. [64] ibid 176. [65] ibid 178 (emphasis added). [66] ibid 177.

[67] See eg the discussion in ch 4 on the influence of *Marbury v Madison* for the establishment of constitutional review in Israel.

The concept of constitutional identity has two dimensions. Particular constitutional identity is close to the experiences of the people but at the same time does not refer directly to public opinions and sentiments. Instead, it is based on more constant evaluative commitments inferred from a host of constitutional practices. General constitutional identity is attached to certain values that are a consequence of the fact that community has a constitution. It is therefore more universal in aspiration and opens a space for the idea that a reflection upon fundamental values of constitutionalism may lead to similar conclusions in different constitutional systems.

2.3.2 South Africa

Similar conclusions follow from the analysis of constitutional practice in South Africa. While the South African constitutional court is famous for its cosmopolitan outlook, it quite often relies on the specific constitutional spirit and local constitutional values to support its moral judgments. Its case law reveals two important features of particular constitutional identity: on the one hand, the reliance on local values is distinct from reliance on public opinions, as it may go against and invalidate legislation that conveys such opinions; on the other hand, it does not proceed from specific constitutional provisions, but from evaluative attitudes that arise in the community and express the spirit of the constitution. The fundamental idea is that constitutional practices are the embodiment and source of the most important values of the constitutional community.

Soon after its inception, the Constitutional Court of South Africa asserted that its authority rests, among other things, on a specific constitutional identity. The first articulation of this vision of constitutional values was in *Makwanyane*, a case involving invalidation of the Criminal Procedure Act that provided for the death sentence.[68] The question of the death penalty was intentionally left out of the constitution, as there was no consensus about it at the time of drafting. The court's reasoning is predominantly ethical, as there was no precedent, original intent (apart from avoidance of the issue), or textual support for deciding either way. The court nevertheless found that the death penalty violated the prohibition of 'cruel, inhuman or degrading treatment or punishment', against public opinion that was supportive of it.[69] As in other cases of ethical arguments, the use of moral concepts in the constitution and the lack of previous precedents and doctrines was perceived as an invitation for the court to make a moral judgment. But the court did not ground its judgment in universal moral principles. Most justices instead underlined the specific constitutional ethos of the South African community.

[68] *S v Makwanyane and Another* (n 4).

[69] ibid para 146 (Chaskalson).

The role of particular constitutional identity is best explained in Justice Mahomed's opinion:

> All Constitutions seek to articulate, with differing degrees of intensity and detail, the shared aspirations of a nation; the values which bind its people, and which discipline its government and its national institutions; the basic premises upon which judicial, legislative and executive power is to be wielded; the constitutional limits and the conditions upon which that power is to be exercised; the national ethos which defines and regulates that exercise; and the moral and ethical direction which that nation has identified for its future. In some countries, the Constitution only formalizes, in a legal instrument, a historical consensus of values and aspirations evolved incrementally from a stable and unbroken past to accommodate the needs of the future. The South African Constitution is different: it retains from the past only what is defensible and represents a decisive break from, and a ringing rejection of, that part of the past which is disgracefully racist, authoritarian, insular, and repressive and a vigorous identification of and commitment to a democratic, universalistic, caring and aspirationally egalitarian ethos, expressly articulated in the Constitution.[70]

Justice Mahomed raises at least two important points. First, he sees the constitution as the embodiment of certain values and aspirational ideals to be protected by the court. This understanding of the constitution suggests that its interpretation will often involve ethical arguments. Second, and more importantly, these values articulate a specific ethos of each nation and may differ from one constitutional system to the other. For Mahomed, the task of the court is to decide on the constitutionality of capital punishment against the 'historical background and ethos'[71] of the South African constitution. In other words, even when constitution is silent on a certain matter the court ought to uphold its spirit, and this spirit is to be found in the specific constitutional commitments and experiences. These commitments and experiences are not relevant because of their universalistic aspiration, but because they are embedded in the local constitutional ethos.

Justice Mahomed thus locates the source of value in the particular constitutional identity which expresses deep evaluative commitments of the constitutional community. This approach unsurprisingly expands into reliance on culturally entrenched moral attitudes to illuminate the contours of constitutional values. For example, Justice Mokgoro—together with many others—grounds its moral judgment in the native concept of 'ubuntu', defined as 'humanness' or 'group solidarity'.[72] In her view, 'when ... courts promote the underlying values of an open and democratic society ... they should recognize that indigenous South African values are not always irrelevant or unrelated to this task'[73] but they can 'form a basis upon which to

[70] ibid para 262 (Mahomed).
[71] ibid para 264 (Mahomed).
[72] ibid para 308 (Mokgoro).
[73] ibid para 300 (Mokgoro).

develop South African human rights jurisprudence'.[74] Mahomed similarly understands 'ubuntu' as an ideal which is able to release 'moral energies' necessary to establish a constitutional order based on the respect for human rights.[75] What Mokgoro and Mahomed try to underline is that the values from the constitution—even if they represent a sharp break with the past—may be shared by the constitutional community; the task of the court is to draw on these values to give more substance to constitutional provisions. To understand the particular constitutional identity, the court will often have to look outside of constitutional practices and have a sense of culturally embedded values of the community. However, this does not mean that the court must follow public opinion.[76] There is a fine balance it seems, when it comes to particular constitutional identity, between relying on deeper commitments that support the values enshrined in the constitution, and succumbing to moral opinions of the day.

But constitutional specificities are often combined with a more general vision of what a constitution should be about, which is relatively independent of the local context. For example, in *Makwanyane*, Justice Ackermann developed his argument from the concept of 'constitutional state' used in the preamble to the constitution. This concept describes the 'new order' to be established by the constitution as a supreme law. At the bottom of the notion of constitutional state, in Ackermann's view, is a commitment to the value of equality.[77] In contrast to particular constitutional identity, which is distilled from the contingently shared evaluative commitments connected to the constitution, the notion of constitutional state infuses judicial analysis with the ideas of reason and universality and detaches judicial reasoning from local experiences. The idea of constitutional state—in Ackermann's view—places importance on 'reason and justification' when rights are being limited, and demands that 'state action must be ... capable of being analyzed and justified rationally'.[78] The implicit universalism of this conception of constitutional state is also visible in Justice Mokgoro's opinion: she argues that the new constitutional order of South African society—in virtue of the fact that its constitution is 'value-based'—enshrines ideals that go beyond the specificities of South African experiences and traditions, and 'commits the state to base the worth of human beings on the ideal values espoused by open democratic societies the world over'.[79] General constitutional identity proceeds from the idea that the constitution as a supreme law commits the society to a distinct approach to moral questions.

The notion of equality is often considered to be central to general constitutional identity. For example, in a case regarding gay marriage, *Minister of*

[74] ibid para 307 (Mokgoro).
[75] ibid para 263 (Mahomed).
[76] See eg ibid para 255 (Madala).
[77] ibid para 155 (Ackermann).
[78] ibid para 156 (Ackermann).
[79] ibid para 313 (Mokgoro).

Home Affairs v Fourie, the South African Constitutional Court used the idea of the moral purpose of a constitution to elucidate the concept of equality. The question was whether a lack of provision that would enable gay couples to marry violated the equal protection clause of the South African Constitution and unfairly discriminated against homosexuals on the basis of their sexual orientation. The decision of the court starts with the observation that the bill of rights contains no general right to marry. The reason for this, Justice Sachs observes, is that marriage was unsuitable for constitutional definition as to avoid 'the questions that relate to history, culture and special circumstances of each society'.[80] For him, this issue must be separated from specific communal experiences, and instead, needs to be addressed from a detached point of view. Sachs finds the critical perspective—from which he can dispose with the particular and contingent moral attitudes—in the protection of minorities as the general purpose of the constitution:

> the fact that the law today embodies conventional majoritarian views in no way mitigates its discriminatory impact. It is precisely those groups that cannot count on popular support and strong representation in the legislature that have a claim to vindicate their fundamental rights through application of the Bill of Rights.[81]

He continues the same thought later on:

> Majoritarian opinion can often be harsh to minorities that exist outside the mainstream. It is precisely the function of the Constitution and the law to step in and counteract rather than reinforce unfair discrimination against a minority . . . The objective of the Constitution is to allow different concepts about the nature of human existence to inhabit the same public realm . . .[82]

The judgment was based on a general purpose of a constitution. After an extensive analysis of several other arguments, the court found that both equality and dignity clauses of the South African Constitution had been violated and ordered the Parliament to enact legislation that would enable homosexual couples to marry. There was little support for this conclusion in the text or precedent. The court interpreted ethical concepts—such as equality and dignity—in light of the fact that minorities ought to be protected in a constitutional framework that contains a bill of rights.

In South Africa—similarly to the United States—particular constitutional identity is based on a set of values shared in the constitutional community, that are at the same time capable of overturning popular moral opinions. General constitutional identity is more universal in aspiration and invokes the notions of rationality, reasonableness, and taking different perspectives

[80] *Minister of Home Affairs and Another v Fourie and Another* (n 5) para 47.

[81] ibid para 74.

[82] ibid paras 94–95.

into account. However—instead of directly relying on the idea of universal and mind-independent moral reasons—it proceeds from a specific perspective of a community governed by a constitution. Constitutional identity is in this sense different from both current moral opinions and ideal morality.

2.3.3 *Germany*

While the constitutional context in Germany is quite different—most notably because it participates in larger European legal structures—the contours of the two dimensions of constitutional identity are similar. Particular constitutional identity aims to preserve the essential, and sometimes idiosyncratic, constitutional values of German constitutional order; general constitutional identity reaches for more universal evaluative sensibilities that hypothetically pertain to any system of constitutional government. In a number of decisions—often as a reaction to competing claims of constitutional authority coming from the Court of Justice of the European Union (CJEU)—the German Constitutional Court (FCC) has articulated its vision of constitutional identity in both its particular and general form. On the one hand, it has protected the inviolable core of constitutional values that are constitutive of specifically German constitutional identity. On the other, it has requested that the EU legal order complies with certain general principles that ought to support its claims of supreme constitutional authority.

The concept of particular constitutional identity has for example played a key role in the FCC's judgment on the constitutionality of the Lisbon Treaty.[83] In this decision, the court set the foundations of the 'identity review' under which it examines whether EU law violates the core of German constitutional identity inferred from the Article 79(3) of the constitution. This article—the so-called 'eternity clause'—prohibits the amendment of certain fundamental and inviolable constitutional principles, including human dignity and democratic character of German constitutional order. These basic principles of German constitutional identity—such as 'democracy, the rule of law, the principle of the social state, the republic, the federal state, as well as the substance of elementary fundamental rights indispensable for the respect of human dignity'[84]—are not entirely unique to German constitutional system. But they are often interpreted in a particular way in German constitutional practice. Such interpretations do not immediately follow from the text of the constitution, but from the gist of constitutional tradition as it develops over time.[85]

[83] *Lisbon Judgment* (2009) 2 BvE 2/08. [84] ibid para 217.

[85] In the same vein, the FCC has established that the judgments of the European Court of Human Rights (ECtHR) need to be incorporated in accordance with the standards pertinent to the domestic

We can focus on the example of human dignity to illustrate this. The FCC has shown that it is prepared to safeguard its specific interpretation of dignity as a part of inviolable constitutional identity. For example, the court resorted to the identity review in a case concerning the European Arrest Warrant,[86] where it did not allow for an extradition of a US citizen to Italy where he was sentenced in absentia because he would not be allowed to have an evidentiary hearing in the appeals proceeding. The court found that this would violate human dignity, because it would not respect the basic fairness of the criminal process. This principle is not derived from the dignity clause by virtue of the strict reading of the constitution, but by virtue of an application of the sense and spirit of German constitutional tradition.

This tradition and the peculiar understanding of human dignity emerged as a consequence of atrocities committed during the Second World War in Germany. The German constitution (Basic Law) of 1949 made constitutional rights foundational in the constitutional order. Unlike the Weimar constitution, which has been widely regarded as responsible for the instability of political institutions that eased Hitler's rise to power and subsequent termination of the constitutional order itself, the primary purpose of the new constitution was to establish a robust system of rights and to stabilize political institutions.[87] At the apex of that order stands Article 1 of the constitution as a reminder that human beings must never again be denied their dignity: 'Human dignity shall be inviolable'.

This simple clause has been transformed through the jurisprudence of the FCC to one of the most far-reaching and yet perplexing doctrines. Human dignity has been treated as an absolute value, which—once implicated in a case—trumps all other concerns or interests that could be balanced. While no comprehensive treatment of the concept of dignity can be found in the FCC's jurisprudence, one particular interpretation has been dominant: dignity entails 'treating persons as ends and not as means to an end'.[88] This understanding of dignity expresses the first principle of German constitutional identity. Its roots are to be found in a collective conscience that strives to prevent persons being treated as means, as was the case during the Second World War. Hence, even dignity—as one of the most universal

constitutional system. See eg *Preventive Detention Case* (2011) 2 BvR 2365/09 part C.I.f. and *Adoption and Custody Case* (2004) BvR 1481/04 para 35.

[86] *European Arrest Warrant Case II* (2015) 2 BvR 2735/14.

[87] See more in Donald P Kommers, 'Germany: Balancing Rights and Duties' in Jeffrey Goldsworthy (ed), *Interpreting Constitutions: A Comparative Study* (Oxford University Press 2007).

[88] See Kai Möller, 'On Treating Persons as Ends: The German Aviation Security Act, Human Dignity, and the Federal Constitutional Court' [2006] Public Law 457.

moral concepts—may obtain a very specific understanding in different constitutional systems.[89]

The application of this interpretation of dignity has had profound consequences on the moral choices the FCC makes. For example, in the *Aviation Security* case,[90] the court ruled that the act, which provided for the possibility of shooting-down airplanes that have been hijacked with a purpose of using them as weapons, violated dignity. The act regulated the situation analogous to the 'trolley problem': succinctly put, the question is whether it is morally justified to sacrifice fewer lives to save more, and, if yes, under which circumstances. The FCC answered the question in the following way: it is justified to sacrifice lives to save more only in the case when terrorists are alone on the plane, for they have taken the responsibility for what could happen; otherwise, it is never justified.[91]

The message of the decision is clear—human dignity combined with the right to life establishes a deontological principle that does not give way to any other concern. The thrust of the argument is the following:

> [Shooting down the plane] ignores the status of the persons affected as subjects endowed with dignity and inalienable rights. Their death becomes a means to save others, they are treated as objects and at the same time deprived of their rights; with their lives being disposed of unilaterally by the state, the persons on board of the aircraft, who, as victims, are themselves in need of protection, are denied the value which is inherent to every human being for her own sake.[92]

There are no exceptions to this rule and no balancing of interests, not even in the case when it is clear that the lives of the passengers are already lost.[93] What explains this unique understanding of dignity is the heritage of the Second World War, and the specific constitutional identity that emanates from it. The FCC has developed a multitude of dignity doctrines and interpretations in its practice and has demonstrated willingness to protect them both internally and externally as a part of the particular constitutional identity.

At the same time, the FCC has used the idea of general constitutional identity to explain its position as to the CJEU's claims of constitutional supremacy. In the famous *Solange I* case, the court found that the transfer of powers to the EU must not amend the 'basic structure of the constitution, which forms the basis of its identity', including the fundamental rights which are

89 See more in Christopher McCrudden, 'Human Dignity and Judicial Interpretation of Human Rights' (2008) 19 European Journal of International Law 655.

90 *Aviation Security Case* (2006) 115 BVerfGE 118.

91 ibid.

92 ibid para 124.

93 Needless to say, the consequences of this understanding of dignity could be immense; for example, it would follow that any order in a defensive war that could jeopardize military personnel's lives would entail treating them as a means to an end (to save other lives).

its 'inalienable essential feature'.[94] It found that the European Community lacked 'a democratically elected parliament' and 'a codified catalogue of fundamental rights', which consequently undermined its supremacy claims.[95] In other words, the FCC demanded that claims of supremacy be backed in certain general—and perhaps even universally applicable—features of constitutional authority. The confirmation of this reading came in the *Solange II* case, where the court declared that it would not review the community legislation as long as it secures fundamental rights in 'substantively similar' manner.[96] The FCC came to a position that there are certain general principles that are capable of establishing constitutional authority which need not fully replicate its domestic constitutional commitments, but nonetheless ought to be applied in any constitutional framework that deserves to be respected and obeyed.

We have seen that in South Africa the argument from general constitutional identity sometimes takes a form of presumption in favor of minorities. A similar notion applies in Germany. For example, in a case concerning the display of crosses and crucifixes in classrooms which was made obligatory by a regulation of the state of Bavaria, the court was faced with a quintessential constitutional dilemma where competing constitutional values point to different directions.[97] On the one hand, there was a positive freedom of the majority of the population to preserve their religion, identity, and culture; and, on the other, the negative freedom of the minority to choose the religious and philosophical setting for the education of their children. Article 135 of the Bavarian constitution—supported by a popular referendum—stated: 'In [public elementary schools] pupils shall be taught and brought up in accordance with the principles of the Christian confessions'.[98] Christian religion was thus made a part of the constitutional identity of the state of Bavaria; moreover, such constitutional identity expressed the moral sentiments of the majority of Bavarian citizens who voted in the referendum.

The FCC refused to defer to such a particularistic conception of constitutional ethics; conversely, it relied on reasoning that could generally apply in systems that are committed to constitutionalism. At its core was an understanding of the boundaries of legitimate authority of the state. The court distinguished between the encounters with religious symbols in everyday life which are not 'inescapable' and the public display of such symbols 'based on a compulsion enforceable where necessary through sanctions'.[99] In the

94 *Internationale Handelsgesellschaft von Einfuhr- und Vorratsstelle für Getreide und Futtermittel* (1974) 37 BVerfGE 271, [1974] CMLR 540 paras 22 and 23.

95 ibid para 23.

96 *Re Wünsche Handelsgesellschaft* (1986) 73 BVerfGE 339, [1987] CMLR 225 para 48.

97 *Kruzifix-decision* (1995) 93 BVerfGE 1.

98 Act amending art 135 of the Constitution of the Free State of Bavaria of 22 July 1968 (GVBl 238).

99 *Kruzifix-decision* (n 97) para C.II.2.a.

concluding paragraph, the FCC expressed its vision of the purpose of constitutional rights: 'The conflict arising cannot be resolved according to the majority principle, for the fundamental right to religious freedom is specifically aimed in a special degree at protecting minorities'.[100] The court found that the purpose of the constitution was to establish safeguards against domination over minorities; consequently, it declared the Bavarian regulation null and void.

To conclude, constitutional identity is a complex concept: one the one hand, it is rooted in local constitutional commitments and, on the other, it presupposes more general constitutional ideals that are detached from the specificities of the concrete constitutional setting. Both dimensions of constitutional identity can go against current moral opinions; at the same time, they do not amount to claims about universal moral principles that ought to apply irrespectively of constitutional context. Let us see how we can make sense of constitutional identity as a source of value.

2.4 VALUE OF CONSTITUTIONAL IDENTITY

Comparative constitutional practice reveals several tendencies. Courts in the United States, South Africa, and Germany understand constitutional identity as generating both specific answers to moral problems based on a particular constitutional tradition, and more general answers about the fundamentals of political authority that presumably apply in all political systems that deserve to be called constitutional. But—while all these courts use the same form of argument—they often reach diverse conclusions. Ethical concepts from the constitution may be understood differently depending on the particular constitutional identity that is accepted in any given constitutional community: for example, the fact that different courts interpret the notion of equality need not mean that they will reach similar judgments. General constitutional identity also does not command a precise outcome of a constitutional decision. It may encourage courts to give more weight to certain positions—such as protection of minorities—but it does not fully specify moral answers to constitutional problems.

Two questions arise at this point. The first one concerns the ethical character of the argument from constitutional identity. The argument from constitutional identity belongs to the range of argumentative options and strategies that the courts have at their disposal as a matter of more or less established practice amongst the most senior legal officials. But although its form is legal, the law does not determine its content. The argument from constitutional identity refers to tendencies, views, and ideas—sometimes

[100] ibid C.II.3.b.

described as the 'spirit' of constitution—which aim to give guidance to a court that is making a moral judgment but do not follow from specific constitutional provisions, legislative enactments, or precedents.

The courts use the argument from constitutional identity to give further content to the ethical concepts from the constitution. These concepts, for example, include equality, dignity, and cruel, inhuman, or degrading treatment or punishment, but also notions that pertain to the value of constitutional government, such as the rule of law, democracy, and fundamental rights. There is most often no clear and settled law that would determine the meaning of these concepts, and the courts—in addition—do not even aim for an interpretation that would discern the textual meaning of legal provisions or intentions of constitution-makers, legislators, and other courts. Instead, they aspire to offer innovative interpretations that would settle constitutional questions in a morally appropriate manner. In so doing, they seek to discern the gist of existing constitutional tradition but without relying on any legal material in particular; they also try to infer constitutional principles from the fact that the society is governed by the constitution and by reference to the purposes and commitments that characterize any constitutional framework. The argument from constitutional identity thus exhibits the paradigmatic elements of all ethical arguments: the entrenchment in legal practice combined with the aim of moral evaluation that transcends any particular previous legal decision.

The second question pertains to the relevance of metaethics for understanding the value of constitutional identity. We have seen that metaethical questions figure prominently in some of the previous attempts to account for the value of constitutional identity. And—as I shall explain—a metaethical explanation of ethical arguments better accounts for the entirety of constitutional ethics and elucidates the connections between different forms of ethical arguments. But even if the argument from constitutional identity is an ethical argument, there could be a compelling normative reason to use constitutional identity as a ground for constitutional judgment. The argument from constitutional identity appears to be more embedded in existing constitutional practice and is strongly attached to the fact that a society has a constitution. It is then reasonable to assume that its value can be explained by reference to legitimate expectations or collective autonomy of the citizens that are committed to a certain constitutional framework of values. These normative ideas go a long way in accounting for the value of constitutional identity, but they ultimately do not offer a complete explanation.

There are two reasons why legitimate expectations or consistency do not fully explain the normative force of constitutional identity. On the one hand, the use of this argument in practice often goes against these normative ideals. The argument from constitutional identity aims at an innovative interpretation that frequently trumps previous legislative or judicial opinions. While it does proceed from the spirit of the constitution, it further specifies constitutional principles and regularly changes the existing law. For example, the US Supreme Court explained in *Bakke* how equality ought to be understood in the context of affirmative action, without there being a firm previous legal understanding of this problem; it also inferred a completely new power to review legislation in *Marbury v Madison*. In *Makwanyane*, the South African Constitutional Court invalidated the Criminal Procedure Act that provided for the death penalty, and in *Fourie* it quashed the common law definition of marriage. The German Constitutional Court developed its ideas about dignity in a way that is not fully predictable, and introduced the identity review of EU legislation that may potentially bring about more uncertainty into the existing legal framework. Judicial arguments based on constitutional identity may thus go against the presumed expectations and do not always aim at consistency with previous decisions.

On the other hand, legitimate expectations and consistency cannot offer a persuasive normative justification of the argument from constitutional identity. If the judicial use of constitutional identity is at least partly motivated by the moral appropriateness of constitutional judgment—and this is most probably so given the fact that they are interpreting ethical concepts without or against previous law—then consistency may only go so far as a justification. Consistency may be pursued in other ways that would generate more certainty, such as following previous law more closely, but it also must give way if there are good moral reasons to reach a judgment that is inconsistent with expectations based on existing law. Consistency is indifferent about the way in which it is achieved, and constitutional identity—which is subject to disagreement and aims to change or develop existing law—may not be the best way to pursue it.

A potentially more convincing normative explanation of the value of constitutional identity proceeds from the idea that it protects the collective autonomy of citizens and the ability of constitutional community to determine its own destiny. However, some of the problems that arise in relation to consistency apply here as well. Collective autonomy may be expressed in constitutions and legislation. But the argument from constitutional identity is not fixed by a reference to either of these instances in which collective autonomy is exercised. On the one hand—as I have explained—this argument regularly overturns legislation which express current moral opinions of the citizens. On the other, the argument from constitutional identity often does not even aim to discern moral pre-commitments articulated in the constitution as a form of more fundamental exercise of collective autonomy. The actual arguments from constitutional identity discussed in the previous section do not rely on the views of constitution-framers or original textual meaning of constitution. The courts use this form of argument to refer to a host of constitutional practices that transcend any particular expression of public will. This is not to say that the process of constitutional engagement between different institutions and citizens—by virtue of which constitutional identity acquires its content—may not itself be seen as an exercise of collective autonomy. But the difference is in the emphasis. If securing collective autonomy were the essence of this argument we could expect that the courts would give much more weight to constitutional text and legislative opinions when they determine the gist of constitutional identity.

The argument from constitutional identity is best understood as referring to a practice by which constitutional community builds upon already existing and develops new moral solutions to constitutional problems. It does not acquire normative force because of the authority of constitution-making or legislative process, but because constitutional practice is itself seen as a value-generating endeavor in a given community and across generations. This practice both locates and creates moral values. Particular constitutional identity refers to existing moral attitudes that developed in the constitutional community over time without treating any particular exercise of collective autonomy as paramount. General constitutional identity reflects upon fundamental constitutional principles and aspires to change or overcome some of the entrenched moral attitudes, including those that could be seen as clear expressions of collective autonomy.[101]

What then explains the value of constitutional identity? It is treated as a source of value which ought to determine answers to moral questions. But constitutional identity—understood as a source of value—is at the same time neither completely attached to current moral values of a constitutional community nor can it aspire to reveal universal and timeless moral answers that are detached from contingent moral commitments of such a community. This raises metaethical questions. On the one hand, the two elements of constitutional identity are in *tension*. In its particular dimension, constitutional identity denotes local and contingent moral commitments; yet, these commitments are different from the prevailing moral opinions expressed, for example, by the legislature. In its general dimension, constitutional identity involves a process of reflection upon and development of these basic constitutional commitments; yet, it is not premised on a claim that this process reveals mind-independent values but only values that are properly ascribed to a community which is governed by a constitution. If we suppose that moral values are mind-dependent, then why ought we rely on constitutional identity as opposed to moral opinions of the citizens? If we suppose that moral values are mind-independent, then why ought we respect constitutional

[101] See eg ibid.

identity as opposed to objectively true moral answers? On the other hand, the two elements of constitutional identity are *limited*. Particular constitutional identity builds upon contingent evaluative commitments and—when these commitments are not clear—it needs to expand into the argument from common sentiment. General constitutional identity incorporates the idea that reflection could reveal more universal evaluative commitments but—to enable a sufficient critical distance—it needs to expand into the argument from universal reason.

The question is then: can constitutional identity be treated as a self-standing source of value? We have seen that some of the previous accounts—starting from the problem of legitimacy—arrive at the conclusion that constitutional identity is as far as a court should stray from the existing law in order to reach a sound moral judgment. The cases discussed in this chapter also demonstrate that the argument from constitutional identity is often considered to be sufficient for elucidating ethical concepts from the constitution. But if the argument from constitutional identity does not remedy the problem of legitimacy of judicial review, and if it cannot be fully justified on the basis of other normative principles such as consistency or collective autonomy, we need to ask whether it makes sense as an approach to moral judgment. The issue is not whether the argument from constitutional identity has an important place in the greater scheme of constitutional ethics. In fact—as I shall explain later—constitutional identity may indeed be of vital importance for the moral judgment of a court.[102] But given the central role it occupies in judicial practice and the claim that it could be a self-standing ethical argument, we need to inquire whether the vision of moral value that is implicit in the argument from constitutional identity can provide an independent basis of moral judgment. So, the issue is narrower at this point: can the argument from constitutional identity map the process in which moral values may be revealed without resort to other types of ethical arguments? It is to this question that we now turn.

2.4.1 *Particular constitutional identity*

Particular constitutional identity locates the source of value in evaluative commitments of a constitutional community. It does not even aspire to offer moral answers that are potentially true irrespectively of these local commitments. Although their societies may face similar moral problems—such as racial segregation—the courts do not proceed from the idea that the solutions to these problems ought to be the same. Justice Powell argues in *Bakke* that affirmative action measures have to pass the strict scrutiny test not

[102] See ch 6.

because he thinks that this might be the best moral solution to be applied universally, but because he trust that the American constitutional history has already taken a distinct approach to this question and that 'the clock ... cannot be turned back'.[103] When they find that the death penalty constitutes 'cruel, inhuman and degrading treatment', the South African constitutional justices rely on evaluative attitudes ingrained in the transformative ambition of the constitution; they proceed from the specific 'historical background and ethos' of the constitution and do not suggest that the moral direction that the constitution has taken applies to all constitutional systems.[104] The German Constitutional Court protects its own vision of dignity not because it may be mind-independently true but because of the promise of the German constitution that people would never again be 'treated as objects and ... deprived of their rights'.[105] Particular constitutional identity cannot be taken to entail something more than a contingent constitutional vision about some of the most difficult moral questions. And given the vast differences between constitutional identities and their evolution over time it is difficult to see how they could be understood as expressions of mind-independent, timeless, and universal values.

At the same time, particular constitutional identity is not to be confused with popular moral opinions. When they determine the content of evaluative commitments that constitute particular constitutional identity, the courts do not try to discern what people actually consider to be the most appropriate moral solution in a given case. Most often there are no references to popular opinions in judgments based on constitutional identity. The discussion of the moral vision of the 14th Amendment to the US constitution in relation to affirmative action does not take into account public opinions about the way in which racial segregation ought to be tackled. The FCC does not consider public sentiments to discern whether people think that their commitment to human dignity prevents the state from shooting down a plane hijacked by terrorists. The South African Constitutional Court is even more explicit: it deems public opinion irrelevant for the question of whether the death penalty is inhuman or degrading. The argument from particular constitutional identity sees morality as being embedded in evaluative attitudes that evolve under the constitutional framework, but it is not concerned with prevailing moral opinions of the people.

There are several reasons why the argument from particular constitutional identity cannot offer a complete picture of morality that is to be applied in constitutional cases. The first concerns the indeterminacy of this argument.

[103] *Regents of the University of California v Bakke* (n 44) 295 (Powell).

[104] *S v Makwanyane and Another* (n 4) para 264 (Mahomed).

[105] *Aviation Security Case* (n 90) para 124.

Although it may allow the courts to discern some tendencies that may give more weight to certain positions, the argument from particular constitutional identity rarely commands a distinct outcome of a constitutional case. It refers to general principles that can be applied in many different ways and that often cannot give enough substance to judicial moral judgment: for example, in the United States affirmative action cases, the dominant idea is that the constitution is 'colour-blind';[106] in South Africa, the notion that is guiding judicial reasoning about death penalty is that the constitution presents a 'vigorous identification of ... democratic, universalistic, caring and aspirationally egalitarian ethos';[107] and in Germany, the view that grounds the court's judgment on shooting down a plane seized by terrorists is that the state should not deny 'the value which is inherent to every human being for her own sake'.[108] It is not surprising that the argument from particular constitutional identity sometimes does find further support in other culturally shared moral opinions. To acquire substance, particular constitutional identity needs to expand into the domain of actual evaluative attitudes that are embedded in a given constitutional community which need not be strongly connected with its constitutional practices. For example, the motivation for the use of 'ubuntu' in *Makwanyane* comes both from the idea that constitutional identity must be connected to evaluative experiences of the people, and from the ambition to further illuminate unclear commitments arising from constitutional identity.

The point about indeterminacy reveals the second problem with the argument from particular constitutional identity. It effectively distinguishes between two sets of mind-dependent moral attitudes. On the one hand, there are deeper or more authentic attitudes that constitute the core of identity of constitutional community. On the other, there are culturally embedded moral attitudes and moral opinions of the day that are either disregarded or not given the same standing in constitutional adjudication. But the grounds of this distinction and its importance are not entirely clear. Which qualities give the commitments from particular constitutional identity priority over current moral opinions? As I mentioned, it is quite plausible that ordinary moral reasoning gives precedence to deeper or more authentic moral attitudes. But the process can go the other way round once we realize that the principle we accepted clashes with our other moral intuitions. Given the imprecise character of commitments stemming from constitutional identity, the disagreement about their application, and the contingent character of both sets of attitudes, the interaction between them needs to be elucidated.

[106] *Plessy v Ferguson* (n 43) 559 (Harlan).

[107] *S v Makwanyane and Another* (n 4) para 262 (Mahomed).

[108] *Aviation Security Case* (n 90) para 124.

This demands an inquiry into the relationship between the argument from particular constitutional identity and common sentiment. We need to explain why the courts can be justified in preferring one over the other set of evaluative attitudes and what makes the commitments from constitutional identity more fundamental. As I will argue later, the importance of the notion of identity within the moral point of view can justify this distinction.[109] Suffice it to say here that—in contrast to the theories discussed in this chapter—the analysis of ethical arguments must then take a more holistic approach and explain the interaction between different elements of constitutional ethics.

The third issue with the argument from particular constitutional identity is that it treats contingent moral commitments as constitutive of the appropriate moral outlook of a court. Because the normativity of this argument cannot be fully explained by reference to other normative ideas—such as consistency or collective autonomy—it is not clear why the courts should prefer it over 'ideal' morality. If there are mind-independent values, then the argument from constitutional identity may be off-track in relation to these values. We have seen that some of the accounts of constitutional identity retain the possibility that it may clash with and must consequently give way to mind-independent values. If this is the case, the normative significance of contingent and idiosyncratic elements of constitutional identity is questionable: social and psychological facts about deep evaluative commitments of a constitutional community may be wrong in relation to mind-independent moral facts and—if this is the case—they ought to be abandoned. But given the importance of this argument for the moral judgment of a court, this would mean that our constitutional practices are confused and that the courts should be seeking mind-independent, timeless, and universal moral answers to constitutional dilemmas instead of searching for deep commitments constitutive of identity. This makes the argument from particular constitutional identity fundamentally unstable: if moral values are mind-dependent, why not take contingent moral opinions into account, and if they are mind-independent, then what is the relevance of contingent constitutional identity?

2.4.2 *General constitutional identity*

While particular constitutional identity rests on local evaluative commitments and expands into common sentiments, general constitutional identity aspires to offer moral solutions that are more detached from the distinctive characteristics of local constitutional framework and shares certain elements with the argument from universal reason. An important feature of general

[109] See ch 6.

constitutional identity is the claim that certain moral principles follow from the very existence of a constitution. The idea is that constitutions have purposes which need not be consumed by intentions and commitments of the people that enacted or are living under the constitution. These purposes are implicit in the decision to be bound by the constitution but do not refer to actual opinions of the people. By virtue of this argument, the courts may sometimes reach similar conclusions notwithstanding the differences in the specific precepts of particular constitutional identity. For example, the US Supreme Court argues that judicial review of legislation is a commitment that pertains to any constitutional framework, and constitutional courts in Germany and South Africa contend that the very fact that there is a constitution with a bill of rights compels the court to take into consideration the interests and views of different segments of society and to grant minorities special protection. General constitutional identity can also invalidate concrete moral commitments of the people and even their particular constitutional identity, as exemplified by the FCC's decision to declare the Bavarian constitution void even though it has been confirmed in a referendum which expresses moral opinions of the majority of its population.

General constitutional identity is thus more universal in its aspiration. We have seen that the US Supreme Court takes into account British constitutional practices to discern the meaning of the rule of law, that the South African constitutional judges argue that the idea of constitutional state implies certain values which transcend domestic constitutional experiences, and that the German Constitutional Court sees the commitment to democracy and fundamental rights as a precondition of any justified claim of constitutional authority. The universalism of the argument from general constitutional identity also incorporates the notion that taking a distance from local constitutional commitments and occupying a detached viewpoint allows the courts to better understand the value of a constitution as such. This reflection may occur through engagement with solutions to similar problems in other constitutional systems (US), in dialogue with other sites of constitutional authority (Germany), or as a consequence of the demand for rational justification of state's actions (South Africa). The argument from general constitutional identity assumes that the existence of a constitutional framework involves a commitment to reflection and reasoning that may counter overly confident moral attitudes of a constitutional community.

But the question is can general constitutional identity provide a self-sufficient basis for the moral judgment of a court and thus an exclusive foundation of constitutional ethics? The first problem with this idea—similarly to particular constitutional identity—is the inevitable indeterminacy of general constitutional identity. While it does add some weight to judicial arguments and allows the courts to reach moral judgments, it rarely commands unique and specific moral answers to constitutional dilemmas. The US Supreme Court based its argument for the establishment of judicial review on the general constitutional commitment to the rule of law and hierarchy of legal sources, but these principles—for example—do not say anything about the kind of judicial review that is appropriate. The South African Constitutional Court inferred from the general commitment to equality that gay marriages ought to be constitutionally protected, but this does not tell us much about the kinds of minority claims that should be considered justified. When it demanded that the CJEU respects democracy and fundamental rights, the FCC did not and could not—based on the idea of general constitutional identity—specify which conception of democracy ought to be established or which understanding of fundamental rights must be protected. This is not to downplay the importance of the idea that constitutional framework incorporates some widely shared principles that require respect, but to suggest that the court typically cannot reach substantive moral conclusions based on general constitutional identity alone.

The second question is whether we could understand the demands of general constitutional identity as being premised upon universal moral values that are true regardless of specific commitments arising from each constitutional framework. There is in this sense an important connection between a concrete constitutional framework and the argument from general constitutional identity. Although it may be presented as a universal feature of all constitutions, it is not the case that *any* constitutional system will require, for example, equal concern for minorities, respect for fundamental rights, or even less so a robust judicial review. There could be constitutional systems that do not entail these kinds of commitments: to use an obvious example, the South African Constitution is an attempt to overcome a previous constitutional setting that did not share allegiance to the principle of equality and minority protection. Even general constitutional identity—although it does transgress the boundaries of a single constitutional system—cannot be seen as being universally accepted. It is then perhaps misleading to think about general constitutional identity as universal, rather than as simply common given the significant overlap between contingent features of most liberal democratic constitutional systems. In addition, it is not clear that the conclusions arrived at by virtue of the argument from general constitutional identity may be understood as expression of ideal or mind-independent moral values. They are attached to the fact that a society has a constitution which is entrenched, guarantees certain rights, and broadly adheres to a plausible conception of democracy. The argument from general constitutional identity is better understood as a mechanism of development of the existing constitutional self rather than as an expression of universally applicable moral principles. It does probe deeper into contingent evaluative attitudes that can be ascribed to the constitutional community as a whole and may bring additional coherence to the moral outlook of a constitutional community that is constituted by such attitudes, but it is difficult to see how, for instance, establishing a system of robust judicial review can be understood as universal moral duty of any constitutional system.

But even if it is understood as stipulating universal moral principles—the claim that could have some plausibility when it comes to values such as dignity, equality, or the rule of law—general constitutional identity will need to resort to particular constitutional identity in order to give further content to these indeterminate principles. And this content varies across constitutional systems. In South Africa, the understanding of equality stems from general constitutional identity and motivates the argument that minorities ought to be afforded special protection; however, the details of this protection in other constitutional systems—as demonstrated by the example of affirmative action in the US—will often be diverse. The moment general constitutional identity needs to solve more specific constitutional problems it will turn to particular constitutional identity that is historically developed and differs from time to time and place to place. The reflection entailed by the notion of general constitutional identity will need to have a strong foothold in the existing constitutional commitments in the specific community in which these problems arose. So, it will not be able to offer sufficient detachment that could completely overcome some of the entrenched moral views in the constitutional community.

Finally, the transformative potential of reflection based on general constitutional identity is limited compared to a moral decision that would seek greater reflective detachment from contingent moral attitudes of a constitutional community and aim to discover mind-independent moral values. If universality of general constitutional identity does suggest mind-independent quality of the moral answers it generates, it would have to rely on a more robust reflection and expand into the domain of the argument from universal reason. In other words, if there are mind-independent values, general constitutional identity will fail to grasp them on its own. And if this is the case, we must question its normativity. Constitutional identity—in both its particular and general form—seems weak as an independent foundation for a normative judgment of a court if we presuppose that there are true moral answers out there.

2.5 CONCLUSION

This chapter introduced the notion of constitutional ethics, as a set of legally embedded patterns of ethical arguments in constitutional reasoning. While these ethical arguments have legal form, they aim to evaluate morally, rather than to discern the meaning of an authoritative directive. This makes them different from usual legal arguments. But ethical arguments are not ordinary moral arguments either: the specific institutional context in which they arise and their legal entrenchment make them quite different from the arguments we typically use in moral discourse. To understand the dual character of ethical arguments, we need to understand morality from the viewpoint of law. Ethical arguments embed a particular vision of moral value: they locate moral value somewhere in our universe and attach it—for example—to our emotions, reasons, local traditions, or humanity.

The chapter discussed some of the existing theories of ethical arguments which identify the notion of constitutional ethics with constitutional identity. While they rely on the plausible intuition that law constrains ethical arguments, they neglect other elements of constitutional ethics and do not adequately account for their metaethical foundations. These theories neither explain why constitutional identity would be a valid source of value nor how it relates to other ethical arguments. Given the claims about its ability to become an independent foundation of constitutional ethics and its importance in constitutional practice, this chapter also examined the argument from constitutional identity in isolation from other ethical arguments. However—as I have argued—the argument from constitutional identity cannot be disconnected from other types of ethical arguments and needs to be understood as a part of a wider framework of constitutional ethics.

The argument from constitutional identity is underdetermined. Constitutional identity may offer a perspective from which popular moral opinions are assessed and brought into coherence, and could have some legitimating power to the extent that it relies on evaluative commitments that people already accept but might fail to observe in their daily moral practice. But the content of constitutional identity is fluid and imprecise. It does give more substance to ethical concepts from the constitution, but often this is only a tendency that gives additional weight to certain interpretations. For this reason, the argument from constitutional identity needs to find additional support in other types of ethical arguments.

Constitutional identity is also intrinsically connected to other elements of constitutional ethics. The argument from constitutional identity has two dimensions. General constitutional identity assumes that constitutions as such entail certain universally applicable values, while particular constitutional identity proceeds from moral commitments that arise in a specific constitutional community. General constitutional identity aspires to offer more universal moral solutions to constitutional problems but falls short of detachment and reflection that would presumably reveal mind-independent values: it thus expands into the argument from universal reason. Particular constitutional identity is contingent upon constitutional practices of a constitutional community, but it is not as specific as other—more tangible and explicit—moral commitments of that community: it thus expands into the argument from common sentiment.

At the same time, it is not quite clear which conception of value is in the background of the argument from constitutional identity. General constitutional identity seeks a more universal understanding of constitutional values and particular constitutional identity stays embedded in a more parochial interpretation of these values. It is thus already nascent in the discussion of the argument from constitutional identity that there is a problem of locating and accounting for the nature of moral value. Is moral value another mind-dependent social fact that differs from system to system, or is it mind-independent and universal?

This problem will become all the more clear when the argument from common sentiment and the argument from universal reason are discussed. The difference between the two tracks the division between particular and universal understanding of values, and between emotions and reason. These divisions threaten to render constitutional ethics incoherent, as they stem from divergent ideas about the sources of normativity. The task of the next two chapters is to focus on ethical arguments from common sentiment and universal reason and reveal their metaethical foundations. Once this is done, I will go on to reconstruct judicial practice in accordance with a sound understanding of moral value.

3

Common Sentiment

3.1 INTRODUCTION

The purpose of this chapter is to analyse the philosophical foundations of ethical argument in constitutional interpretation which holds that moral sentiments of the people in a particular community constitute the right solution to moral problems; it seeks to reveal the underlying commitments of this type of argument and subject them to critique. The chapter thus contains two sections. The first attempts to sketch the contours and general features of the argument from common sentiment by analysing legal doctrines in three different constitutional systems. The second exposes the argument to philosophical analysis.

The argument from common sentiment looks at existing moral feelings, internal dispositions and psychological tendencies to discover solutions to moral problems. As such, it has at least one obvious advantage: a powerful moral epistemology. It is—most of the time—obvious what we are inclined to do when faced with moral problems, guided by our gut feelings. Moreover, there is nothing metaphysically mysterious in saying that our emotions exist, for we feel them all the time and we are aware of their normative and motivational pull. We need not populate the world with suspicious 'moral facts', whose existence is 'utterly different from anything else in the universe', as Mackie would put it.[1] Therefore, we seem to have an easy answer to both the moral question before us, and to a larger metaphysical problem. But if we are inclined to do something—inflict the death penalty, legalize gay marriages, prohibit abortions—can we just go for it? Is this the *right* thing to do? What else is needed to reach a *moral* decision? Must we analyse, re-evaluate, or justify our initial reactions? What—if anything—does this process entail and does the argument from common sentiment obstruct it?

As we have seen, the argument from common sentiment is not the only type of ethical argument in constitutional reasoning; however, I analyse it separately from other types, as a stand-alone argument. The reason is this.

[1] John L Mackie, *Ethics: Inventing Right and Wrong* (2nd edn, Penguin 1990) 38.

The nature of law, as a path-dependent social practice, entrenches particular ways of seeing morality in legal doctrines. This leaves the question of initial motives for using the argument less important, as the doctrine acquires a force of its own, and thus at times precludes other types of ethical arguments. It tends to consume the realm of constitutional ethics and become exclusionary: courts often claim that the only argument that applies to a case—legally speaking—is the ethical argument from common sentiment. In this chapter, I wish to illustrate these views and show that at their foundation lies an inadequate moral ontology. This is not to say that such arguments never makes sense politically, legally, or even morally. The courts may be motivated in different ways, it can be politically wise or morally justified to leave the moral issue for others to decide, or it may be legally sound to follow previous patterns of interpretation strictly. But I shall argue that, to the extent to which the ethical argument from common sentiment excludes other types of arguments, it loses much of its appeal because it does not capture the way moral questions need to be approached. The argument from common sentiment does not leave space for reflective endorsement and justification of our moral feelings.

3.2 ELEMENTS OF THE ARGUMENT FROM COMMON SENTIMENT

To understand the argument from common sentiment, it is useful to distinguish it from a related, but different idea of popular constitutionalism. In the domain of constitutional adjudication, the notion of popular constitutionalism has been used as an explanation of the ways in which constitutional change occurs outside the formal constitutional revision procedure,[2] as a manner in which a shared deliberation between courts and citizens can constitute a foundation of constitutional authority,[3] and as a normative thesis about an attractive mode of constitutional interpretation.[4] These accounts are motivated by the debate about the 'counter-majoritarian' difficulty: the possibility of courts overturning the decisions of a democratically elected majority.[5] In contrast to this, I analyse a particular regime of ethical arguments in constitutional reasoning, which holds that the moral sentiments of

[2] Bruce A Ackerman, *We the People: Foundations* (Belknap Press 1991).

[3] See Robert Post and Reva B Siegel, 'Democratic Constitutionalism' in Jack M Balkin and Reva B Siegel (eds), *Constitution in 2020* (Oxford University Press 2009).

[4] Larry Kramer, for example, argues that the citizens are 'a higher authority out there with a power to overturn [Court's] decisions'. Larry Kramer, *The People Themselves: Popular Constitutionalism and Judicial Review* (Oxford University Press 2004) 253.

[5] See Alexander M Bickel, *The Least Dangerous Branch: The Supreme Court at the Bar of Politics* (Bobbs-Merrill 1962).

the members of one community determine how moral dilemmas are to be resolved. There are two central components of this argument: the *emotional reaction* of the people in a *particular community*.

Because the idea of popular constitutionalism appears to be in the neighbourhood of the argument from common sentiment, I shall differentiate them by answering an immediate objection that could arise. One may argue that the argument from common sentiment is not about its background metaethical assumptions, but about the legitimacy of judicial review, or simply about letting different institutions do what they do best. In other words, the objection states that explaining these arguments as metaethically grounded misses their point, because they are motivated by the *legitimacy* of judicial review, or by the comparative *institutional choice*, and hence popular constitutionalism presents a better theoretical framework to understand them. There are many reasons why something like popular constitutionalism may be a more legitimate way to deal with problems raised by the indeterminacy of constitutions. One reason for deference to real or hypothetical popular opinion could be the lack of democratic legitimacy of the courts, which may be further supported by the fact that there seems to be a less stark moral disagreement about the fairness of the democratic procedure, than about the substantive moral issues at stake before the courts.[6] Furthermore, there are many institutional advantages of legislators over courts. Legislators, for example, can be better placed to make these choices because they do not block the policy process, unlike courts, which may incur more political and legal costs in changing the decision later, especially if there is an entrenched constitution in place.[7]

I do not take issue with these arguments—they indeed seem plausible—but there are two ways in which I distinguish the ethical argument from common sentiment from the idea of popular constitutionalism (which starts from the concerns over legitimacy and questions about institutional competence). The ethical argument explained here is both narrower and broader. First, it is *narrower* because it does not claim that each instance of deference to representative branches can be traced back to an implicit metaethical position. In other words, I deal with a set of cases where deference to legislatures, juries, or popular opinion could be connected with certain views about morality, and these cases by no means explain all the reasons the courts may have to be deferential. Second, the concept is *broader*, because the argument from common sentiment may not lead the courts to respect legislative, juries' or

[6] See Jeremy Waldron, 'The Core of the Case against Judicial Review' (2006) 115 Yale Law Journal 1346 and Jeremy Waldron, *Law and Disagreement* (Clarendon Press 1999).

[7] See Neil K Komesar, *Imperfect Alternatives: Choosing Institutions in Law, Economics, and Public Policy* (University of Chicago Press 1994) and Neil K Komesar, *Law's Limits: The Rule of Law and the Supply and Demand of Rights* (Cambridge University Press 2001).

popular opinions. As the examples below will show, the courts also use this kind of reasoning to decide the issue themselves, or to take into account other courts' decisions. Therefore, there is no correlation between this type of ethical argument, and deference to popular will because of legitimacy or institutional concerns. This implies that there may be other reasons and motives at play that determine the institutional choice—such as democracy, fairness, self-government, respect for precedents—which could lead to the same result as the ethical argument from common sentiment. Nevertheless, it is possible to analyse its metaethical foundations, as long as we are aware of the fact that we can infer little about its nature from the institutional choice as such.

In this sense, the understanding of ethical argument from common sentiment does depart from the debate about popular constitutionalism, if the latter is perceived as a plea for giving more power to interpret the constitution to the people. This may leave conceptual space for arguing that popular constitutionalism is still sound or not, on the basis of some independent reason. Yet, while I do not deny that there may be other arguments for letting the people decide on these issues, I do hope to show that the institutional deference to legislatures or juries often does follow from a particular metaethical perspective, entrenched in a constitutional doctrine.

To understand what exactly is the argument from popular constitutionalism we need to take a closer look at some cases from comparative constitutional practice. In order to crystallize the underlying common denominators and central commitments of this argument—and show why the legitimacy of judicial review is not the appropriate framework to analyse them—I shall rely on cases from different institutional settings, that involve diverse ways of determining public opinion, with varying backings in precedents or text, and dealing with heterogeneous legal and moral issues. The case studies are chosen to show the same pattern of reasoning which leads to different institutional consequence, so that our focus can remain with the metaethical foundations of these arguments. They neither exhaust all the instances of the use of ethical argument from common sentiment, nor are they intended to be representative of all constitutional cultures; they do, however, intend to be illustrative enough to support some general conclusions. The examples I shall use are: the United States Supreme Court decisions on the death penalty; the European Court of Human Rights obscenity doctrine; and the Canadian Supreme Court's extradition jurisprudence.

Let me briefly introduce common elements of all three examples which show that we are dealing with the same type of argument. First, in all cases the question before the court depends on moral judgment. There is no dilemma that the issue is not fully determined by text, previous precedent, or in any other intrinsically legal manner, while the courts explicitly search for moral solutions to these issues. Second, the conventions of interpretation do not exclude—at least initially—other types of ethical arguments. In all these cases, there is a dispute whether the argument from common sentiment is the only way to deal with the problem, with one side to the dispute claiming that it is. Third, and centrally, in all these cases courts understand morality as consisting in the emotional reactions of a particular community. Fourth, regardless of the same moral foundation, the arguments lead to different institutional consequences. This shows that the issue is not simply a matter of institutional choice, but of something analytically separate and prior to that.

3.2.1 United States

As I have already mentioned, the 8th Amendment to the US Constitution amendment prohibits 'cruel and unusual' punishment,[8] and this phrase—as the Supreme Court has held since its landmark decision in *Trop v Dulles*—'must draw its meaning from the evolving standards of decency that mark the progress of a maturing society'.[9] To answer whether the death penalty is cruel and unusual, the Supreme Court thus needed to grapple with the question of how these standards of decency are to be determined, and which 'maturing' society is relevant. While there is some textual support both in the Amendment itself ('unusual' punishment), and in the *Trop* test for understanding these standards of decency as based on socially shared values and currently dominant opinions, the question is still a matter of dispute among justices. On the one hand, some of them believe that the task of the court is to defer to moral opinions of legislatures and juries. On the other, subjection of popular opinion to reason-based evaluation has never been ruled out completely.[10] The interpretation of the clause is hence open to different approaches: there is no immediate resolution on the basis of textual or doctrinal argument, but there are competing conventions of interpretation that can guide the court's analysis.[11]

[8] It reads: 'Excessive bail shall not be required, nor excessive fines imposed, nor cruel and unusual punishments inflicted'.

[9] *Trop v Dulles* 356 US 86 (1958) 100–101.

[10] This is even true of justices who in other decisions subscribe to the ultimate relevance of popular intuitions. An example is Justice Stevens. He argued that '[i]t is of vital importance to the defendant and to the community that any decision to impose the death sentence be, and appear to be, based on reason rather than caprice or emotion' (*Gardner v Florida* 430 US 349 (1977) 358), and he subsequently supported a doctrine which implicates judicial moral judgment when there are 'reasons to disagree' with popular and legislative judgment which otherwise holds sway in the 8th Amendment analysis. See his opinion in *Atkins v Virginia* 536 US 304 (2002), but also *Coker v Georgia* 433 US 584 (1977) and *Enmund v Florida* 458 US 782 (1982), where the doctrine was developed.

[11] See eg Justice Scalia in *Atkins v Virginia* (n 10) and *Roper v Simmons* 543 US 551 (2005).

The current of judicial reasoning that is relevant here takes emotional reactions as fundamental for diagnosing what is cruel and unusual. How this came to be the prominent interpretation of the 8th Amendment is well-known. Ever since it faced a robust legislative response to a split decision in *Furman v Georgia*,[12] the Supreme Court took legislative and jury opinions as the starting point of the 8th Amendment analysis. Justice Stewart captured this attitude in *Gregg v Georgia*:

> [i]t is now evident that a large proportion of American society continues to regard [the death penalty] as an appropriate and necessary criminal sanction ... The most marked indication of society's endorsement of the death penalty for murder is the legislative response to Furman ... In the only statewide referendum occurring since Furman and brought to our attention, the people of California adopted a constitutional amendment that authorized capital punishment ... The jury also is a significant and reliable objective index of contemporary values because it is so directly involved.[13]

Notwithstanding the causal explanation of such reading of the 'cruel and unusual' clause—as a consequence of institutional deference in the aftermath of a significant popular backlash—there is a justification which parallels such reading, provides a philosophical framework to support it, and puts the institutional choice in a moral perspective. This philosophical framework takes the emotional reactions of the community as the bedrock of moral evaluation.[14]

[12] *Furman v Georgia* 408 US 238 (1972). Having failed to deliver a controlling opinion on the matter in *Furman*, the court faced an unprecedented legislative response that supported the imposition of the death penalty: the Congress and thirty-five state legislatures regulated the death penalty between *Furman* and *Gregg v Georgia* 428 US 153 (1976).

[13] *Gregg v Georgia* (n 12) 179–81. Stewart considered values to be socially-based and dependent in some way on the reaction of the American people to a particular moral problem. But even more interesting is the way he understood this response as a matter of weighing different emotions, which presents the embryonic version of the argument from common sentiment. On the one hand, Stewart held that 'capital punishment is an *expression of society's moral outrage* at particularly offensive conduct', and—citing Furman—that '*the instinct for retribution is part of the nature of man*, and channeling that instinct in the administration of criminal justice serves an important purpose in promoting the stability of a society governed by law' (ibid 183, emphasis added). On the other hand, he found an emotional counterbalance to this: 'the reluctance of juries in many cases to impose the sentence may well reflect the *humane feeling* that this most irrevocable of sanctions should be reserved for a small number of extreme cases' (ibid 182, emphasis added). Since *Coker v Georgia* (n 10) the jurisprudence of the court has involved determining whether there is a consensus among the states to abandon capital punishment for certain crimes or offenders. While over time the relative weight given to legislative opinion has arguably decreased—as the court has placed more emphasis on legislative tendencies and has balanced them against criminological or substantive moral concerns—the view that moral opinions of citizens in some way determine the answer has remained a part of the court's jurisprudence. This changing trend is particularly observable in *Atkins v Virginia* (n 10), *Roper v Simmons* (n 11), and *Kennedy v Louisiana* 554 US 407 (2008). For example, in *Kennedy*, the court ignored the inclination of several legislatures, including the Congress, to prescribe capital punishment for child rape.

[14] David Garland also connects the trend of institutional deference to local authorities with the idea that justice is determined by community sentiments: 'the Court came to insist that justice ... required that

Expressions of this view often take on a similar form, which can be exemplified by Justice Stevens' opinion from *Spaziano v Florida*.[15] The petitioner in this case, Mr Spaziano, was found guilty of first-degree murder in Florida. The jury proposed life imprisonment, but the trial court refused to follow the recommendation and sentenced Spaziano to death. This was possible under Florida law because juries' opinions were only advisory in the sentencing process, and once the case reached the Supreme Court the main question became whether the 8th Amendment allows for overriding of juries' decisions by judges. Stevens argued that the practice was not constitutional and, in so doing, he relied on a particular conception of morality that affected the institutional choice between juries and courts in the sentencing process. Thus, the first step in his reasoning was to make the question of the imposition and constitutionality of the death penalty *moral*, both given the issue at stake and the previous doctrine which directs the court to engage in moral reasoning. As Stevens puts it, 'in the final analysis, capital punishment rests on not a legal, but an ethical, judgment'.[16]

The second step in the argument is crucial and offers a conception of morality: a particular metaethical grounding of moral judgments. Morality is defined by two elements: it consists in the *emotional*, intuitive response of a specific *community* to a moral problem at hand. For Stevens, the death penalty 'is ultimately understood only as an expression of the community's outrage—its sense that an individual has lost his moral entitlement to live'.[17] He argues that the deterrence rationale cannot fully justify the death penalty, and that 'the question whether the death sentence is an appropriate, non-excessive response to the particular facts of the case will depend on the retribution justification' connected to 'society's moral outrage'.[18] Notice that even if the death penalty may only be causally explained by outrage, it does not follow that such explanation is not morally deficient.[19] But given that Stevens starts his moral analysis from the feeling of outrage—and granted his view that nothing more can be said to justify the death penalty—it follows for him that we ought to surrender our moral judgments to socially shared moral commitments that find expression in emotional reactions to a particular set of facts: the constitutionality of capital punishment—as Stevens puts

juries alone might impose death sentences, since juries best understood the community sentiments that made such sentences justifiable'; 'The court systematically empowered local figures—governors, state legislators, district attorneys, state judges, and local juries: most of them elected, all of them responsive to community sentiment—to decide the questions of life and death that capital cases entailed'. David Garland, *Peculiar Institution: America's Death Penalty in an Age of Abolition* (Oxford University Press 2010) 273.

[15] *Spaziano v Florida* 468 US 447 (1984). [16] ibid 481 (Stevens). [17] ibid 469 (Stevens).

[18] ibid 480 (Stevens) citing *Gregg v Georgia* (n 12) 183–84.

[19] For a defence of the retributivist-emotivist view of punishment see Michael S Moore, *Placing Blame: A Theory of the Criminal Law* (Oxford University Press 1997) ch 3.

it—'critically depends upon whether its imposition in a particular case is consistent with the *community's sense of values*'.[20]

This step in Stevens' reasoning thus performs another role as well. Not only ought communal sentiments prevail when the sanction is imposed—because of the retributivist character of the death penalty—but they also determine the constitutionality of the practice as a whole. The logic is this: if morality is the same phenomenon, and if it informs both the infliction of the death penalty in a particular case and the constitutionality of the practice in general, then to be consistent about morality we must take into account the communal moral sentiments on both of these levels. He justifies the death penalty as an individual sanction and as a general practice with the same argument: the moral sense of the community demands it. For Stevens, the fact that all state legislatures, except the ones that abolished the punishment, have at some point involved juries in this process demonstrates 'a strong community feeling that it is only decent and fair to leave the life-or-death decision to the authentic voice of the community—the jury—rather than to a single governmental official'.[21] According to him, we must also question whether assigning '[t]he decision whether or not an individual must die' to 'governmental officials, and not juries, is consistent with the community's moral sense'.[22] The constitutionality of the practice does not follow from the ideal of democratic legitimacy, but from a conception of morality based on communal feelings.

This point is further evidenced by the third and final step of Stevens' argument, where he focuses on *institutional choice*, and grounds his analysis in the capacity of certain institutions to stay true to a community's moral sentiments:

> if the decision that capital punishment is the appropriate sanction in extreme cases is justified because it expresses the community's moral sensibility—its demand that a given affront to humanity requires retribution—it follows, I believe, that a representative cross-section of the community must be given the responsibility for making that decision.[23]

Again, the argument has bifurcated effects: not only do moral sentiments determine the imposition of the death sentence in particular cases, but they also determine its constitutionality. Stevens believes that moral sensibility is best expressed by juries, and that both legislatures and courts are deficient in mapping it. Although the legislative opinion is a 'logical starting point'[24] for the analysis of a community's sentiments, it will often be distorted by the implications of judicial decisions. Stevens thus searches for something like

[20] *Spaziano v Florida* (n 15) 489 (emphasis added).
[21] ibid 469 (Stevens).
[22] ibid 476 (Stevens).
[23] ibid 481 (Stevens).
[24] ibid 472 (Stevens).

pure, unbiased or pre-theoretical communal sentiment; for example, he considers the legislative response to *Furman v Georgia* as 'not entitled to the same presumption of validity' because it fails to represent a genuine 'community sentiment'.[25] Similarly, judges themselves are a deficient litmus test for communal values as compared to juries which 'reflect more accurately the composition and experiences of the community as a whole, and inevitably make decisions based on community values more reliably, than can that segment of the community that is selected for service on the bench'.[26] As a consequence, Stevens found that the imposition of the sentence in Spaziano's case was unconstitutional because it removed the sentencing power from the jury and thus did not reflect the moral sentiment of the community.

This kind of reasoning provides a philosophical and moral justification to the conclusion from *Gregg* quoted above, which directs the Supreme Court to look for consensus on the issue among legislatures and juries when interpreting the 8th Amendment. And such logic is also evident in cases when the court shows readiness to depart from popular opinion on the constitutionality of the death penalty. When this happens, the dissenters are usually quick to point out not only that democratic concerns should lead to more judicial restraint, but also that moral judgments—predicated upon feelings and intuitions—are better exercised by the representative branches of government. In other words, opposition to judicial activism often relies on the philosophical argument that puts communal moral sentiments at the centre of the moral system. For example, when the court departed from popular opinion in *Roper v Simmons* to reach the moral conclusion through its own reasoning, Scalia dissented and argued that the conception of morality that is dictated by precedents excludes the independent moral decision of the court on this issue. According to him, if the test for morality are:

> '[t]he evolving standards of decency' of our society, it makes no sense for the Justices then to prescribe those standards rather than discern them from the practices of our people. On the evolving-standards hypothesis, the only legitimate function of this Court is to identify a moral consensus of the American people.[27]

Similarly, in *Atkins v Virginia*, Scalia expresses the idea that if the moral sentiments are dispositive of moral judgment, then the court should exercise restraint. As he explains:

> Beyond the empty talk of a 'national consensus,' the Court gives us a brief glimpse of what really underlies today's decision: pretension to a power confined *neither* by the moral sentiments originally enshrined in the Eight Amendment (its original meaning) *nor even* by the current moral sentiments of

25 ibid 475 (Stevens).

26 ibid 486–87 (Stevens).

27 *Roper v Simmons* (n 11) 616 (Scalia).

> the American people ... [P]resumably ... really good lawyers have moral sentiments superior to those of the common herd, whether in 1791 or today ... [I]t is the *feelings* and *intuition* of a majority of the Justices that count ...[28]

The gist of his argument is again the same: given that moral sentiments are fundamental to the decision, there is no reason to believe that the moral sentiments of justices are worthier than anyone else's. And indeed, if we subscribe to the first premise and believe that moral sentiments are all there is to moral judgment, it is probably cogent to defer on this issue to legislatures and juries, who are arguably also well informed about morally relevant facts, but are more representative of the community at the same time. In other words, if we accept the moral ontology the issue becomes merely epistemic: given that morality is about moral sentiments, what is the best way for us to learn about them?

Let me sum up what I have tried to demonstrate here. The argument from common sentiment—as it appears in one important strand of the 8th Amendment jurisprudence—relies on a vision of morality which consists of two elements. First, it is the *emotional response* that determines moral judgment. Second, the emotional response is limited to a society: in other words, it is *community-bound*. While deference to popular emotions could be explained by textual interpretation or reasons of political prudence, the argument is analytically premised on a specific understanding of morality. The court may be right to defer on these issues to other branches of government for all kinds of reasons, but here the conclusion follows from the contingent and emotional nature of values, tied to a particular society at a particular time.

3.2.2 *European Convention on Human Rights*

The obscenity jurisprudence of the European Court of Human Rights (ECtHR) shares the same conception of morality with the 'cruel and unusual' punishment doctrine in the US.[29] However, it shows that the institutional consequence of such a conception of morality may be deference to other courts or constitutional systems, and not only to legislatures and juries. It demonstrates that there is no direct link between this particular metaethics and democratic values: they may coincide in terms of institutional consequences, but are not necessarily connected. Once the moral ontology is in place, the institutional issue becomes epistemological, a matter of the most

[28] *Atkins v Virginia* (n 10) 348 (Scalia), references omitted.

[29] The system of the European Convention shares many features of a modern constitutional system: for example, an entrenched bill of rights protected by a judicial body in a legal procedure. At the same time, the court often engages with national constitutional practices, and thus touches upon the issue of constitutional reasoning even in the strict sense of the term.

reliable way of getting the community's sentiment right. Another contrast with the US example is the text of the clause which is interpreted, as the ECtHR is explicitly called on to reflect on the concept of morality by the European Convention on Human Rights (ECHR): 'morals' is one of the possible justifications for the restriction of free speech.[30] The court therefore must have a conception of morality, for without it the analysis of limitations to the freedom of speech cannot get off the ground.

The ECtHR first developed its conception of morality in the context of free speech in *Handyside v UK*.[31] In this case, the applicant was convicted of obscenity for publishing a book whose audience were mainly children and which took an 'uncritical' stance towards sexual intercourse, pornography, masturbation, and the like. The same book was published without any legal problems in several other European countries, as well as in some parts of the UK; consequently, the court needed to tackle the question of how universal the conception of morality is. If morality is at least partially relative to different communities, it is possible that freedom of speech protection varies; if it is universal, then the protection should be the same. In the first case, morality is contingent and diverse, while in the latter it is universal and uniform. The court famously opted for the first view:

> [i]t is not possible to find in the domestic law of the various Contracting States a uniform European conception of morals. The view taken by their respective laws of the requirements of morals varies from time to time and from place to place, especially in our era which is characterised by a rapid and far-reaching evolution of opinions on the subject. By reason of their direct and continuous contact with the vital forces of their countries, State authorities are in principle in a better position than the international judge to give an opinion on the exact content of these requirements . . .[32]

In this passage, the ECtHR effectively declared morality contingent, dependent on (legal) consensus, and prone to change over time. In the development of the argument, the institutional point ('in a better position to decide') follows from the conception of morality. Because there is divergence in moral opinions in Europe and within the UK itself, the court thinks that national authorities can have better access to values because of their direct engagement with the community which generates them. Thus—while variation between communities can be explained in other ways, such as factual circumstances or flawed reasoning—the court opts to accommodate these differences within the conception of morality. In so doing, it makes two logically

[30] 'The exercise of [freedom of speech] . . . may be subject to such formalities, conditions, restrictions or penalties as are prescribed by law and are necessary in a democratic society, in the interests of . . . the protection of health or morals . . .'. See ECHR art 10(2).

[31] *Handyside v United Kingdom* (5493/72) [1976] ECHR 5 (7 December 1976).

[32] ibid para 48.

separate points: it defines morality, but it also—given such definition—exercises restraint and deference to national authorities.[33]

Even though the doctrine has not completely precluded interpretations of free speech which rely on an autonomous judicial understanding of morals,[34] the account of morals from *Handyside* has been at least the most dominant one in the ECtHR's obscenity jurisprudence. But this socially-based conception of morality has acquired further content over the years. In subsequent cases, the ECtHR's conception of morality incorporated two elements of the argument from common sentiment: the doctrine focused on the *emotional response* of a particular *community*.

Such interpretation became prominent in *Müller v Switzerland*. The applicant in this case—Joseph Felix Müller—was a painter who took part in an exhibition in Fribourg (Switzerland). The exhibition was publicly advertised and open to all, and the participating artists were called to create their art on the spot. Mr Müller produced three paintings which depicted scenes of homosexuality and bestiality, causing complaints and harsh reactions from the people attending the exhibition. Before long, the paintings were removed and seized on the order of an investigating judge. The ECtHR needed to decide whether Mr Müller's freedom of speech was justifiably limited on the basis of 'morals'.

The ECtHR's analysis was primarily informed by the domestic courts. Since the Swiss criminal law contained no precise definition of obscenity, the Federal Court in Switzerland defined it as follows: 'any works or items which offend, in a manner that is difficult to accept, the sense of sexual propriety, are obscene; the effect may be to arouse a normal person sexually or to disgust or repel him'.[35] While the reference to a 'normal person' was meant to provide the element of objectivity, the test in fact contained no precise criteria for settling the issue. The only evident specification of the test was its emotivist basis: at the bottom, it was a question of the 'sense' of sexual propriety, 'disgust', and 'repellence'. Guided by such a test, Swiss courts did

[33] Notice that there is a competing explanation of the doctrine, but one which ultimately fails to account for the court's argument. One could argue that the institutional consequence follows from the court's concerns regarding its position in a supra-national system of rights-protection. Similarly to the US example, what *caused* the court to exercise restraint was a concern about its legitimacy in the political and legal system. This may be true, but had there not been a claim about the nature of morality, the argument would have been deficient as it stands. Why would the state authorities be in a better position to determine the demands of morality if morality were universal? The court argued that *because* requirements of morality are determined nationally, and they thus vary 'from time to time and from place to place', deference to national authorities is warranted. The argument was not that disagreement justifies caution, but that the best explanation of disagreement is a contingent and parochial conception of morals.

[34] See eg Judge Mosler's separate opinion in *Handyside v United Kingdom* (n 31).

[35] *Müller v Switzerland* (10737/84) [1988] ECHR 5 (24 May 1988) para 20, citing judgments of the Swiss Federal Court (ATF), vol 83 (1957), pt VI, 19–25; vol 86 (1960), pt IV, 19–25; vol 87 (1961), pt IV, 73–85.

not justify their decision with a separate moral argument, but tried to get to the core of the emotional reactions of the majority of the population in their community.

Domestic courts accepted the two elements of the argument from common sentiment. First, what is moral is determined by the *emotional reactions of the majority* of the people. Sarine District Criminal Court, for example, held the following view: 'The subjects [of the paintings]—sodomy, fellatio, bestiality, the erect penis—are obviously morally offensive to the vast majority of the population'.[36] Similarly, the Fribourg Cantonal Court described these emotions as 'generally accepted views'.[37] Second, these moral reactions are temporally and spatially *relative*, and are hence neither timeless nor universal. Again, the district court wrote that 'allowance has to be made for changes in the moral climate',[38] and the cantonal court how 'public general views on morality and social mores … vary at different times and different places'.[39] In short, morality is dependent on the emotional reactions of the majority in a certain community.

The ECtHR confirmed this understanding of morality, reiterating its margin of appreciation doctrine.[40] It proclaimed that 'conceptions of sexual morality have changed in recent years', and accepted the analysis of the Swiss courts based on the 'sense of sexual propriety' of the average person.[41] The court also accepted that the test would render divergent results depending on the community in question. It thus held that morality is distinct for each community which shows a convergence of emotions. In *Müller*, for example, the relevant 'sense' of appropriateness varied across different Swiss regions. The exhibition was prohibited in the canton of Fribourg, but not in Basel.[42] Hence, morality is not necessarily attached to a state, but even to communities on a sub-state level.

Again, we may try to explain the court's decision to defer to the national and sub-national conception of morals by its institutional position in the pan-European system where many different traditions exist, or by the doctrine of the margin of appreciation which tied the court's hands in later cases. But at least initially—when it was forced to reflect upon the concept of

[36] ibid para 14. [37] ibid para 16. [38] ibid para 14. [39] ibid para 16.

[40] In a nutshell, the margin of appreciation denotes a leeway allowed for the member states to regulate issues affected by the Convention (ECHR) when there is no consensus on the European level.

[41] *Müller v Switzerland* (n 35) para 36.

[42] ibid para 36. Similarly, in *Otto-Preminger v Austria*—a case dealing with a forfeiture of a blasphemous film—the ECtHR respected the conclusion of Austrian courts which had found the film offensive for the community in Tyrol, while a theatre play with the same content could be staged in Vienna. In this case, the court further clarified its margin of appreciation doctrine by saying that 'even within a single country such conceptions [of the significance of religion] may vary'. *Otto-Preminger-Institut v Austria* (13470/87) [1994] ECHR 26 (20 September 1994) para 50. For similar issues see also *Wingrove v United Kingdom* (17419/90) [1996] ECHR 60 (25 November 1996) and *Murphy v Ireland* (44179/98) [2003] ECHR 352 (10 July 2003).

morality—the ECtHR developed a type of ethical argument based on the emotional reactions of the majority of people in a particular community.

3.2.3 Canada

Another example of the argument from common sentiment appears in Canadian extradition jurisprudence. Under Section 7 of the Canadian Charter of Rights and Freedoms, 'everyone has the right to life, liberty and security of the person and the right not to be deprived thereof except in accordance with the principles of fundamental justice'. The Canadian Supreme Court interpreted this clause as preventing the deportation of individuals to countries where their rights would be infringed in a way that goes against 'fundamental justice', which thus became the crucial concept for deciding extradition cases. To understand this concept—similarly to previous examples—the Canadian Supreme Court relied on the emotional, intuitive element of the comprehension of fundamental justice. Furthermore, the understanding of this concept put to the forefront the question of the relative character of values, because of the cross-border nature of extradition. As in the case of the US Supreme Court and ECtHR, one important strand of judicial reasoning tied the understanding of fundamental justice to the values of Canadian society alone. However, although the understanding of morality was similar, the institutional consequence was not; instead of deferring to legislatures, juries or other courts, the Canadian Supreme Court decided the issue itself, paying only loose attention to public opinion.

The issue first arose in *Canada v Schmidt*, a case dealing with an appeal from Ms Schmidt, a Canadian citizen, who was to be extradited to the United States.[43] Ms Schmidt abducted a two-year-old girl, acting in the belief that the girl was her granddaughter who lived in inappropriate conditions. She was tried, found not guilty, and subsequently acquitted in the US for the federal offence of kidnapping. At the same time, she faced charges for the state offence of 'child-stealing' in Ohio. Once released by the federal court, she fled to Canada, where she was arrested and where extradition proceedings were put in motion.

Writing for the majority, Justice La Forest examined the case in light of the concept of fundamental justice from Section 7 of the Charter.[44] To explicate the concept, he dwelled on two issues in particular: the test for determining its substantive content, and the leeway to be left for foreign systems. The first issue tied the concept of fundamental justice to emotions, and the second generated a gap between the Canadian and American sense of justice, making them community-relative. To determine the content of

[43] *Canada v Schmidt* [1987] 1 SCR 500.

[44] ibid para 45.

fundamental justice, La Forest proceeded by way of giving examples of what would amount to its violation,[45] but at the bottom of his reasoning was a litmus test consisting in an emotional reaction to extradition. Starting from what he understood to be a paradigmatic example of fundamentally unjust treatment—torture—La Forest set out the doctrine in the following manner:

> Situations falling far short of [infliction of torture] may well arise where the nature of the criminal procedures or penalties in a foreign country sufficiently shocks the conscience as to make a decision to surrender a fugitive for trial there one that breaches the principles of fundamental justice enshrined in s. 7.[46]

Apart from torture, he added some examples to shed further light on what 'shocks the conscience': for instance, lack of procedural safeguards or presumption of innocence does not 'shock' it, while a recurring prosecution for the same offence does.[47] However, La Forest did not say much about what connects these different cases or what could be a principle that would guide the future application of the 'shocks the conscience' test. The foundation of the test was the feeling of 'shock', an *emotional reaction* to a possible extradition.

The second element of La Forest's conception of fundamental justice is *relational*, which at the foundation makes the question of value *relative*. Fundamental justice is a matter of going to the core of our intuitions about justice, and then comparing them with the values of other societies. Not all cases where Canadian law is different from the law of other countries fall within the conception of fundamental justice. Only the most central values are protected. But the core of these values is not to be found in some abstract and universal procedure: they are contingent and parochial. They are protected not because of their universal worth, but because of their worth for Canadians.[48]

A confirmation and development of such a reading of fundamental justice came about in *Kindler v Canada*, when the court had to decide on the constitutionality of the extradition of convicted offenders to the US, where they would face the death penalty.[49] Joseph Kindler fled to Canada after the jury

[45] ibid. Being convinced that in this case the possibility of double jeopardy is not real for Ms Schmidt—because the two crimes she had been charged with 'involve quite different elements'—La Forest was not compelled to give a clear-cut definition of the concept (ibid para 57). However, the test is supposed to have real bite and is not satisfied in all legal systems a priori. See *Canada v Schmidt* (n 43) para 47.

[46] ibid para 47. [47] ibid paras 48 and 56.

[48] From this understanding of value—as the intuitive, emotional reaction of members of a society—follows La Forest's view that the courts should defer to the executive. The executive is better placed to know morally relevant facts, which in this case include the intricacies of foreign systems. At the same time, everyone should be shocked in the same way if they were aware of all the relevant facts, and courts have no a priori better standing in this regard. See *Canada v Schmidt* (n 43) para 49.

[49] *Kindler v Canada (Minister of Justice)* [1991] 2 SCR 779.

in Pennsylvania recommended a death penalty for him, because of murder, conspiracy to commit murder, and kidnapping. Before the sentencing court reached the decision, Mr Kindler escaped from prison and was subsequently arrested in Canada. The Supreme Court had to decide whether extradition to the US would violate his rights under the Charter.

In *Kindler*, La Forest tied the 'shocks the conscience' doctrine more firmly to the 'Canadian community' and 'conscience of Canadians', but refused to equate the test with public opinion of the day. In his view, while polls can give us access to the concept of fundamental justice defined by the feeling of shock, we are not justified in proceeding on the basis of the feelings of the majority only: 'I do not think the courts should determine unacceptability in terms of statistical measurements of approval or disapproval by the public at large, but it is fair to say that they afford some insight into the public values of the community'.[50] What determines the feeling of shock is the fact that, for example, the legalization of torture is 'unimaginable' in Canadian society, while reinstatement of the death penalty is not completely out of the question. The properties that differentiate between similar feelings are their firmness and patent irreversibility; this leaves some conceptual space for public opinion to be wrong, even if values are socially and emotionally contingent. For example, in *United States v Allard*, La Forest was also unable to explain the nature of these immutable moral feelings with more precision, and described them as 'simply unacceptable'.[51]

Justice McLachlin further dwelled on the relationship between public and judicial opinion, and tried to redefine what 'simply unacceptable' means in *Kindler*. For her, the sense of justice is tied to the Canadian community, but she thinks that the only way to objectify it is to defer to the feelings of majority:

> At the end of the day, the question is whether the provision or action in question offends the Canadian sense of what is fair, right and just ... In determining whether, bearing all these factors in mind, the extradition in question is 'simply unacceptable', the judge must avoid imposing his or her own subjective views on the matter, and seek rather to objectively assess the attitudes of Canadians on the issue of whether the fugitive is facing a situation which is shocking and fundamentally unacceptable to our society.[52]

McLachlin's account, however, does not explain how the court should 'assess' the attitude of Canadians: if the objectivity is dependent on what the majority of people feels, it is hard to imagine how judges can 'correct' that feeling to be more objective.[53]

50 ibid (La Forest). 51 *United States v Allard* [1987] 1 SCR 564, 572.

52 *Kindler v Canada* (n 49) (McLachlin).

53 Sopinka confronted these views with an argument that much resembles the argument from constitutional identity. He argued that the source of value is the Charter itself, and that the court ought not to

This approach to public opinion was amended and clarified in *United States v Burns*. Apart from including more concerns in the balancing exercise when deciding on the principles of fundamental justice, the court also rejected blind deference to public opinion, arguing that 'the phrase "shocks the conscience" and equivalent expressions are not to be taken out of context or equated to opinion polls. . . . The words were not intended to signal an abdication by judges of their constitutional responsibilities in matters involving fundamental principles of justice'.[54] Perhaps this is because the feeling of shock will always occur when the principles of fundamental justice are violated: 'The rule is not that departures from fundamental justice are to be tolerated unless in a particular case it shocks the conscience. An extradition that violates the principles of fundamental justice will always shock the conscience'.[55] However, it is again not clear how judges can access the principles of fundamental justice more objectively than people themselves. Presumably, the idea here is that people can be guided by different emotions, and judges can correct this either by discovering truly moral emotions, or emotions of particular strength.

To sum up: the 'shocks the conscience' doctrine relied to a significant extent on the outrage that Canadians feel when confronted with an extradition which is against the principles of fundamental justice. Who has the best insight into these feelings is a function of the knowledge of relevant facts and the ability to differentiate between feelings of moral outrage on the basis of their strength and centrality in our emotional apparatus. Institutional consequences depend on weighing these different concerns. While people may reflect popular sentiments more reliably, they can both be deluded in differentiating between truly central, irreversible feelings about 'simply inconceivable' injustices and surface feelings which are not firmly established. We see that, in this version, the argument from common sentiment comes close to the argument from constitutional identity. The relativity of feelings to a certain community connects them to the identity of such a community; there is also the idea that there is a cluster of more central and deeper commitments that give the court the standpoint from which to assess the dominant moral feelings. However, it is still the communal feelings and popular opinions that are central to this argument, and not the identity evolved through engagement with the constitution. We can thus note these interconnections between different types of ethical arguments—which will be

surrender to public opinion: 'the requirement that the fugitive face a situation that is "simply unacceptable" must entail more than a simple consideration of majority opinion. It must be interpreted in light of the values underlying s. 7'. See *Kindler v Canada* (n 49) (Sopinka).

[54] *United States v Burns* [2001] 1 SCR 283 para 67. [55] ibid para 68.

explored later—and focus on the elements of the argument from common sentiment.

3.3 MORAL ONTOLOGY OF COMMON SENTIMENTS

Let us now abstract from the contextual differences, and see whether in these examples there are three dots that make a line. As I mentioned at the beginning, the examples include different lines of cases, with diverse positions of the courts vis-à-vis other branches of government, divergent textual and doctrinal backing, and varying institutional consequences. However, in all of them the common denominator is a particular understanding of morality with two defining features: an *emotional* response of a specific *community*.

We can call the first element of the argument from common sentiment the *emotivist element*. In all of the above cases, the communal opinion equals an emotion. So, for example, in the US context, capital punishment is the expression of 'moral outrage', and its constitutionality must conform with 'the community's moral sense'. The ECtHR supports Swiss courts in relying on the emotions of 'repugnance and disgust' and on the 'sense of sexual propriety'. Finally, the Canadian Supreme Court invokes the feeling of 'shock' and 'sense' of what is moral. The second component of the argument we can label the *relativist element*. Morality is considered as community-bound, but the relevant communities differ: the US Supreme Court relies on a national consensus, or defers to the states; the ECtHR seeks a supranational, European consensus or otherwise it respects even a sub-national convergence of emotions; the Canadian Supreme Court accepts only national consensus as relevant.

To unpack these elements further, we need to see whether they establish an epistemic or ontological claim. If the argument from common sentiment is an *epistemic* or heuristic device, the emotional reaction of a particular community to a moral problem would be a way to know the solution to that problem. This explanation is metaethically plausible; for example, there is no reason to deny that moral duties are at the very least reflected in corresponding moral feelings on the part of duty-bearers. Even Kant—who prototypically constructed his moral theory from reason and independently of experience—accepted a role for the moral feeling of 'respect' in his aetiology of moral action. For him, the feeling of respect is induced in us by the universal moral law. Once we cognize the moral law, this feeling follows. Given that this feeling is, as Kant says, 'the representation of a worth', it may have some epistemic value.[56] For other strands of non-naturalist cognitivism, the

[56] Immanuel Kant, *Groundwork for the Metaphysics of Morals* (Allen W Wood (tr), Yale University Press 2002) 17 and 76. See also Paul Guyer, 'Moral Feelings in the Metaphysics of Morals' in Lara Denis (ed), *Kant's Metaphysics of Morals: A Critical Guide* (Cambridge University Press 2010).

epistemic worth of moral emotions is obvious. Intuitionism, for example, holds that there are moral facts which are knowable-in-themselves. It presupposes a special faculty—moral intuition—by virtue of which we are able to grasp non-inferential moral facts. GE Moore makes this famous analogy: 'good is a simple notion, just as yellow is a simple notion; that, just as you cannot, by any manner of means, explain to anyone who does not already know it, what yellow is, so you cannot explain what good is'.[57] We do not learn what is good through an inference from reasons, but in a way analogous to our sense-based cognition of external reality.[58] Finally, the epistemic connection between feelings and morality comes naturally for an emotivist. Emotivism implies internalism about the relationship between moral judgment and action: characterizing an action as wrong presupposes a motivation not to do it. In this view, moral judgment *is* the desire to act upon it. For example, in a strong version of this view, Hare thought that one's true principles were only revealed by what one had actually done.[59]

The issue, however, is more complicated, both as a matter of moral theory and as a matter of judicial practice. Not every motivational attitude is a moral attitude.[60] Most of the time it seems obvious to us that we can recognize something as morally wrong and still do it. This could, for example, be a part of the explanation for the lack of convergence in our reactions to moral problems. But then the epistemic question becomes pressing and needs to be tied to a conception of value: how can we know which emotional reactions count? Take a closer look at how different courts establish the existence of a particular emotion. In our examples, the US Supreme Court mostly relies on juries and legislatures, the ECtHR takes into account the whole institutional and social reality (including courts), and the Canadian Supreme Court seems to be confident in its own intuitions about the issue. The apparently epistemic decision must depend on a prior conception of value. For example, the Canadian court may think that because of a weakness of will citizens fail to make good moral judgments; however, this implies that there is a conception of good moral judgment which determines the choice of the court to correct public opinion.

[57] GE Moore, *Principia Ethica* (Thomas Baldwin (ed), 2nd edn, Cambridge University Press 2000) 59.

[58] See eg Henry Sidgwick, *The Methods of Ethics* (7th edn, McMillan 1962); Henry Sidgwick, *The Methods of Ethics* (Macmillan 1874); WD Ross, *The Right and the Good* (Clarendon Press 1930); Robert Audi, *The Good in the Right: A Theory of Intuition and Intrinsic Value* (Princeton University Press 2004).

[59] 'If we were to ask of a person "What are his moral principles?" the way in which we could be most sure of a true answer would be by studying what he did'. See RM Hare, *The Language of Morals* (Clarendon Press 1952) 1.

[60] Peter Railton, 'Realism and Its Alternatives' in John Skorupski (ed), *The Routledge Companion to Ethics* (Routledge 2010) 304.

A purely epistemic account of the argument from common sentiment would also demand a redescription of the cases. First, even if a reason-based theory of morality such as Kant's can accommodate the feeling of duty or respect, its epistemology is radically different. In the most minimal sense, feelings could not form an exclusive way of knowing moral duties; we would, for example, be able to reach the true moral decision through a reflective process or by taking a particular point of view. But as we have seen, the argument from common sentiment is frequently considered as the only valid ethical argument. When faced with a different type of argument, the courts resort to the legal character of interpretive conventions. Recall for example Scalia's argument that morality is a matter of sentiment, and that the Court's own understanding of it is not epistemologically valid. Justice Rehnquist, for example, argued that foreign law is immaterial to the decision whether something is cruel and unusual: 'if it is evidence of a *national* consensus for which we are looking, then the viewpoints of other countries simply are not relevant'.[61] Such arguments make little sense if we subscribe to a reason-based and universal conception of moral value.

Second—and connected to this—these views cannot accommodate the analytic precedence of having the concept of morality. If the constitution contains concepts such as 'cruel', 'fundamental justice', or 'morals', then where one looks for their content—under the circumstances of discretion—depends on what one considers as moral. You may believe that someone is in a better position to know something or reach a decision of a certain kind, but you need first to have at least a rough idea of what that something is. Suppose, for example, I broke the headlights on my car and went to a car wash to fix it. The failure of my practical rationality follows from a false idea of what constitutes my problem and who can solve it, not from the lack of desire to repair the headlights. This shows that even an institutional reference saying, for example, that legislatures will take all affected interests better into account, follows from a notion that all affected interests ought to be heard and accommodated. This is consistent with references made by courts to what morality *is*. In all three cases, the courts offer views on this issue that are a far cry from saying that morality is independent of our moral feelings. Quite the opposite: their understanding is that emotional communal reactions are constitutive of morality.

Third, divergent institutional consequences of the argument from common sentiment testify that epistemology follows from the understanding of the nature of value (which is a natural way to think about this relationship in general). If the argument were epistemic, we would expect that the ways of knowing morality would be the same in all these cases. If it is not epistemic,

[61] *Atkins v Virginia* (n 10) 325 (Rehnquist).

then we have one explanation for all examples.[62] Given the answer of what morality is, the courts opt for different ways of knowing it: by tracking popular opinions, deferring to those who are closer to the community that generates moral feelings, or through a combination of introspection about their own feelings verified against popular intuitions. All of these ways of knowing morality make sense if, at their foundation, there is a conception of morality as contingent and dependent on communal feelings; on the other side, if there were no specific understanding of morality to support these epistemic consequences, they would remain far more mysterious. The argument from common sentiment becomes harder to explain: while it maybe makes sense to check our moral judgments against the gut reactions of our community, it is not a natural place to start and finish moral inquiry if we do not hold this specific metaethics.

That said, even if all these reasons do not convince completely that the argument from common sentiment implies particular metaethics, at a minimum they justify analysing the argument more closely as an ideal type. Whatever the best explanation of the argument is, the path dependency of law and the exclusivity of the argument that follows from it warrant the need to treat the argument as an ontological claim. The *ontological* claim of the argument from common sentiment—a claim about what morality is—takes the emotional reaction of the people in a particular community about a moral problem as constitutive of the solution to that problem, and not as a way of knowing the solution. The distinction is subtle, but highly relevant. In our examples, such an ontological account would mean that there is nothing more to morality than the moral sense of the people on issues of capital punishment, free speech, or extradition. Treating the argument from common sentiment as ontological is justified mostly because it becomes entrenched as a convention of interpretation excluding other ways of approaching the issue. The iterative practice of law forecloses other types of ethical arguments, and they by implication come to be considered as misconceptions of morality.

If understood as an ontological position, the argument from common sentiment—given its defining elements—suggests a vision of morality that is emotivist and relativist. Because of this, it ultimately depends on the plausibility and compatibility of emotivism and relativism: the ontological claim of the argument from common sentiment is true if and only if emotivist and relativist elements can both be plausible at the same time. There are thus two hurdles this type of argument needs to pass: on the one hand, it depends on the plausibility of both emotivist and relativist elements taken separately,

[62] Notice that this argument is plausible only if the phenomenon is the same. I hope that the explanation given at the beginning suffices to demonstrate that the cases are indeed relevantly similar.

and on the other, it is conditional upon their compatibility. Because of this the analysis has the following structure: I will first provide arguments for the most tenable versions of emotivist and relativist elements, and then I shall evaluate their mutual coherence.

3.3.1 *The emotivist element*

There is something puzzling about the use of the ethical argument from common sentiment. The soundness of ethical arguments in general depends upon the (at least minimal) practical relevance of morality. This is a normative assumption, but I think a justified one. If a judge is sceptical about morality's relevance and uses ethical arguments, there is an inconsistency in her views that we may find unacceptable. We don't want our judges to be cynical about the evaluative perspectives they take, and we don't want their argumentative practices to be based on flawed or insincere premises. A judge that uses ethical arguments thus should also believe that morality is important, that it is not just a matter of different tastes. The pressing issue here is: does the emotivist element entail subjectivism about value which is in tension with the practical relevance of morality? And, if this is so, does the moral ontology of common sentiments collapse under the pressure of its own internal incoherence?

The view that judicial moral judgments are subjective is sometimes openly expressed. For example, when the US Supreme Court decided on the constitutionality of the death penalty for minors in *Roper*, Justice O'Connor wrote that the Court 'should not substitute its own "inevitably subjective judgment" on how best to resolve this difficult moral question for the judgments of the Nation's democratically elected legislatures',[63] and Justice Scalia argued that 'the meaning of our Eighth Amendment' should not 'be determined by the subjective views of five Members of this Court'.[64] Similarly, McLachlin wrote in *Kindler* that 'the judge must avoid imposing his or her own subjective views on the matter, and seek rather to objectively assess the attitudes of Canadians on the issue'.[65] O'Connor, Scalia, and McLachlin thus believe that judicial moral judgments are 'subjective', while legislative moral views are presumably 'objective'. The fact that they express this issue in the language of objectivity is revealing: it is evident that leaving the issue to legislatures can help us move from less to more democratic *legitimacy*, but it is far from clear how we could get more moral *objectivity*.

[63] *Roper v Simmons* (n 11) 607 (O'Connor), citing in part her opinion from *Thompson v Oklahoma* 487 US 815 (1988) 854.

[64] *Roper v Simmons* (n 11) 608.

[65] *Kindler v Canada* (n 49) (McLachlin).

Even more telling is the fact that the argument from common sentiment sometimes implies the inability to explain, systematize, or justify our moral emotions. For instance, in *McCleskey v Kemp*, Justice Powell finds no hazard in the fact that juries' moral judgments 'defy codification' and are 'often difficult to explain'.[66] The Swiss District Court in *Müller* denies the need to reflect upon our initial emotional reactions to obscene material: 'Comment on the confiscated works is superfluous; their vulgarity is plain to see and needs no elaborating upon ... Nor can a person of ordinary sensitivity be expected to go behind what is actually depicted and make a second assessment of the picture independently of what he can actually see ...'.[67] In Canada, La Forest refused to make a principled argument as to what 'shocks the conscience' or amounts to 'simply unacceptable' treatment; he struggled to articulate the role of courts in the assessment of people's emotions on the basis of their 'strength' or 'immutability', precisely because it is not obvious why these properties should themselves be valued.

A particularly vivid expression of the view that emotional reactions escape and exclude reason-based judgment is Scalia's opinion from *Lawrence v Texas*, dealing with homosexual sodomy:

> One of the benefits of leaving regulation of this matter to the people rather than to the courts is that the people, unlike judges, need not carry things to their logical conclusion. The people may feel that their disapprobation of homosexual conduct is strong enough to disallow homosexual marriage, but not strong enough to criminalize private homosexual acts—and may legislate accordingly.[68]

For Scalia, it is a virtue of people's moral judgment that it is based on a feeling of disapprobation which need not be coherent, rational, or logical: he praises popular opinion for not being subject to laws of reason. Notice that the deference to legislature is here not a consequence of democratic reasons as such, regardless of the consequences. Instead, Scalia argues that the best moral judgment will be made in the process that relies on emotive moral disapproval of the people, for there is nothing more to such judgment and certainly nothing reason-related. This is the same view as the one held by—already mentioned—Justice Marshall in *Furman*, where he claimed that the test for cruel and unusual punishment depends on the 'subjective, emotional reactions of informed citizens' which are not 'required to act rationally'.[69] Again, this is not to say that democratic concerns are discredited by this metaethics. In fact, I will argue later that democracy must be central to any plausible conception of constitutional ethics. Rather, the argument from

[66] *McCleskey v Kemp* 481 US 279 (1987) 311 references omitted.

[67] *Müller v Switzerland* (n 35) para 14.

[68] *Lawrence v Texas* 539 US 558 (2003) 604 (Scalia).

[69] *Furman v Georgia* (n 12) 360–62 (Marshall).

common sentiment can have institutional consequences which may seem to be a mere outcome of democratic sensibilities, and thus conceal its metaethical foundations.

It also does not follow from this argument that judges necessarily subscribe to the subjectivism of moral judgments. For example, if the moral ontology of common sentiments is correct, and there is nothing more to moral judgments than emotional reaction to a set of facts, we may be cautious and check our own emotional reactions against such reactions of the community. Moreover, it is understandable that moral agents need not be able to offer a sophisticated theory of morality to make moral judgments; one, in other words, doesn't have to be a moral philosopher to make the difference between right and wrong. However, the casual expressions of scepticism by judges may actually track a deeper conceptual problem. There is a thin line between saying that moral judgments are constituted by emotional reactions, and denying the possibility to curb our moral sentiments at all. The question is how to find the Archimedean point from which we can say that something is good or bad, apart from what we subjectively feel.

This problem is pertinent to *sceptical emotivism*, which holds that the function of moral language is not to describe facts, but to express pro and con attitudes.[70] According to this strand of emotivism, to utter a moral judgment of the sort 'the fact that you tortured babies for fun was wrong' reports the fact that you tortured babies for fun and adds nothing to it except an expression of disapproval of the action. It can be translated into two distinct utterances without anything being lost: 'you tortured babies for fun' plus 'boo torturing babies for fun'. The former presents a belief in a fact, and the latter reports a value which can only correspond to the speaker's subjective state of mind (attitude, intention, etc). The purpose of such a statement is to influence someone's behaviour.[71] Since only beliefs about facts can be objectively true or false, evaluative statements lack truth-conditions and are thus not truth-apt. And if moral statements are not truth-apt, they cannot be objective. They guide our behaviour in so far as we internalize the feeling set out in moral expressions, but saying that we have an objective moral duty external to our psychological apparatus is nonsensical.[72]

While the references to subjectivity made by judges may be understood in a more relaxed, institutional sense, the emotivist foundation of their moral judgments cannot be easily squared with objective moral values, so there may be some deeper truth in O'Connor's stipulation that moral judgments

[70] See AJ Ayer, *Language, Truth, and Logic* (2nd edn, V Gollancz 1946) ch 6 and Charles L Stevenson, *Ethics and Language* (Yale University Press 1944).

[71] Ayer, *Language, Truth, and Logic* (n 70) 107.

[72] Bernard Williams, *Moral Luck: Philosophical Papers, 1973–1980* (Cambridge University Press 1981) ch 8.

are 'inevitably' subjective. If emotivist-sceptical metaethics is the only possible background framework to such views, the attempts to justify our moral judgments invite infinite regress. Because moral emotions are merely expressions of our perspectival preferences, we have no objective grounds for looking at emotions in the first place. In other words, what establishes the value of emotions themselves is mysterious, but—given that on this view it can only be another subjective emotion—we are left with a sceptical view.

To go back to our examples, translated to the sceptical emotivist explanation of moral language, our emotions about the constitutional issues at stake would amount to 'boo/hooray capital punishment', 'boo/hooray obscenity', and 'boo/hooray extradition'. A restatement of the court's arguments (in the case of capital punishment, but this can be translated to all the examples) would then take the following form:

(i) the emotion that the majority of people expresses ought to determine whether there should be capital punishment
(ii) the majority of the people expresses the emotion 'boo capital punishment'
(iii) there should be no capital punishment.

But how can the proposition (i) be justified or explained? Notice that (i) contains a normative statement which translates as 'hooray majority's boo or hooray', amounting to just another subjective expression of a preference. Therefore, O'Connor and Scalia must be mistaken to think that deference to representative bodies can be motivated by moral objectivity, because the value on which such deference is based is just another subjective preference. They cannot conceptually escape what they wish to avoid most: imposing their own subjective views on the majority of people.

The controversial part of the argument from common sentiment—given its emotivist background—is internal inconsistency. Simon Blackburn describes this as 'schizoid attitude': having a moral commitment from (i) and at the same time thinking of it as ungrounded.[73] Let me explain this attitude using one of the examples we introduced earlier. Imagine a judge who thinks that the feeling of an individual citizen concerning what is obscene amounts only to this citizen's personal preference. Now, why would she think these personal preferences matter? She would have two options. One would be to say that this is because the majority of the people have a feeling that their personal preferences on this issue are important. Nonetheless, it is not clear how this feeling would amount to anything more than yet another personal

[73] Simon Blackburn, *Spreading the Word: Groundings in the Philosophy of Language* (Oxford University Press 1984) 197.

preference. The fact that many people feel something provides no obligation for others to follow. For example, many people like ice cream, but it does not follow that I must like it as well. The other option would be to say that it is her personal preference that what the majority feels should be the answer. If she does think that it is only her subjective emotional attitude to respect the majority's view on what is obscene, she would then either have to pretend that it is not only her preference to impose the views of the majority on this issue (hence she would contravene the practical relevance of morality), or she would have to commit herself to the view that her emotion is somehow different from the other emotions people express (hence she would have the schizoid attitude). To simplify: if a judge is aware that morality is about subjective feelings *only*, she should reject it altogether, because then it is her own view that the first premise in her reasoning is just her preference.[74]

Whereas we may think of the worry about the objectivity of judicial moral judgments expressed by O'Connor, Scalia, or McLachlin as a rhetorical tool to articulate a concern about legitimacy, or as an expression of a value of democratic governance, the problem becomes real when we want to situate that value in a coherent philosophical system. Similarly, the inability to articulate justifications for our moral judgments that Powell, La Forest, and Swiss courts do not find troubling may signal a more profound instability in their general conception of morality. The value with which their moral choice is justified is subject to the same criticism of subjectivity they wish to avoid. Justice Steven's opinion in *Spaziano* is a prime example of such circularity. His argument is that the community's moral sentiment dictates

[74] The problem is not that emotivism accuses reasoning in morality of being mistaken, but that such reasoning is applied in constitutional interpretation while believing it is erroneous to do so. The difficulty lies in the inability of sceptical emotivism to account for the functions which moral judgments have in conditional contexts. This has been known as the Frege-Geach problem. (See PT Geach, 'Assertion' (1965) 74 Philosophical Review 449) Consider an imaginary example based on the Canadian extradition cases. The example includes a combination of two intertwined arguments from two different cases, so that the conclusion of the second argument changes the premise of the first: (i) Extradition from Canada to countries where convicts face the death penalty is always morally justified; (ii) If extradition from Canada to countries where convicts face the death penalty is always morally justified, then extradition of Mr Burns to the United States is morally justified; (iii) However, extradition of Mr Burns to the United States is not morally justified; (iv) Therefore, extradition from Canada to countries where convicts face the death penalty is not always morally justified. This argument seems valid but the statement 'Extradition from Canada to countries where convicts face the death penalty is always morally justified' in the emotivist account has a different semantic role in assertive (i and iii) than in conditional contexts (ii and iv). For an argument to be valid, the meaning of identical statements must be the same in all premises. Therefore, if sceptical emotivism is true, reasoning like this is flawed. For if the meaning of the statement 'Extradition from Canada to countries where convicts face the death penalty is always morally justified' in (i) is not truth-apt, then we cannot make a conclusion in (ii) because such a conclusion can only follow from a statement which is true. Similarly, we cannot infer that (i) is not true in virtue of (iv), because it was not true in the first place. Again, it is open for an emotivist to reject the application of logic to morality as an illusion; however, a judge cannot then rely on this kind of reasoning and reject it at the same time. There needs to be some other way to explain the role of reasoning and the normativity of feelings. For a more recent discussion and rejection of the problem, see Paul Horwich, 'The Frege-Geach Point' (2005) 15 Philosophical Issues 78.

deference to branches which express the community's moral sentiment better. But what directs us towards the community moral sentiment in the first place? Or consider La Forest's argument that emotions have a property of strength or immutability which allows courts to evaluate them further. But is this property also valuable because someone feels it to be valuable? In short: because the subjectivist thinks that the objects in reality do not have a property of being valuable, but we only ascribe that property to them, there is no obvious way in which such ascriptions can gain objectivity, and we also must have an independent argument why only these ascriptions count as moral.[75]

The judges seem to think that the existence of convergence may grant us the vantage point to talk *as if* they were objective. This is also a familiar emotivist strategy, and probably the best for someone who implicitly relies on desire-based moral theories, but at the same time wishes to reject scepticism. Crucial to any such strategy is either to presuppose a convergence that enables us to talk as if moral values are objective or—failing that—to provide tools already present in our emotive framework of values to overcome disagreements.[76] The main tools for overcoming disagreements are reflection and reasoning, which are precluded by the emotive, pre-reflective, and irrational foundation of argument from common sentiment. This means that the argument must eventually suppose a high level of moral agreement.

This is not necessarily a problem: while there is a lot of focus on moral disagreements, these disagreements exist and make sense only against the background of a much greater moral agreement.[77] For example, while we may disagree all the time about the best welfare policies, no one probably thinks that torturing babies for fun is acceptable. But the question is whether this agreement is enough to support—in the emotivist account—the objectivity of moral talk without the backing of reflection and reasoning. To uncover whether this venue is really open for the argument from communal sentiments, let us look more closely to David Hume's moral theory as a classic

[75] Sceptical emotivism equalizes our moral feelings with all other psychological dispositions, and thus must offer an account of a prior and objective delineation between moral and immoral; the problem is that this definitional delineation must already have evaluative content. Hence—as Philippa Foot observes—such a view does not rule out 'bizarre so-called "moral judgments" about the wrongness of running around trees right handed or looking at hedgehogs in the light of the moon'. Philippa Foot, 'Does Moral Subjectivism Rest on a Mistake?' (1995) 15 Oxford Journal of Legal Studies 1, 2.

[76] One strategy, discussed in ch 5, is to suppose that metaethical questions about the nature of value are in fact first-order normative questions. See in particular Allan Gibbard, *Wise Choices, Apt Feelings: A Theory of Normative Judgment* (Clarendon Press 1990) and Simon Blackburn, *Ruling Passions: A Theory of Practical Reasoning* (Clarendon Press 1998).

[77] See eg Waldron, *Law and Disagreement* (n 6). Each theory based on disagreement must not only presuppose that there is agreement on how to overcome disagreements, but it also needs to show *why* agreement is normatively and non-sceptically relevant.

example of *non-sceptical emotivism*. While there are countless variations of similar emotivist strategies—many of which I analyse in Chapter 5—Hume's own theory is both paradigmatic and salient in this particular case: it allows us to explore how far the argument from common sentiment can go as a stand-alone argument before collapsing under its own weight, for it nicely illustrates the tension between its emotivist and relativist limbs.

Even though the basis of a moral system for Hume was not reason but moral sentiment, it does not follow that practical rationality is irrelevant for moral judgments and that there can be no moral system. In a famous passage, Hume says '[r]eason is, and ought to be the slave of the passions, and can never pretend to any other office than to serve and obey them'.[78] The question is: how does it serve and obey them? Hume's view is that ought claims are hypothetical imperatives. So for example, if you say 'I want a nice bagel and I'm going to a hairdresser to get it', I can tell you that you should not go to a hairdresser to get a bagel but to a bakery. Hypothetical imperative—the reason to go to a bakery and not to a hairdresser—is an instruction that already presupposes the existence of your desire. It only tells you what is the most rational or prudent way of fulfilling it. Given that you already want a bagel, it is reasonable for you to go to a bakery. But your desire to have a bagel is uncorrectable by reason, for there is no unreasonable desire. This is strikingly similar to the argument from common sentiment. Because there cannot be reasons external to our psychological emotional sets, our moral reasons must also be internal motivational dispositions.[79]

However, if I have no reason, as Hume says, to 'prefer the destruction of the whole world to the scratching of my finger',[80] how is it possible that there is a system of morality? This is conceivable because Hume presupposes a specifically moral motive which all humans share: the other-regarding sentiment of sympathy. Because actions which follow from sympathy are moral, this motive allows us to delineate moral motives and actions; also, sympathy enables us to evaluate both particular acts and general norms. For Hume, 'natural virtues'—kindness, benevolence, generosity, and the like—advance welfare directly and are not socially contingent, they flow straight from sympathy. However, our moral conventions also play a role. Hume calls these socially generated norms 'artificial virtues' (justice, property, etc). Each instantiation of artificial virtue may not contribute to the general welfare and satisfaction directly, but overall the system will benefit everyone, and as such it will produce the feeling of satisfaction. Natural virtues cannot do the

[78] David Hume, *A Treatise of Human Nature* (LA Selby-Bigge and PH Nidditch (eds), 2nd edn, Clarendon Press 1978) 415.

[79] The best explication of this view is Williams, *Moral Luck: Philosophical Papers* (n 72) 101–13.

[80] Hume, *A Treatise of Human Nature* (n 78) 416.

trick in a large society: the human condition is marked by a scarcity of goods and self-interest, and hence we need artificial virtues as well.

Notice that both artificial and natural virtues are ultimately supported by (universally human) sympathy:

> [a]s the means to an end can only be agreeable, where the end is agreeable; and as the good of society, where our own interest is not concerned, or that of our friends, pleases only by sympathy: It follows, that sympathy is the source of the esteem, which we pay to all the artificial virtues.[81]

This is not to say that justice cannot be supported by a specific feeling. But this feeling can be traced back to sympathy, which is a part of human nature. John Stuart Mill's explanation of the process is revealing: 'What was once desired as an instrument for the attainment of happiness, has come to be desired for its own sake. In being desired for its own sake it is, however, desired as *part* of happiness'.[82] The appropriate analogy here is between there being a desire for some pleasure which money can buy, and developing a desire for money itself. The latter may occur, but comes only as a consequence of having the initial desire.[83]

The question then is what ultimately gives us the sense of ought? This model does not work if we do not presuppose a shared inter-subjective common ground which gives us the platform of normativity. It is thus absolutely central for morality that there is a *convergence in feelings*, for this explains the *illusion of objectivity*.[84] A common feeling shared by all enables inter-subjective agreement because it mimics the objective truth, while the normativity of morality still depends on the initial emotion of sympathy. As Hume puts it himself: 'The notion of morals implies some sentiment common to all mankind, which recommends the same object to general approbation, and makes every man, or most men, agree in the same opinion or decision concerning it'.[85]

Now let us suppose that a judge in one of our examples shares this illusion of objectivity. Recall that the problem of the 'schizoid attitude' persists if the judge shares the illusion in the first premise and not in the second. On a Humean reading, this problem does not seem insurmountable. The second premise becomes not an expression of the attitude such as 'boo capital

[81] ibid 577.

[82] John Stuart Mill, 'Hedonism' in Russ Shafer-Landau (ed), *Ethical Theory: An Anthology* (2nd edn, Blackwell 2013) 261.

[83] ibid.

[84] Or, as we have seen, a way of confirming our convictions or overcoming disagreement through reflection and reason, which are excluded by the very nature of the argument from common sentiment.

[85] David Hume, *Enquires Concerning the Human Understanding and Concerning the Principles of Morals* (LA Selby-Bigge (ed), 2nd edn, Clarendon Press 1902) 272.

punishment' but an emanation of the common moral feeling of sympathy. The judge can make the inference because she is in the same kind of illusion as other citizens who express this emotion. Someone may object that, since the judge must not recognize the illusion, and because the second premise (knowing to look for emotions only) still reveals that the illusion is known to her, she could not in turn hold it important and must resist this kind of reasoning. I will deal with this objection and schizoid attitude in general at length in Chapter 5, but here we can set the objection aside, because—given that there is a convergence of desires—the judge is able to conclude what is the most reasonable way of fulfilling them (thus generating a hypothetical imperative for these desires). So we can assume for present purposes that the objection is not valid, because the illusion is supported by the factual circumstance of overlap in feelings and attitudes: it can be, in other words, an illusion all the way down.

The critical part here is the agreement or convergence of feelings. Not any convergence will do—while there may be some people who are incapable of having moral feelings or who get the facts wrong and thus their relevant beliefs are false—the vast majority of people ought to feel the same (as Hume says 'every man, or most men'). Now the distinction between artificial and natural virtues becomes important. In the case of artificial virtues (social conventions), it is plausible that judges ought to look at the moral conventions of their society and the feelings invoked by them. But because sometimes (and in controversial constitutional cases perhaps even often) there is no absolute convergence, the only thing a judge can do is to fall back on the general feeling of sympathy and natural virtues. If there is no convergence in our emotions about social conventions, we can only rely on this universal feeling.

However, this universalizing tendency of non-sceptical emotivism is directly opposed to the community-bound character of the argument from common sentiment.[86] The illusion of objectivity in all instances of reasoning is too demanding on the other element of this type of argument: the relativist element. In other words, because there is a common human nature that determines what is moral, the emotivist element clashes with the relativist element, rendering the ontological claim inadequate. The argument from communal sentiments can thus only go so far: if the convergence is fractured, the objectivity slips through the cracks of disagreement. This is because the moral ontology of this argument stops at the unreflective feelings of the people in one society; according to the argument from common

[86] Recall here that the ontological claim of the argument from common sentiment requires exclusiveness, that is to say it demands to be the only paradigm of ethical arguments. I will deal with the interaction between different regimes of ethical arguments later.

sentiment, it is the only thing that matters. There is no reflection, reason, or process of justification to overcome disagreement, and there is no agreement to maintain the impression of objectivity. But we are now crossing the line between the emotivist and relativist element, and the latter deserves treatment on its own.

3.3.2 The relativist element

Even though the argument from common sentiment is now in doubt, we may start from the other end and see whether we can work our way back to support it. I have so far expressed scepticism about the possibility of combining unrefined and unreflective emotivism with relativism into a sound metaethics.[87] There are also good reasons to do so, for relativism seems to rebut the moral ontology that is based on sentiments only. While emotivism understands moral statements as non-truth-apt, relativism holds that moral statements *are true* but only *in relation* to a specific frame of reference; moral statements could then be true from the standpoint of one frame of reference and not from the other. As such, relativism negates both universal objectivism and the version of emotivism that informs the argument from common sentiment: if such emotivism is true then relativism is false, and vice versa.[88]

But what does this mean exactly? Why deny that our emotional reactions can be collective as well as individual? Couldn't we just say that if people believe something—where 'believing' includes having converging desires or false beliefs in the truth of that something—then we should respect their opinion? Is this fact enough to generate the normativity of public moral opinions? While this view could make sense as a normative commitment within one's framework of values, we need to eschew it as an ontological position, for it leads to a rather *banal* version of relativism.

To explain why this view is not defensible, let us—following David Lyons—introduce a distinction between agent and appraiser relativism.[89] Agent relativism is the view that standards relevant for moral judgments are relative to the person (or society) that is being judged, and appraiser relativism takes as relevant the moral standards of the person (or society) that is making the

[87] For the defence of a version of emotivist relativism see Jesse J Prinz, *The Emotional Construction of Morals* (Oxford University Press 2007). For the view that emotivism leads to relativism and that this is—broadly speaking—a tension within this view see: Philippa Foot, *Moral Dilemmas and Other Topics in Moral Philosophy* (Oxford University Press 2002) ch 2; Russ Shafer-Landau, *Moral Realism: A Defence* (Oxford University Press 2003) ch 1.

[88] Nicholas L Sturgeon, 'Relativism' in John Skorupski (ed), *The Routledge Companion to Ethics* (Routledge 2010) 356.

[89] David Lyons, 'Ethical Relativism and the Problem of Incoherence' (1976) 86 Ethics 107.

judgment. What I have labelled 'banal' relativism is in fact a distorted form of agent relativism.

If one is to ask people in the street what relativism is, the answer would probably be something to this effect: 'there is nothing more to morality than the socially shared values of the members of a particular culture'.[90] So in our examples agent relativism—together with the emotivist element which identifies moral values with emotional reactions—would mean: 'capital punishment/obscenity/extradition is good or bad because people in the society which is being judged feel it is good or bad'. The courts infer from this that we ought to conform to the views of the majority of people in societies that are being judged. Recall for instance the ECtHR's margin of appreciation doctrine here: different moral compacts in Europe must be respected unless there is a pan-European consensus. This is—at least up to a point—an agent-relativist view.[91] On the other hand, the Canadian 'shocks the consciousness' doctrine is probably better understood as a version of appraiser relativism: what is relevant is how we feel about the question and not the societies we are judging.

Even if we suppose that cultures are bounded in this way and that the one-person-one-culture view is correct, there is still a problem with this reasoning from the perspective of agent relativism. To reject it we need not presuppose the existence of mind-independent and universal moral truths, for this type of relativism entails a universalist premise to which it initially denied relevance. From the fact that there are differences in moral views between cultures and societies, the universal conclusion that we ought to respect the majority's view in these cultures cannot follow. Such a conclusion can only be supported by a value internal to the evaluative framework from which the judgment is made.

The wrongness of the inference lies in the implicit move from agent to appraiser relativism. This is analogous to a false conclusion that the value of tolerance follows if morality is a culturally embedded phenomenon. According to this argument, because we are aware that cultures are different, we ought to respect them equally. But this could also be true only in relation to a particular culture; that is, it cannot hold universally because we start from the premise that all moral opinions are culturally constrained and not universal. This condition would only obtain if such a view is widely held within a given appraiser culture, and it would bind solely members of that particular culture. The ECtHR's margin of appreciation doctrine cannot

[90] Harry Gensler, 'Cultural Relativism' in Russ Shafer-Landau (ed), *Ethical Theory: An Anthology* (2nd edn, Blackwell 2013).

[91] One could, of course, see this position as being a part of the evaluative framework of the court making this judgment and thus as coherent. I will discuss these issues at length in chs 5 and 6 and I will show how this view might make sense in a more refined version.

follow from the fact of diversity—as it is often presented—but from a specific agreement on the appropriate moral attitude to deal with such diversity. Therefore, the relativist element can only be supported by some version of appraiser relativism.

Sophisticated relativism must thus reject the agent relativist view, but at the same time the question remains whether *our* (appraiser's) emotions are the *only* thing that matters. Recall that we are still dealing with the ontological thesis, that is, with the question of what morality is, and not how can we know it. There are two possible ways in which the thesis can be defended. One avenue would be to claim that it is actually people's belief that their feelings are the only things that matter. The other could be to claim that there is nothing more to our practice than emotions; that is, by looking closely at moral practice—and regardless of what the people believe—we can see that the truth of moral claims is established by moral practice that consists only of emotional responses to moral problems. Both defences are implausible.

Consider an example which teases out the conceptual problem with the first response. Within a culture, it is usually the case that moral principles like 'torturing babies for fun is wrong' are understood as 'torturing babies for fun is wrong regardless of the majority's opinion'. People do not believe that this question is appropriate for some kind of referendum. It is a part of—at least our—culture that some moral issues are removed from majoritarian decision-making.[92] If this is true, we face a self-contradiction by taking the first defence: we believe that our beliefs on this issue do not matter, hence if we take our beliefs to be important, we ought at the same time to abandon the view that they are important. This reveals the vicious circle this kind of explanation eventually must face.

This leads us to the second line of defence the emotivist appraiser-relativist can take. In this case, the claim is that the best explanation of the moral practice of uttering things like 'capital punishment should be abolished', 'this is obscenity' or 'extradition in this case is not justified' is that by so doing we express our emotions *only*. But this argument is not sound for two reasons: first, it fails to account for the role of reflection and reasoning in our moral talk; and second, even if it can offer a causal account of how we came to adopt certain moral opinions, it is not attentive enough to the practical relevance of morality and cannot make its normativity intelligible. Ronald Dworkin conveys this point elegantly: 'What is shocking and wrong

[92] While some argue that moral disagreements about rights justify the abolishment of judicial review of legislation (eg Waldron, 'The Core of the Case against Judicial Review' (n 6)), the facts are saying the opposite: judicial review has been the most successful project of modern constitutionalism and the idea that the majority's opinion ought to be curtailed is perhaps the one thing that most constitutional systems agree about.

is not [the] idea that the community's morality counts, but [the] idea of what counts as the community's morality'.[93]

The main point is this: there is reason to doubt the position of an appraiser relativist judge who subscribes to the ontology of common moral sentiments, because—when her thesis about morality is qualified with the emotivist element—it cannot account for the ways in which morality actually functions. As David Wong observes, this kind of argument for relativism cannot explain moral reasoning and criticism:

> Whatever is communally judged to be the case, the argument goes, actually comes to be the case ... The question with this argument, however, is whether we can accept that custom determines in a strong sense what is fine and ugly, just and unjust. It may influence what people *think* is fine and just. But it is quite another thing for custom to determine what *is* fine and just. Customs sometimes change under the pressure of moral criticism, and the argument seems to rely on a premise that contradicts the phenomenon.[94]

As we have seen, in ordinary moral discourse we do not believe that some questions are a matter of different feelings or opinions. This need not be the case because there are some universal and mind-independent facts of the matter about this issue, but taking solely feelings as the basis of our society's moral commitments is actually not our society's moral commitment.

A sophisticated appraiser relativist who is attracted to emotivism needs to explain the role of moral reasoning in our moral practice. When we take the moral point of view, we do not rely solely on other people's emotions. Resolving moral questions from our examples—capital punishment, obscenity, extradition—does not simply amount to counting our common feelings on the matter. We think of our moral judgments as justified when we are able to offer an argument for them starting from a value (that we presumably all accept), and using the basic rules of moral reasoning. In this process, we may also rethink our values, even if we are committed to the view that values are socially shared commitments to certain goals. This is because we also take into account actions that would make our lives go better, we are sensitive to the aims of our society, we compare our moral judgments with other values we believe in to reach a balanced decision, etc. Relativists may be right that all values are contingent; however, a pure emotivist relativism neglects important parts of our practice that are necessary—even on the relativist account—to make moral claims justified.[95]

[93] Ronald Dworkin, 'Lord Devlin and the Enforcement of Morals' (1966) 75 Yale Law Journal 986, 1001.

[94] David Wong, 'Relativism' in Peter Singer (ed), *A Companion to Ethics* (Blackwell 1991) 443.

[95] Even if we assume that appraiser relativism would accept that our society could become a society that highly values torturing children, what would make this morality warranted is not a simple fact that we

Take for example some claims made about events, geographically and temporally outside of our immediate culture: 'What Hitler did to Jews was wrong'; 'Slavery was a morally appalling practice'; 'We should have prevented genocide in Rwanda'. By uttering these sentences, we do not imply that it is *our* feeling *now* that these conducts were wrong. This would describe the situation with 'one thought too many',[96] for we condemn these practices simply because we think they were wrong. If someone were to claim otherwise, we would expect an argument for that claim. Similar problems arise in cases which rely on the argument from common sentiment and reach conclusions that are morally unacceptable, for then we may ask the same question: what is the argument for such conclusions? Take an example. In *McCleskey v Kemp*, Justice Powell used the argument from common sentiment to refuse to address the fact that African Americans in Georgia had a much greater chance of being sentenced to death. He held that the objective demonstration of communal values is to be found in legislative and juries' opinions, and that there would need to be 'exceptionally clear proof before [the Court] would infer that the discretion has been abused'.[97] What this opinion lacks is a realization that discretion was abused, but—more importantly—a clear conception of what would amount to an abuse. If, for example, morally wrong or racist decisions of representative bodies present the abuse of discretion, this demands a prior idea of what moral answers are; it would demand an argument that could decide either way. But if these answers are consumed by communal emotions, then the court lacks the resources to address the fact that the death penalty remains concentrated in the American South and imposed mainly on black people.[98]

This brings us to the problem that will prove to be central for the conception of value developed in Chapter 5. One could take an external perspective of the practice and say: what causally explains our feeling that this is wrong is that we came to learn that conduct such as this would have devastating consequences for us so we became committed to preserving peace, equality, and other values; moreover, given the importance of these values, we transmit them through cultural means to future generations as ultimate, unchangeable, and universal. The question is how much purchase these external and causal statements ought to have on our internal ethical perspective. We do experience the world in both causal and normative terms.

all came to cherish the value of child-torturing, but that we came to cherish it following the rules of our moral practice.

[96] Williams, *Moral Luck: Philosophical Papers* (n 72) 18. Williams used the expression to criticize utilitarianism, but the same objection applies here.

[97] *McCleskey v Kemp* (n 66) 297.

[98] See Garland, *Peculiar Institution: America's Death Penalty in an Age of Abolition* (n 14) 280–82.

But—while causal explanations can tell us how we came to believe and act in certain ways—normative explanations account for our actions as morally appropriate or not.[99] This is the source of what we have earlier identified as the 'schizoid attitude'. Much of the appeal of relativist and emotivist positions come from the force of causal perspective on morality, but we need to be cautious about its impact in the normative domain. The argument from common sentiment could be an example of this: it might draw its force from the observation of factual differences between moral frameworks and the role of emotions in our moral judgments, but it is not sufficiently attentive to the normative domain and practical relevance of morality. It fails to give both causal and normative perspectives their due.

In fact, relativism itself need not deny that there is also a framework of values that we contingently share in the world. Even if this contingent agreement on values is partial and too thin to resolve the most difficult moral dilemmas, there is no reason to suppose that it is not there. While this common framework of values might be contingent and relative—perhaps most obviously in the temporal sense—there is no reason to accept relativism in a crude and empirically inaccurate form that sees different constitutional systems as constitutive of completely idiosyncratic moral commitments.[100] The big question is, of course, where to derive the normativity of these idiosyncratic commitments if they are not universally true, but we need not answer this question yet. Suffice it to note at this point that a version of relativism which is based solely on emotions is not credible. It falsely presupposes that morality is a set of emotional solutions to concrete problems, but—even on socially based and relativist conception of morality—this is not enough. Even if we accept the empirical assumption that our moral practices are community-bound, they neither include the commitment to the relativity of moral truth nor the belief that emotions are the only basis of moral judgments. To conclude: any defensible sophisticated relativism is in fact a

[99] See eg Thomas Nagel, *The View from Nowhere* (Oxford University Press 1986) 140–44. For a discussion of the interplay between these two perspectives in the context of law see Dennis Patterson, 'Normativity and Objectivity in Law' (2001) 43 William and Mary Law Review 325.

[100] Relativists often assume that there are some variations between cultures, but also stipulate a threshold that socially based codes must pass to qualify as moral. Most of these accounts depart from assumptions about human nature and similarities in the human condition. For example, David Wong starts from the practical function of morality as a regulatory tool for resolving conflicts of interest under the circumstances of scarcity to develop universal limits to particular moralities, so that morality may be inadequate in relation to this function. See David Wong, *Natural Moralities: A Defense of Pluralistic Relativism* (Oxford University Press 2006). David Copp thinks that a moral code is justified only if it would be rational for people to choose it in the society in question, a notion which partly depends on the specific and contingent moral values of the society, but also on their basic natural needs. David Copp, *Morality, Normativity, and Society* (Oxford University Press 1995). The problem with these views, however, is that they assume a normative premise in their account of morality which then serves as a universal yardstick for assessing the appropriateness of any moral code.

version of appraiser relativism which in addition must relax (if not abandon) the constraint of the emotivist element to the moral ontology of the argument from common sentiment.

3.4 CONCLUSION

In this chapter, I have tried to demonstrate that the argument from common sentiment consists in an emotional response of a particular community to a set of morally relevant facts. To the extent to which it functions as an exclusive type of ethical argument in constitutional reasoning that precludes other ways of expounding moral concepts, it relies on a moral ontology which is not plausible. The immediate consequence is this: there may be other types of ethical arguments that can be compatible with the argument from common sentiment, for the latter cannot enjoy an ontologically privileged status.

The argument from common sentiment underappreciates the role of reason in moral judgments. From the emotivist standpoint, the lack of reflection and reasoning in moral practice fails to support the illusion of objectivity in the face of moral disagreements. From the relativist standpoint, the lack of reflection and reasoning fails to account for the actual ways in which our moral framework—even if relative and contingent—operates. Both, however, face a common objection: how do the descriptive facts about our contingent moral attitudes gain any normative traction? The typical response to these kinds of concerns is to turn to the role of reason and its ability to generate universal moral imperatives. This kind of metaethical underpinning is present in another ethical argument: the argument from universal reason. Let us then explore this type of argument further and see whether starting from universal moral reasons can get us further in moral inquiry.

4

Universal Reason

4.1 INTRODUCTION

The previous chapter concluded that an inadequate moral ontology underscores the argument from common sentiment, and that it cannot serve as a self-sufficient constitutional approach to moral problems. This type of argument does not account for the role of reasoning in moral judgment, and does not explain why moral inquiry necessarily stops at the borders of a community. This chapter explores another type of ethical argument that inverts both elements of the argument from common sentiment; in other words, the argument which is neither emotivist nor relativist, but reason-laden and universalistic. On the one hand, it relies on the idea that morality is *universal*, or at least more detached from particular communal, cultural, or individual experiences. It presupposes that the value will appear to us if we take the 'view from nowhere',[1] and that the moral point of view requires removing the layers of contingency induced in us by our lives here and now. On the other hand, this argument assumes that moral requirements are attainable though *reason*, and are not dictated by emotions; instead of sentiments, it uses the language of reflection, reason, and argument.

This chapter argues that these elements—universality and reasonableness—are present in judicial reliance on foreign law when they interpret domestic constitutional provisions. Both case law and academic commentary share the notion that the use of foreign law has to do with the idea of reasoned judgment in morally sensitive issues, and that this phenomenon depends on a more cosmopolitan understanding of the nature of value. I will thus call the use of foreign law in constitutional interpretation *the argument from universal reason*.

Universality and reasonableness promise to give moral values solid grounds: instead of being subject to whim and caprice, they would be rooted in universally human reasons. If successful, such an argument could

[1] See Thomas Nagel, *The View from Nowhere* (Oxford University Press 1986) chs 8 and 9.

overcome the limitations of the argument from common sentiment. First, by introducing the possibility of moral reflection and reasoning it would remedy the lack of convergence in moral feelings; it would both help us fine-tune our own moral point of view and provide the argumentative tools to convince others. Second, it would account for the intuition that at least some values are universal. But this could also create inconsistencies in the judicial approach to the nature of value. The argument from common sentiment implies an unrefined version of emotivism that forecloses the possibility of arriving at moral judgments by reason (or by reason *only*), so how can we explain the role of reason-based ethical arguments within the same jurisdiction, by the same court, or even in the same judgment? Similarly, if the value is revealed by the emotional reaction of the community to a certain set of morally relevant facts, how can the judgments of courts in other jurisdictions be relevant? There are two ways to proceed: the argument from common sentiment is either to be replaced or supplemented with the argument from universal reason.

The chapter argues that the argument from universal reason ought to supplement and not replace the argument from common sentiment. This is because the most plausible account of the argument from universal reason actually fits well with the argument from common sentiment. On this account, universality is not an absolute and timeless property of values, but a mere recognition of contingent interconnections between moral codes in the world; reasonableness does not presuppose a robust relation between reasoning and categorical moral truths, but involves a reflective process through which we become aware of normatively relevant concerns. The argument from universal reason thus gives up on the foundational role of reason in moral judgments and attributes to it only a correctional function. It allows our contingent moral attitudes and emotive intuitions—present in the arguments from constitutional identity and common sentiment—to feed into moral judgments and does not completely eliminate the parochial and emotional character of constitutional ethics. This, however, leaves the normativity of constitutional ethics unexplained, and Chapters 5 and 6 therefore deal with this issue in more depth.

This chapter follows a similar structure to the previous one. The first part identifies the elements of argument from universal reason in comparative constitutional practice, and the second analyses its philosophical foundations. However, instead of showing the internal inconsistency in this ethical argument, it tries to reveal distinct ways in which the use of foreign law can be connected with the idea of universal reason. The chapter attempts to demonstrate that there is such a link, but that the idea of universal reason implicit in the use of foreign law is rather modest.

4.2 ELEMENTS OF THE ARGUMENT FROM UNIVERSAL REASON

This chapter asks why the non-mandatory use of foreign law in difficult constitutional matters is valuable, and seeks to explain the connection between the use of foreign law and moral value. There are two possible ways to do this: direct and indirect. The first aims to establish a *direct* connection between advancing a specific moral value and the use of foreign law. The nature of value is not vital for this argument; it is enough that we are roughly certain that such a value—be that liberty, equality, welfare, happiness, or pleasure—is considered normatively important. Jeremy Waldron, for example, puts forward a direct normative argument for the use of foreign law. In his view, there is reason to prefer global consistency in legal policies that is partly independent from their moral correctness, because people legitimately expect similarity in the rules that determine their basic status.[2] However, the reach of this argument is limited.[3] Consistency may be appealing when there is epistemic uncertainty about specific moral requirements, while at the same time some substantive moral threshold is secured. But epistemic uncertainty is typically connected to the moral insignificance of the issue. For instance, we may opt for convergent traffic rules between countries so long as we are not sure which rules bring about better results in terms of reducing the number of accidents, but once we discover that these rules are increasing the number of accidents, then we should change them regardless of consistency. If the issue is not insignificant, we ought not to be indifferent about it, and there are no reasons to defer to foreign consensus without substantive moral backing. The direct justification for the use of foreign law on the basis of consistency is therefore weak: it pertains to a small fraction of cases when there is an expected convergence in morally less significant policies. More generally, it is rather challenging to show the worth of the use of foreign law with reference to any particular value. Foreign law may substantively differ and develop over time, and so its effects can vary as well.

The second way to justify the use of foreign law is *indirect*. It inserts an intermediary step between the use of foreign law and the substantive values to be attained, for it argues that this process could make us cognizant of value as such. The worthiness of the process does not directly depend on the empirical link between the use of foreign law and a specific valuable outcome, but makes this connection intelligible by demonstrating that—given a particular understanding of the nature of value—the process is apt to lead us

[2] Jeremy Waldron, *'Partly Laws Common to All Mankind': Foreign Law in American Courts* (Yale University Press 2012) ch 5.

[3] Waldron admits that the argument is 'pretty modest'. ibid 141.

to better answers to moral dilemmas. Notice that the indirect justification is not completely independent from the results it delivers, but that the connection is subtler: if a process is generally able to deliver good results, then we have reason to place trust in it even when we are uncertain about its each and every particular instance. So, while the direct approach focuses on the realization of some value in *particular*, it is best to think of the indirect approach as providing means to attain value in *general*. To make sense of the abstract connection between foreign law and moral value, the indirect approach must rely on a conception of value against which the use of foreign law will be epistemologically trustworthy.

Most of the existing normative accounts of the use of foreign law are of the indirect type. Mark Tushnet aptly observes that the issue has been framed as a 'disagreement between those who believe that human experience reflects and seeks to realize universal values, and those who are said to take a more relativistic view'.[4] The universalist strand of thinking about the use of foreign law is well captured by Harold Koh's metaphor of a 'global community of reason and rights'; the central idea is that constitutional interpretation ought to be in line with converging practices in international and comparative law, which present the earthly embodiment of universal values based on reason.[5]

The critics reject these metaethical premises. For instance, Richard Posner—in line with many others—argues that the use of foreign law relies on the discredited idea of natural law which is universal and consequently represented in foreign law.[6] According to Posner, the notion that such natural law principles ought to constrain positive law is implausible, primarily because it does not take into account moral disagreement and violates democratic values.[7] But neither Posner nor other critics of the use of foreign law offer an alternative conception of value that is capable of avoiding these pitfalls.[8] For example, it is not clear why democratic values are not subject to the same disagreement objection. For consider: either the judges who use foreign law disagree with Posner about the relevance of democratic

[4] Mark V Tushnet, 'Referring to Foreign Law in Constitutional Interpretation: An Episode in the Culture Wars' (2006) 35 University of Baltimore Law Review 299, 310–11. See also Sanford Levinson, 'Looking Abroad When Interpreting the U.S. Constitution: Some Reflections' (2004) 39 Texas International Law Journal 353.

[5] Harold Hongju Koh and William Michael Treanor, 'Keynote Address: A Community of Reason and Rights' (2008) 77 Fordham Law Review 583.

[6] Richard Posner, 'Foreword: A Political Court' (2005) 119 Harvard Law Review 32, 85.

[7] ibid 84–90.

[8] See Eric Engle, 'European Law in American Courts: Foreign Law as Evidence of Domestic Law' (2007) 33 Ohio Northern University Law Review 99, 103; Roger P Alford, 'In Search of a Theory for Constitutional Comparativism' (2005) 52 UCLA Law Review 639; Roger P Alford, 'Roper v. Simmons and Our Constitution in International Equipoise' (2005) 53 UCLA Law Review 1, 16–21.

values, or he is building a straw-man; in the former cases democratic values are subject to the same disagreement problem, in the latter his argument is confused.[9] The critics, however, do raise a credible point that the connection between foreign law as a contingent occurrence in the world and the realm of value is not clear.[10] This is the connection that needs to be elucidated if the argument from universal reason is to gain normative traction: we need to see why the use of foreign law is a reliable or trustworthy method to find moral answers.

To do this we need to have a better sense of the actual patterns of judicial arguments and then analyse their implicit metaethical commitments. The argument from universal reason shares some common traits with other ethical arguments. First, it is used to support moral judgment: foreign law is brought to illuminate ethical concepts from the constitution, often developing the understanding of these concepts beyond the constitutional text, previous precedents, or original intentions. Second, over time it may become an entrenched way of interpreting the constitution.[11] Third, the use of foreign law need not result in a judgment that goes against the legislative will, and this argument cannot be adequately discussed only in terms of the legitimacy of judicial review.[12]

In contrast to the argument from common sentiment, the argument from universal reason rests on the idea that values are not confined to a specific community and that moral judgment is not complete without reasoning and reflection. To discern these implicit metaethical assumptions behind this argument, I will turn to the constitutional practice of the United States, South Africa, and Israel. The choice of cases is appropriate because it illustrates several different attitudes towards both foreign law and the nature of value: in the United States there has been a lot of opposition to the use of foreign law and values are often seen as local, but when foreign law is cited the

[9] This argument from disagreement to democracy is invoked in many other articles in the debate without recognizing this problem. See eg Rosalind Dixon, 'A Democratic Theory of Constitutional Comparison' (2008) 56 American Journal of Comparative Law 947, 958–59.

[10] Joan L Larsen, 'Importing Constitutional Norms from a "Wider Civilization": *Lawrence* and the Rehnquist Court's Use of Foreign and International Law in Domestic Constitutional Interpretation' (2004) 65 Ohio State Law Journal 1283, 1322–26.

[11] It may also become relevant through a single precedent. For example, because the court mentioned the law of England, Scotland, India, and Ceylon when establishing the rule against self-incrimination during the police interrogation in *Miranda v Arizona* 384 US 436 (1966) 486–90, Justice O'Connor argued in a subsequent case (*New York v Quarles* 467 US 649 (1984) 672–73) that the law of these countries is relevant for the determination of the scope of this rule.

[12] For example, even though the practice of reference to foreign law had had a very long history before *Trop v Dulles* 356 US 86 (1958), this was the first case to use foreign law in striking down legislation. See Steven G Calabresi and Stephanie Dotson Zimdahl, 'The Supreme Court and Foreign Sources of Law: Two Hundred Years of Practice and the Juvenile Death Penalty Decision' (2005) 47 William and Mary Law Review 743, 846–47.

elements of universality and reasonableness are quite robust; South Africa is the most open to foreign law, but regardless of the strong cosmopolitan and reason-based rhetoric, the elements of universality and reasonableness are modest; in Israel, the vision of value is more parochial and context-sensitive, and the use of foreign law is constrained by the specific local identity, but the results of the use of foreign law are often universalistic.

4.2.1 United States

There are several reasons why the argument from foreign law in the United States is best understood as an *ethical* argument. First, the cases in which the justices of the Supreme Court used foreign law were ground-breaking and decided some of the most important moral dilemmas of their era. To mention but a few: *Dred Scott v Sandford* (denying citizenship rights to African Americans);[13] *Reynolds v United States* (upholding anti-polygamy laws notwithstanding the freedom of religion);[14] *Lochner v New York* (invalidating a working hours limit on the basis of liberty of contract);[15] *Roe v Wade* (establishing the right to abortion);[16] *Washington v Glucksberg* (denying the right to die);[17] *Bowers v Hardwick* and *Lawrence v Texas* (respectively upholding and striking down sodomy laws);[18] *Trop v Dulles, Coker v Georgia, Enmund v Florida, Thompson v Oklahoma, Atkins v Virginia*, and *Roper v Simmons* (determining the meaning of 'cruel and unusual' punishment).[19]

Second, justices use foreign law to expound ambiguous moral concepts from the constitution: the practice occurs most frequently when the court interprets the prohibition of 'cruel and unusual' punishment from the 8th Amendment and the substantive component of the due process clauses from the 5th and 14th Amendments, which prohibit the deprivation of 'life, liberty, or property, without due process'. Both clauses enable the court to enrich the constitution with new interpretations beyond the strict reading of its text, and—in the case of the substantive due process doctrine—to protect new rights on the basis of the notion of liberty.

Third, the attitude towards foreign law is very different from the attitude towards authoritative legal materials. As Justice Kennedy explained in *Roper v Simmons*: 'The opinion of the world community, while not controlling our outcome, does provide respected and significant confirmation for our

[13] *Dred Scott v Sandford* 60 US 393 (1856).

[14] *Reynolds v United States* 98 US 145 (1878).

[15] *Lochner v New York* 198 US 66 (1905) 71–72 (Harlan).

[16] *Roe v Wade* 410 US 113 (1973).

[17] *Washington v Glucksberg* 521 US 702 (1997).

[18] *Bowers v Hardwick* 478 US 186 (1986); *Lawrence v Texas* 539 US 558 (2003).

[19] *Trop v Dulles* (n 12); *Coker v Georgia* 433 US 584 (1977); *Enmund v Florida* 458 US 782 (1982); *Thompson v Oklahoma* 487 US 815 (1988); *Atkins v Virginia* 536 US 304 (2002); *Roper v Simmons* 543 US 551 (2005).

own conclusions'.[20] This is a different vocabulary from the one attached to sources of law: foreign law does not produce immediate outcomes, but carries a certain normative weight. The idea is that foreign law will help judges reach a better judgment, and not that they are authoritatively compelled to consult foreign sources.[21]

The justification of this idea typically arises from the conception of value premised upon two interconnected elements: reasonableness and universality. Let me illustrate this by using *Roper* as an example. In this case, the court found capital punishment to be 'cruel and unusual' if the offender was less than 18 years old when he committed the crime. The decision undoubtedly included a *moral judgment* on the part of the court. Justice Kennedy, writing for the majority, explicitly took a moral perspective ('[f]rom a moral standpoint it would be misguided to equate the failings of a minor with those of an adult')[22] confirming a line of cases which consider moral judgment as inevitable for the 8th Amendment analysis.[23] This analysis includes a two-tier test: first, the court seeks to establish what the national moral consensus is, and then evaluates the *reasonableness* of the punishment, or—as Justice O'Connor puts it—its 'moral proportionality'.[24] While common moral sentiments feed into the first part of the test, the majority in *Roper* used foreign law in the second part, to determine the reasonableness of the practice.[25] The connection between reasonableness and foreign law holds in other cases as well: all capital punishment cases that use foreign law adopt the two-tier analysis that includes court's evaluation of the reasonableness of the community's moral consensus.[26]

In this context, reasonableness means that the punishment must be proportionate to the harm inflicted and to the blameworthiness of the offender.[27] But more importantly, the idea is that common sentiments could be morally wrong, and that the court is there to provide a check on these sentiments with the assistance of foreign law; the underlying thought is that if enough people in the world reflect enough about the morality of a punishment they will reach a solution that is more 'reasonable', 'civilized', and

20 *Roper v Simmons* (n 19) 578.

21 Bosko Tripkovic, 'Judicial Comparativism and Legal Positivism' (2014) 5 Transnational Legal Theory 285.

22 *Roper v Simmons* (n 19) 570.

23 The court rejected both the substantive holding from *Stanford v Kentucky* 492 US 361 (1989), and the approach from that case which denied the relevance of the court's own moral judgment to 8th Amendment analysis. The alternative view—that the court's moral judgment is indispensable—is for example taken by the plurality in *Coker v Georgia* (n 19) 597.

24 *Roper v Simmons* (n 19) 587 (O'Connor).

25 ibid 575–78.

26 *Coker v Georgia* (n 19) 597; *Enmund v Florida* (n 19) 796; *Thompson v Oklahoma* (n 19) 833–38; *Atkins v Virginia* (n 19) 312–13.

27 *Enmund v Florida* (n 19) 815.

'proportionate' than are the unreflective sentiments of the population. The notion of reasonableness thus stands in an uneasy relationship with the contingent moral sentiments: it hovers above these sentiments and is able to render them inappropriate, but it is at the same time unclear how the property of reasonableness can be different in kind from what the people themselves think is reasonable.

The second element of this conception of value is *universality*. International materials confirm or rebut the court's own reasonableness analysis, so moral values are not seen as confined to parochial traditions and sentiments. Justice Breyer once defended the use of foreign law in a case pertaining to the death-row phenomenon by describing it as a 'not technically legal, but rather law-related human question' or 'human problem'.[28] This captures the spirit in which foreign law is used: judges aim to answer how we ought to live, believe that all humans share these deep moral dilemmas, and trust that true answers to these dilemmas are not limited to the existing law.

An expression of both elements of the argument from universal reason is found in O'Connor's dissent in *Roper*:

> this Nation's evolving understanding of *human dignity* certainly is neither wholly isolated from, nor inherently at odds with, the values prevailing in other countries. On the contrary, we should not be surprised to find *congruence between domestic and international values*, especially where the international community has reached clear agreement—expressed in international law or in the domestic laws of individual countries—that a particular form of punishment is inconsistent with fundamental human rights. At least, the existence of an international consensus of this nature can serve to confirm the *reasonableness* of a consonant and genuine American consensus.[29]

O'Connor's reasoning starts from a moral concept with a particularly cosmopolitan flavour: human dignity. She then argues that the convergence in the world about the meaning of this value must be telling of the value itself. Finally, the existence of consensus is attached to the idea of reason: the fact that others have reached the same conclusion can confirm the reasonableness of local American sentiments.

O'Connor's argument also illustrates the tensions between the argument from universal reason and the argument from common sentiment. For O'Connor, if there is no local agreement, and if the court is unable to independently justify its own moral decision, the global consensus has no normative weight.[30] Apart from doctrinal and legitimacy reasons, this is

[28] Norman Dorsen, 'The Relevance of Foreign Legal Materials in U.S. Constitutional Cases: A Conversation between Justice Antonin Scalia and Justice Stephen Breyer' (2005) 3 International Journal of Constitutional Law 519, 528. Breyer was referring here to *Knight v Florida* 528 US 990 (1999).

[29] *Roper v Simmons* (n 19) 605 (O'Connor) (emphases added).

[30] ibid.

because O'Connor's conception of value is ambivalent about the relationship between the local and global, and emotions and reason: if the consensus is reasonable, and reasonableness is a property of true moral values, then why doesn't the consensus trump misguided local opinions? What follows—normatively speaking—from the sociological fact that 'we shouldn't be surprised to find congruence' between international and domestic values? To answer these questions, we need a clear conception of the connection between comparative law, reason, and moral value.

Similar issues arise in other opinions that make use of foreign law. In a number of cases the court deduces evaluative conclusions from the fact of a widespread consensus in comparative law. For example, in *Trop v Dulles* the court found that forfeiture of citizenship was a 'cruel and unusual' punishment. The plurality opinion written by Chief Justice Warren also approached the problem from the perspective of human dignity,[31] and understood it as a requirement that penal practices must be exercised 'within the limits of civilized standards'.[32] Warren assumed that comparative law would reflect such standards and found that '[t]he civilized nations of the world are in virtual unanimity that statelessness is not to be imposed as punishment for crime'[33] and that '[t]he United Nations' survey of the nationality laws of 84 nations of the world reveals that only two countries, the Philippines and Turkey, impose denationalization as a penalty for desertion'.[34] While Warren also argued that banishment was 'universally decried by *civilized* people' and that statelessness was 'deplored in the international community of *democracies*'[35]—thus attaching the relevance of foreign law to a set of values shared with the American society—in the final analysis the power of the argument was statistical: only two out of eighty-two countries used revocation of citizenship as a punishment for the crime of desertion. Another example of the statistical use of foreign law is *Coker v Georgia*, where the court found capital punishment unconstitutional for the crime of rape. In the plurality opinion Justice White followed the *Trop* approach and took convergence in foreign law ('the climate of international opinion') as a reliable testimony about value, noticing that 'out of 60 major nations in the world surveyed in 1965, only 3 retained the death penalty for rape where death did not ensue'.[36] There is a nascent idea here, used later on in many other cases, that true values will be recognized even by the regimes that are not strongly committed to fundamental rights protection, or that values will somehow affect their contingent, worldly practices.

But from *Coker* onwards, the universality element in this argument has not been monolithic: some cases have continued to take the pervasiveness

[31] *Trop v Dulles* (n 12) 100. [32] ibid. [33] ibid 102. [34] ibid 103. [35] ibid 102.

[36] *Coker v Georgia* (n 19) 596 n 10.

of widespread consensus as relevant, and others have restricted the use of foreign law to countries that share common values with the United States. In *Atkins v Virginia*, the majority led by Justice Stevens held that execution of the mentally challenged is a cruel and unusual punishment, and argued that 'within the world community, the imposition of the death penalty for crimes committed by mentally retarded offenders is overwhelmingly disapproved'.[37] This finding supported the majority's conclusion 'that there is a consensus among those who have addressed the issue',[38] signalling that the value will reveal itself to those that reflect enough about the problem.

Similarly, the majority in *Roper* relied on the widespread convergence in comparative law. Justice Kennedy, who wrote the opinion, noticed that 'the United States is the only country in the world that continues to give official sanction to the juvenile death penalty'.[39] Kennedy explicitly mentioned that even regimes that are not considered to be moral forerunners had abolished the death penalty for minors, such as Iran, Pakistan, Saudi Arabia, Yemen, Nigeria, the Democratic Republic of Congo, and China.[40] Even though Justice Kennedy did focus on English law as historically relevant,[41] he evidently also held the view that foreign legal practices will transcend their contingent differences and echo universal moral values. The connection between contingent evaluative attitudes and moral values is here quite robust: what is valuable will find its way into attitudes not *because* of similarities but even *in spite of* differences.

In contrast, another strand of jurisprudence has continued to rely on the abridged consensus, pertinent to countries that share the evaluative framework with the United States. But this approach has not been applied consistently. In *Enmund v Florida*, the court found that capital punishment for a vicarious felony murder was unconstitutional, and cited the law of Commonwealth countries, continental Europe, England, India, and Canada in support of its conclusion, without explaining why these countries would be relevant.[42] In *Thompson v Oklahoma* the court concluded that the death penalty was unconstitutional for minors under 16 years of age, and that this conclusion was consistent with laws of the 'nations that share our Anglo-American heritage' and the 'leading members of the Western European Community'.[43] Probably, the idea was that a common heritage would lead to similar evaluative attitudes, and that this fact bears normative consequences. However, the court also stated that '[j]uvenile executions are also prohibited in the Soviet Union', indicating that common heritage may not be all that

[37] *Atkins v Virginia* (n 19) 316 n 21. [38] ibid. [39] *Roper v Simmons* (n 19) 575. [40] ibid 577.

[41] ibid. English law was also relevant because the text of the 8th amendment has roots in the English Bill of Rights of 1689.

[42] *Enmund v Florida* (n 19) 796 n 22. [43] *Thompson v Oklahoma* (n 19) 830.

matters.[44] Likewise, Justice Breyer took this 'mixed' approach to foreign law in his dissent in *Knight v Florida*, where he considered the constitutionality of extended delays in execution of the death sentence and discussed decisions of the Privy Council of the United Kingdom (in a case dealing with the Jamaican constitution), Supreme Court of India, European Court of Human Rights, and the Supreme Court of Zimbabwe;[45] for Breyer, these decisions were 'useful even though not binding'[46] because they 'considered roughly comparable questions under roughly comparable legal standards'.[47] However, even if legal standards were similar, the framework of values in Zimbabwe was different from that in the United States, so we find traces of unrestricted universalism in this opinion as well.

Part of the confusion about the scope of the universality element of the argument from universal reason arises from its nature as a legally embedded ethical argument. The approach of the court in *Coker* illustrates how the ethical argument from universal reason becomes entrenched through a precedent: a dictum from the plurality opinion in *Trop* found its way to *Coker*, and the use of foreign consensus became the accepted approach to moral dilemmas. The pair of sodomy cases in the context of the substantive due process—*Bowers* and *Lawrence*—demonstrates a similar pattern. In his concurrence in *Bowers*, Chief Justice Burger claimed that there is no right to homosexual sodomy, and he further asserted that the '[c]ondemnation of [homosexual] practices is firmly rooted in Judeo-Christian moral and ethical standards'.[48] In *Lawrence*, the court overturned *Bowers* and held that consensual homosexual conduct falls within the scope of protected liberty under the due process clause. Justice Kennedy, in the majority opinion, specifically rebutted the claim from Burger's concurrence in *Bowers* that Western civilization unequivocally condemns homosexual sodomy: to support the rebuttal, Kennedy mentioned the jurisprudence of the ECtHR and British legislative history.[49] In both *Coker* and *Lawrence*, the court followed a previous case in its use of foreign law: while in *Coker* the court looked at the global consensus, in *Lawrence* it used only the laws of the countries that share the cultural background of the United States.

To sum up: the argument from universal reason brings foreign law to bear on moral issues. The argument is premised upon the belief that foreign law reflects reasonable solutions to moral issues. It also assumes that values are shared beyond national borders. One strand of thinking connects such values to humanity as a whole, and the other ties it to a common cultural background. Much of the ambivalence in the conception of value follows from the way in which foreign law has been used in preceding cases; however, it

[44] ibid 831. [45] *Knight v Florida* (n 28) 995–97. [46] ibid 998. [47] ibid 997.

[48] *Bowers v Hardwick* (n 18) 196. [49] *Lawrence v Texas* (n 18) 571–73 and 576–77.

also means that there is no clear idea about what makes foreign law normatively significant. The connection between moral value and foreign law thus needs to be explained.

4.2.2 *South Africa*

In contrast to the United States, the specific socio-legal context made the South African Constitutional Court very much open to foreign influences: both post-apartheid constitutions drew heavily on foreign constitutional solutions,[50] the newly established court did not have domestic human rights jurisprudence to build upon, and the court was motivated to identify with liberal democratic jurisdictions in order to renounce the authoritarian heritage of the society.[51] Furthermore, the South African Constitution explicitly allows for the use of foreign law in interpretation of the bill of rights and—simultaneously—calls for its moral reading: 'When interpreting the Bill of Rights, a court ... must promote the values that underlie an open and democratic society based on human dignity, equality and freedom ... and ... may consider foreign law'.[52]

The constitution confers a duty upon the court to promote moral *values* and authorizes it to consider *foreign law*. There is thus no doubt that the use of foreign law is an ethical argument, as the constitution itself connects it to the interpretation of moral concepts such as dignity, equality, and freedom. The court relies on foreign law to improve its own moral judgment: when so doing, it admits to be exercising the law-making function and frequently decides against popular opinion. Let me explain.

The existence of an explicit constitutional warrant to engage in value-based reasoning affects the court's interpretive methods: while the US Supreme Court typically meets with criticism for its activism, the South African Constitutional Court is comfortable in its role as a vehicle of moral change.[53] Justice Mokgoro's opinion from *S v Makwanyane* illustrates this approach: in her understanding, constitutional interpretation entails a 'reference to a system of values extraneous to the constitutional text',[54] while ethical arguments are inescapable, as the interpretation of moral concepts from

[50] DM Davis, 'Constitutional Borrowing: The Influence of Legal Culture and Local History in the Reconstitution of Comparative Influence: The South African Experience' (2003) 1 International Journal of Constitutional Law 181, 181–89.

[51] Ursula Bentele, 'Mining for Gold: The Constitutional Court of South Africa's Experience with Comparative Constitutional Law' (2009) 37 Georgia Journal of International and Comparative Law 219, 228–30.

[52] Constitution of the Republic of South Africa of 1996 section 39(1). See also Constitution of the Republic of South Africa of 1993 (Interim Constitution) s 35(1).

[53] See eg *S v Zuma and Others* 1995 (2) SA 642 para 15.

[54] *S v Makwanyane and Another* 1995 (3) SA 391 para 302.

the constitution draws the court 'into the realm of making necessary value choices'.[55] When the court makes such value choices, it does not shy away from rejecting the argument from common sentiment and replacing it with its own moral judgment. Justice Chaskalson's remark from *S v Makwanyane* captures this attitude succinctly: 'If public opinion were to be decisive there would be no need for constitutional adjudication'.[56] Hence, the court accepts that constitutional interpretation may go against the will of the people and that it sometimes entails making moral calls in the name of the whole society.

The court's value choices are regularly based on the analysis of foreign law. Foreign law appears in at least half of its judgments,[57] and justices openly admit that it serves to assist their law-making function. The idea is that references to foreign law improve domestic law. In *K v Minister of Safety and Security*, Justice O'Regan explained: 'Our courts will look at other jurisdictions for enlightenment and assistance in *developing our own law*'.[58] In her view—shared by many other justices[59]—rejecting the input of foreign law deprives the 'legal system of the benefits of the learning and wisdom to be found in other jurisdictions'.[60] The usefulness of foreign law is most typically seen as epistemic: there is knowledge about values to be gained when one consults foreign legal sources.

The epistemic worth of foreign law depends on views about the nature of moral value, which rest on the elements of *universality* and *reasonableness*: the belief that at least some values are universal and can be grasped by virtue of reason. A typical exponent of such a view is Justice Ackermann, who trusts that the use of foreign law can reveal the universal norms that emerge in the process of reasoning:

> In construing and applying our Constitution, we are dealing with fundamental legal norms which are steadily becoming more *universal* in character. ... we have regard to these findings [of foreign courts], not in order to draw direct analogies, but to identify the underlying *reasoning* with a view to establishing

[55] ibid para 303. In making these value choices—as Mokgoro puts it—'foreign precedent may be instructive'. ibid para 302.

[56] ibid.

[57] Constitution of the Republic of South Africa of 1993 (Interim Constitution) 33(1); Christa Rautenbach, 'South Africa: Teaching an "Old Dog" New Tricks? An Empirical Study of the Use of Foreign Precedents by the South African Constitutional Court (1995–2010)' in Tania Groppi and Marie-Claire Ponthoreau (eds), *The Use of Foreign Precedents by Constitutional Judges* (Hart Publishing 2013) 194.

[58] *K v Minister of Safety and Security* 2005 (6) SA 419 para 35 (emphasis added). See also Justice Chaskalson in *S v Makwanyane and Another* (n 54) para 37 and *Mistry v Interim National Medical and Dental Council and Others* 1998 (4) SA 1127 para 3.

[59] See generally in Bentele, 'Mining for Gold: The Constitutional Court of South Africa's Experience with Comparative Constitutional Law' (n 51).

[60] *K v Minister of Safety and Security* (n 58) para 35.

> the norms that apply in other open and democratic societies based on freedom and equality.[61]

While Ackermann's universalism is curtailed by a reference to a common liberal democratic evaluative framework, he believes that precisely these values are universally human and that constitutional law ought to uphold them: 'constitutional law … is not wholly nationalistic and exclusively historical enterprise, but embodies a certain universally normative minimum core'.[62] In his opinion, the use of foreign law serves to facilitate the acceptance of cosmopolitan values and to side-line cultural relativism; the goal of the practice is to enable 'a greater universalising of these values as enforceable rights'.[63] However, regardless of the rhetoric that is optimistic about the existence of universal moral truths revealed through the faculty of reason, the actual patterns of the use of foreign law demonstrate a less ambitious universalism and incorporate a thinner conception of reason.

Although the court does make references to global legal consensus,[64] most of the time the element of universality is restricted. Quantitatively, justices have cited cases from Canada, United States, United Kingdom, European Court of Human Rights, and Germany much more than any other jurisdiction.[65] More importantly—qualitatively—foreign precedents have not been accepted at face value; the court often distinguishes between them on the basis of differences in constitutional text and spirit, or because of distinctive social circumstances. The approach to foreign law has thus been careful in two different senses. Externally, concerning foreign law, the court has been—in the words of Justice Kentridge—sensitive to 'legal history, traditions and usages of the country concerned' in order to understand 'the purposes of its constitution'.[66] Internally, in weighing the appropriate influence of foreign law, the court has tried to—as Chaskalson puts it—pay 'due regard to our legal system, our history and circumstances, and the structure and language of our own Constitution'.[67]

[61] *Ferreira v Levin; Vryenhoek v Powell* 1996 (1) SA 984 para 72 (emphasis added).

[62] Laurie WH Ackermann, 'Constitutional Comparativism in South Africa: A Response to Sir Basil Markesinis and Dr Jörg Tiedke' in Basil Markesinis and Jörg Tiedke (eds), *Judicial Recourse to Foreign Law: A New Source of Inspiration?* (UCL Press 2006) 274.

[63] ibid 286.

[64] See eg *S v Makwanyane and Another* (n 54) para 33 and *National Coalition for Gay and Lesbian Equality v Minister of Justice and Others* 1999 (1) SA 6 para 52.

[65] See Rautenbach, 'South Africa: Teaching an "Old Dog" New Tricks? An Empirical Study of the Use of Foreign Precedents by the South African Constitutional Court (1995–2010)' (n 57) 197.

[66] *S v Zuma and Others* (n 53) para 15 (Kentridge). Justice Kentridge also explained in *Du Plessis and Others v De Klerk and Another* 1996 (3) SA 850 para 127, that: '[t]he survey [of foreign law] is conducted from the point of vantage afforded by the South African Constitution, constructed on unique foundations, built according to a unique design and intended for unique purposes'.

[67] *S v Makwanyane and Another* (n 54) para 39 (Chaskalson).

This approach has, for example, been prominent in the equality jurisprudence, where the heritage of systemic inequalities prompted the court to adopt a more substantive and remedial understanding of equality.[68] For instance, in *National Coalition for Gay and Lesbian Equality v Minister of Justice*—a case that declared the prohibition of sodomy unconstitutional—the South African Constitutional Court rejected the reasoning of the Supreme Court of the United States in *Bowers v Hardwick*. The court compared sodomy laws which target a group based on sexual orientation to apartheid laws which target racial groups, and concluded that these kinds of differentiations are no longer a part of South Africa's constitutional identity;[69] it then argued that the constitutional situation in South Africa was very different from the one in the United States on which *Bowers* relied, and that the domestic constitution more explicitly demands the protection of privacy, dignity, and equality.[70] Similarly, in *Prince v President*, the court rejected the reasoning of the majority in a US Supreme Court case *Employment Division v Smith*,[71] finding the minority opinion in that case to be 'more consistent' with the South African constitution.[72] The question in *Prince* was whether the denial of access to the legal profession based on the previous use of cannabis for religious purposes is constitutional. While the majority in *Prince* refused to make an exception for the religious use of prohibited substances, reaching the same conclusion as the *Smith* majority, it did so on different grounds and by employing a more stringent test. The *Smith* majority effectively denied any religious exception to general and formally neutral laws;[73] in contrast, Justice Ackermann followed the minority in this case that held the state intervention justified only if it is narrowly tailored to achieve a compelling state interest.[74] Thus, in both *National Coalition* and *Prince*, the court rejected the relevance of the mainstream American approach to equality on the basis of the specific evaluative commitments of South African society.

Universalism has also been circumscribed through judicial localization of moral concepts. In some cases, justices have preferred to rely on traditional South African values that—although similar in content to moral concepts used in other jurisdictions—better express the specificities of local moral practices. For example, Justice Moseneke used a local concept of 'regstellende aksie' to underline South African commitment to substantive equality,

[68] See eg *President of the Republic of South Africa and Another v Hugo* 1997 (4) SA 1 para 41; *Minister of Home Affairs and Another v Fourie and Another* 2006 (1) SA 524 para 60 (Sachs).

[69] *National Coalition for Gay and Lesbian Equality v Minister of Justice and Others* (n 64) para 28 (Ackermann).

[70] ibid para 55 (Ackermann).

[71] *Employment Division v Smith* 494 US 872 (1990).

[72] *Prince v President of the Law Society of the Cape of Good Hope* 2002 (2) SA 794 para 122 (Ackermann).

[73] *Employment Division v Smith* (n 71) 879.

[74] *Prince v President of the Law Society of the Cape of Good Hope* (n 72) paras 122 and 128–29.

according to which remedial measures aimed at alleviating inequalities are not a deviation but an integral part of the notion of equality.[75] On the basis of this concept, Moseneke distinguished American equality jurisprudence as 'inapt', notwithstanding the similarities in constitutional texts.[76] Similarly, in *Makwanyane*, several justices used the local concept of 'ubuntu' to argue for the abolition of the death penalty.[77] As I have previously explained—in Justice Mokgoro's interpretation—'*ubuntu* translates as *humanness*' and underlines 'group solidarity on survival issues';[78] as such, it incorporates both the right to life and human dignity.[79] The concept of ubuntu has served to express a universalistic value of dignity in the local vocabulary, but also to underline that constitutional values arise from indigenous evaluative experiences.[80]

Analogously, the element of *reasonableness* has been modest. The court has not supposed that there is a strong connection between the reasoning of foreign courts and true moral values, and has been cautious about deducing direct normative conclusions from facts about foreign law. Justice Sachs explains this method by saying that the court should 'look for rationales rather than rules' in foreign law.[81] This approach implies that the court should find foreign reasoning 'persuasive' if it is to be applied.[82] To be persuaded by a rationale is to realize that an evaluative judgment is appropriate, without being aware of it before or without being able to articulate it clearly. Notice that this conception of reasonableness—emerging from the process of persuasion and reflection—need not suppose that foreign law contains universal moral truths external to the evaluative framework from which the court is assessing the issue; instead, to be persuasive, reasoning must fall on fertile ground and trigger some of the presuppositions or evaluative commitments that are implicit in the evaluative outlook of the court that is being persuaded. While the 'persuaded' court may in the process change some of its initial evaluative intuitions, it will do so with support from a range of other assumptions that are internal to its own framework of values.

Justice Ackermann describes this element of reasonableness as 'critical rationalism', which entails a process of reflection in order to minimize the influence of one's own 'personal preferences and dangerous intuitions'.[83]

[75] *Minister of Finance and Another v Van Heerden* 2004 (6) SA 121 paras 29–30.

[76] ibid para 29.

[77] *S v Makwanyane and Another* (n 54) paras 130–31 (Chaskalson), 223–27 (Langa), 240–44 (Madala), and 306–12 (Mokgoro).

[78] ibid para 307.

[79] ibid paras 310 and 312.

[80] See the discussion of the notion of ubuntu in ch 2.

[81] *Coetzee v Government of the Republic of South Africa, Matiso and Others v Commanding Officer Port Elizabeth Prison and Others* 1995 (4) SA 631 para 57.

[82] *K v Minister of Safety and Security* (n 58) para 35 (O'Regan).

[83] Ackermann, 'Constitutional Comparativism in South Africa: A Response to Sir Basil Markesinis and Dr Jörg Tiedke' (n 62) 285.

The idea here is not that reflection will generate knowledge of some external reality or make moral judgment robustly and universally objective through a complete detachment from the personal point of view, but that the process—as he describes it—will probably lead to a more stable equilibrium within one's own evaluative outlook. Ackermann lists a number of ways in which foreign law may be useful: to identify the problem, detect the methodology to approach it, recognize its different aspects and implicated concerns, and understand possible hazards attached to different solutions.[84] The purpose, as Ackermann sees it, is to avoid the 'tunnel vision' where '[o]ne's thinking becomes unimaginative',[85] and—at the same time—to be 'ruthless' about one's own presumptions in order to find 'the limits of one's own understandings'.[86] Instead of incorporating the solutions from foreign law directly, the approach of the South African constitutional court involves a process of raising self-awareness about the core evaluative commitments of the domestic constitutional system, and about the best ways to realize these under given social circumstances.

To conclude, regardless of the rhetoric of universalism and reasonableness, the South African Constitutional Court uses foreign law in a way that is sensitive to the local factual and evaluative specificities. In so doing, it does not seem to suppose that external normative truths can be attained through the faculty of reason, but it does assume that reflection is valuable in exposing the limits of one's imaginative horizons and presumptions. In this approach—even if the reflective exercise is conducted—local and contingent values feed into the final moral judgment.

4.2.3 Israel

Israeli Supreme Court has a long history of value-based reasoning entangled with the use of foreign law. On the one hand, foreign law has traditionally had strong influence in Israel, as the new legal system has been developed with limited local sources.[87] On the other hand, the lack of a canonical constitutional text and a complete bill of rights has moved the court towards

[84] ibid 277. [85] ibid 278.

[86] Justice Ackermann, cited in Bentele, 'Mining for Gold: The Constitutional Court of South Africa's Experience with Comparative Constitutional Law' (n 51) 232.

[87] See Suzie Navot, 'Israel: Creating a Constitution: The Use of Foreign Precedents by the Supreme Court (1994–2010)' in Tania Groppi and Marie-Claire Ponthoreau (eds), *The Use of Foreign Precedents by Constitutional Judges* (Hart Publishing 2013) 130–32; Miron Gross, Ron Haris, and Yoram Schachar, 'References Patterns of the Supreme Court in Israel: Quantitative Analysis' (1996) 26 Hebrew University Law Review 115; Chanan Goldschmit, Miron Gross, and Yoram Schachar, '100 Leading Precedents of the Supreme Court: A Quantitative Analysis' (2004) 7 Haifa University Law Review 243, 267; Iddo Porat, 'The Use of Foreign Law in Israeli Constitutional Adjudication' Paper presented in a Conference on Israeli Constitutional Law (Tel Aviv, May 2010) http://www.clb.ac.il/uploads/Porat%20-%20Foreign%20Law%20-%20May%204.pdf (last accessed 16 July 2014).

value-based reasoning without the constraints of originalism and textualism.[88] When exercising its law-making authority, the court has used foreign precedents in two principle ways: first, to protect values and rights that have not been explicitly guaranteed before; and, second, to expand its power of rights-based review.[89] Thus, the use of foreign law as an *ethical* argument has both served to read new moral values into the constitution and to secure the position of the court as the guardian of these values.

The justification of this ethical argument has been embedded in the discourse of *reasonableness*.[90] The views of the former President of the Supreme Court Aharon Barak can illustrate this. In his opinion, '[c]omparative law can help judges determine *the objective purpose of a constitution*'.[91] The emblem of Barak's interpretive approach is a belief that constitutions and legislative acts have objective purposes, which transcend national boundaries and are distinct from the contingent intentions of their framers. The objective purpose is determined by 'the intention of the *reasonable* legislature'.[92] It is thus a normative concept discernible through reason and not a socio-historical fact: the objective purpose denotes 'the interests, values, objectives, policy, and functions that the law should realize in a democracy'.[93] The role of the judge is to determine these hypothetical intentions and find the objective purpose of the constitution: it is up to the court to add the element of reason to ordinary legislative intentions. [94]

The objective purpose of the constitution acquires substance with the assistance of foreign law. However, for Barak, the *universalism* of the argument from foreign law is restricted: the use of foreign law is 'only proper if there is an ideological basis common to the two legal systems and a common allegiance to basic democratic principles'.[95] The idea is that constitutional orders which share a similar evaluative framework also have similar 'functions' or 'purposes',[96] which can be discerned by attending closely to foreign practices.[97] The elements of universality and reasonableness are in this interpretation similar to the commitments arising from general constitutional identity.

[88] Menachem Mautner, *Law and the Culture of Israel* (Oxford University Press 2011) ch 4.

[89] The key cases in this regard are HCJ 73/53 *Kol Ha'am v Minister of Interior* (1953) and CA 6821/93 *United Mizrahi Bank Ltd v Migdal Cooperative Village* (1995), discussed below.

[90] Ran Hirschl, *Comparative Matters: The Renaissance of Comparative Constitutional Law* (Oxford University Press 2014) 63. See also Steven M Mazie, *Israel's Higher Law: Religion and Liberal Democracy in the Jewish State* (Lexington Books 2011) 37–40.

[91] Aharon Barak, *The Judge in a Democracy* (Princeton University Press 2006) 200 (emphasis added).

[92] ibid 136.

[93] ibid 138. See also Aharon Barak, *Purposive Interpretation in Law* (Princeton University Press 2005) ch 7.

[94] Barak, *The Judge in a Democracy* (n 91) 138 and 149. [95] ibid 201. [96] ibid 200.

[97] ibid 200–204.

This understanding of the use of foreign law has deeper roots. In the seminal *Kol Ha'am v Minister of the Interior* case, the court for the first time established that administrative action must conform with values and rights implicit in Israel's commitment to democracy.[98] The question was whether the Minister of the Interior exceeded his authority by ordering a temporary suspension of two newspapers for publishing materials which could endanger public peace. Justice Agranat, writing for the court, relied almost exclusively on foreign law to tease out the relevant concerns surrounding the restrictions to free speech in a democracy.[99] His reasoning was as follows. First, he argued that the 'understanding of the democratic regime inevitably leads ... to the enforcement of the freedom of expression in every state where such a form of government exists'.[100] Second, he analysed foreign precedents to reveal the justifications and restrictions of freedom of expression in other democracies.[101] Third, Agranat found that Israel is 'a state founded on democracy' and that although there was neither constitutional review of legislation nor an explicit textual guarantee of the freedom of expression, 'the law of people must be studied in the light of its national way of life', which he understood to be fundamentally democratic.[102] Fourth, once the link between the values of other democracies and Israel was established, Agranat developed a balancing test that allowed limitations of speech in the case of imminent danger to public peace, which closely resembled the American 'clear and present' danger test.[103] The idea was that there is a non-parochial common framework of values shared by all democracies, and that—consequently—foreign law discloses these values.

Another example of this approach is Aharon Barak's opinion in the *Mizrahi Bank* case. The question was constitutionality of measures aimed at alleviating the consequences of economic crisis in the agricultural sector that could interfere with creditor's claims.[104] But more importantly, in this case, the court conferred constitutional status upon the basic laws and proclaimed its right to conduct judicial review of legislation.[105] This came up as a consequence of the adoption of two basic laws, which guaranteed certain fundamental rights, but did not provide for a formal hierarchy of laws supervised by the court.[106] In 'Basic Law: Human Dignity and Liberty' the Knesset established

[98] *Kol Ha'am v Minister of Interior* (n 89).

[99] The case cites 9 American, 8 English, and only 3 Israeli cases.

[100] *Kol Ha'am v Minister of Interior* (n 89) s A. [101] ibid ss A–E. [102] ibid s E.

[103] ibid ss F(4) and G. For the American test see *Schenck v United States* 249 US 47 (1919) 249.

[104] *United Mizrahi Bank Ltd v Migdal Cooperative Village* (n 89).

[105] For context see Gideon Sapir, 'Constitutional Revolutions: Israel as a Case-study' (2009) 5 International Journal of Law in Context 355.

[106] Navot, 'Israel: Creating a Constitution: The Use of Foreign Precedents by the Supreme Court (1994–2010)' (n 87) 130–38.

that '[t]here shall be no violation of rights under this Basic Law except by a law befitting the values of the State of Israel', and that '[a]ll governmental authorities are bound to respect the rights under this Basic Law'.[107]

Justice Barak understood these laws as nothing short of a watershed constitutional moment and enthusiastically proclaimed that Israel has 'joined the community of democratic countries' and has 'become part of the human rights revolution'.[108] Nonetheless, the gist of his opinion is not universalistic, and Barak's arguments are couched in the idea that a constitution is a 'reflection of national experience'.[109] Values protected by the court do not arise from global norms but from 'national consciousness'[110] and a 'social contract'[111] reflected in the best understanding of Israel's history. Barak's attitude towards foreign law followed from this understanding of the nature of value. While he did cite foreign law extensively, he also argued that a judge must do so carefully, because the 'scope of the constitutional right is derived from society's understanding of its importance', and the balance between a right and public interest is determined by 'society's attitude towards national interest' and the 'unique outlook of Israeli society'.[112] Hence—as in *Kol Ha'am*—the route to foreign law in Barak's *Mizrahi* opinion was not direct, but emerged from Israel's own constitutional identity and the profound moral commitments of the local community.

The basic law defines the values of the State of Israel as both 'Jewish and democratic',[113] and Barak's approach to foreign law followed this dualism: on the one hand, his strategy was to make analogies with democratic jurisdictions and infer conclusions for domestic law; on the other, he refuted the direct import of foreign law when it collided with local values. In a more cosmopolitan manner, Barak used American cases to show that 'true democracy cannot exist without the limitation of the power of majority'[114] and relied on German and Canadian law to confirm that the legislature must be obliged to respect fundamental rights.[115] He also cited *Marbury v Madison* together with the wide acceptance of constitutional review in comparative law to support his argument that such a review is the 'soul of the constitution', which is indispensable to a system that respects the separation of powers, rule of law, and democracy.[116]

The elements of universalism and reasonableness are also visible in Barak's lengthy references to foreign jurisdictions in relation to the proportionality

[107] Basic Law: Human Dignity and Liberty of 17 March 1992, ss 8 and 11.

[108] *United Mizrahi Bank Ltd v Migdal Cooperative Village* (n 89) Introduction (Barak).

[109] ibid para 38 (Barak). [110] ibid. [111] ibid para 50 (Barak). [112] ibid para 88 (Barak).

[113] Basic Law: Human Dignity and Liberty (n 107) s 1a.

[114] *United Mizrahi Bank Ltd v Migdal Cooperative Village* (n 89) para 47 (Barak).

[115] ibid para 69 (Barak). [116] ibid paras 78 and 75–80 (Barak).

analysis, which in his opinion 'does not reflect a unique social history' but a 'general analytical position'.[117] Because Barak understands judicial authority as an exercise in 'reason and not power',[118] it is not surprising that he saw proportionality analysis as an expression of reason and universally applicable method of moral reflection. But this idea of reason is modest. Instead of thinking that reasoning will inevitably lead to convergence on right moral answers, proportionality analysis need not command any particular outcome or lead to consensus; it figures in Barak's analysis as a reflective device that may lead to different conclusions depending on local evaluative commitments. For example, Barak distinguished between the lenient American approach to economic freedom of the state and the forbearing Canadian treatment of legislative infringement of property rights, on the basis of the specific Israeli evaluative outlook in which economic rights can be constitutionally protected, and in which the right to property is specifically guaranteed.[119] In sum, Barak's approach to the nature of value from *Mizrahi* is not universalistic, but it is not parochial either: he accepts the relevance of foreign law, to the extent that there is a shared evaluative outlook. His understanding of the role of reason is similar: while Barak acknowledges that a proper evaluative judgment entails reflection, this does not mean that it will be completely detached from the evaluative experience of the local community.

Not surprisingly, the tensions on the borderline between the universal and the local dimension of value abound in this approach. An evaluative judgment can be widely accepted but at the same time may collide with deeper moral commitments implicit in the constitutional allegiance to democratic government. It is up to the court then to argue that—on reflection—these widely shared moral judgments fail to live up to more fundamental values. Such arguments often attempt to show that there is a blind spot in the set of domestic moral concerns that can be illuminated through the analysis of foreign law; the counter-arguments in turn try to demonstrate the inappropriateness of foreign law for the specific domestic needs and values.

We can illustrate these tensions and the reflective process they generate with the divergent opinions of Justices Barak and Cheshin in *Adalah v Minister of Interior*.[120] In this case, the court by a 6–5 split judgment upheld the constitutionality of amendments to the Law on Citizenship and Entry into Israel. On the basis of the security rationale and fear of terrorist attacks, the law instituted a blanket prohibition of granting residency permits and

[117] ibid paras 94, and 83–107 (Barak). See also Zeev Segal, 'The Israeli Constitutional Revolution: The Canadian Impact in the Midst of a Formative Period' (1997) 8 Forum Constitutionnel 53.

[118] *United Mizrahi Bank Ltd v Migdal Cooperative Village* (n 89) para 81 (Barak).

[119] ibid paras 102–103 (Barak).

[120] HCJ 7052/03 *Adalah Legal Centre for Arab Minority Rights in Israel v Minister of Interior* (2006).

citizenship to residents of the Occupied Territories who are family members of Israeli citizens.[121] Since the citizens who had family ties with Palestinians were predominantly members of the Arab minority, the prohibition raised concerns regarding both their right to family life and equality. But the basic law on dignity and liberty did not guarantee these rights explicitly, and the court itself had to interpret and balance Israeli values in order to reach the judgment.

Justice Barak made two crucial moves in his minority opinion, both with extensive support from foreign law. First, he derived the right to family life and, consequently, to family reunification from the right to dignity. Foreign law served to show that all the countries that respect human dignity also guarantee the right to family life and that these two are intrinsically connected; it followed for him that in Israel family rights are also protected by virtue of human dignity.[122] Second, he underlined the centrality of proportionality analysis to the democratic constitutional system and its elements by a lengthy examination of foreign law;[123] in particular, Barak put much trust in the last part of the proportionality analysis—where the values are balanced against one another—as giving 'expression to the concept of reasonableness'.[124] This approach enabled Barak to define the scope of the right to family life broadly, note the infringement of the right, and place the weight of scrutiny on the balance between the individual right and collective security concerns within the proportionality analysis. Ultimately, he found the law 'inconsistent with the character of Israel as a democratic freedom-seeking and liberty-seeking state'.[125]

In contrast, Justice Cheshin accepted that the right to family life follows from the commitment to human dignity, but he argued that it need not be realized on the territory of Israel. There are two distinct threads in his reasoning in terms of the nature of value. On the one hand, Cheshin acknowledges the existence of universal 'natural' rights that can be discerned from foreign law, but finds their application problematic in the specific social context. He accepts that the right to family life follows from the natural right to human dignity, and that 'the state merely embraces what is already there by wrapping natural law in the garb of law and constitution',[126] but he contrasts this demand with the 'basic principle in the law of the countries in the world' according to which '[e]very state has a natural

[121] The ban was later extended to citizens of 'enemy states' (Iran, Lebanon, Syria, and Iraq). In another divided judgment (6:5), the court upheld these amendments. See HCJ 466/07 *MK Zahava Gal-On (Meretz-Yahad) v Attorney General* (2012).

[122] See *Adalah Legal Centre for Arab Minority Rights in Israel v Minister of Interior* (n 120) paras 33–38 (Barak).

[123] ibid. See in particular paras 54–75 (Barak).

[124] ibid para 74 (Barak).

[125] ibid para 93 (Barak).

[126] ibid para 71 (Cheshin).

right ... to determine who will be its citizens'.[127] Cheshin finds that when these two universal rights are balanced against each other and applied to the 'reality of life' in Israel, there is no obligation of the state to allow family reunification by granting residency or citizenship to Palestinians.[128] As he puts it, 'on the basis of this logical deduction, a deduction that is common to all human beings and to all human peoples, it has been determined in international law that when there is dispute between nations, a nation may prohibit the nationals of the foreign nation, as such, from entering or immigrating to it'.[129] The process of inference from foreign and international law is here deductive: there are universally true principles expressed in global consensus, but their outcomes vary depending on the factual circumstances.

On the other hand, Cheshin's second layer of reasoning assumes that not all values are universally and timelessly true. He distinguishes between universal rights that should be imported from other constitutional systems and 'specific arrangements that are not universal'.[130] Because there is no consensus in the world regarding a right of a citizen to have his foreign spouse immigrate or acquire residency, it follows that this is not a basic natural right.[131] At that point, local values ought to prevail.[132] The specific arrangements fall outside of the scope of natural rights, and there is no analogy between foreign and Israeli law.[133] Cheshin thus adopts the view that within this non-universal margin 'every constitution expresses its own unique hierarchy of social values' and foreign law has little worth.[134] Justice Cheshin thus has a two-track vision of value: there are universal and 'natural' rights that enjoy the supreme status and find expression in foreign and international law, but when these rights are silent or ambiguous, local and contingent arrangements take precedence.

To conclude, foreign law enters the Israeli constitutional system when it shares common evaluative commitments with the domestic system. This generates qualms regarding the nature of value and the substance of local evaluative commitments. For example, Justice Cheshin thinks that there exist both transcendent and contingent values, and that the latter take precedence when the former are ambiguous. Justice Barak sees values as local and historically embedded, but the outcome of his analysis is more in line

[127] ibid para 51 (Cheshin). [128] ibid para 71 ff (Cheshin). [129] ibid para 188 (Cheshin).

[130] ibid para 39 (Cheshin). [131] ibid para 57 (Cheshin).

[132] 'The constitution of the United States is for the people of the United States, the German constitution is for Germans and the Basic Laws in Israel are for Israelis'. ibid para 62 (Cheshin).

[133] ibid para 63 (Cheshin).

[134] ibid para 63 (Cheshin) citing *United Mizrahi Bank Ltd v Migdal Cooperative Village* (n 89) para 69(b) (Shamgar).

with universal trends. They also disagree about the content of Israeli constitutional identity: while Cheshin believes that security threats prevent Israel from enforcing liberal democratic rights to the fullest, Barak thinks the commitment to human rights is stronger than security concerns. They both, however, use foreign law to illuminate these differences and tease out intuitions about the moral commitments of Israeli society.

4.3 NORMATIVITY OF FOREIGN LAW

There is a multitude of different approaches to foreign law in comparative practice. Some of the US Supreme Court judgments rely on a robust conception of universality and reasonableness, which includes a belief that people who reason about values would eventually converge on moral truths regardless of their cultural background; in other cases, this link is weaker and the court takes convergence into account when there is a common evaluative framework between constitutional systems. In South Africa, the dominant approach is universalistic but not automatic: while there is trust in universally human values, foreign law is reflected upon and rejected when it does not fit local evaluative commitments. In Israel, foreign law is introduced with a reference to domestic constitutional identity; but since this identity is sometimes contested, foreign law also modifies it and reinforces cosmopolitan values.

The conception of value behind the use of foreign law always incorporates the elements of reasonableness and universality; however, these elements take different forms. On the one hand, some instances of the use of foreign law assume that foreign law and moral answers bear a direct, robust connection. Call this the *deductive view*. According to the deductive view, we are able to discern some principles from foreign law, which we can legitimately apply to domestic constitutional cases. The knowledge we gain is external to our system and we have reasons to accept it at face value. We are open to such knowledge because it fulfils certain conditions which give us enough reason to believe that what we learn from it is correct. On the other hand, the connection between moral knowledge and foreign law is sometimes more relaxed or indirect, for it only facilitates a reflective state in which we recognize the balance and consequences of our values more easily. Call this the *reflective view*. In the reflective view, foreign law has no direct claim on us because it carries no immediate link to moral truth. The knowledge acquired by engagement with foreign law is about ourselves: it may be implicit, latent, or dormant but not alien to us. The reflective view sees the use of foreign law as the perfection of self-understanding. In that sense, we do not, strictly speaking, learn moral answers but become aware of them with assistance from foreign law. Both views have difficult questions to answer. For the deductive view, it is the question of the precise relationship between moral values and foreign law. For the reflective view, it is the manner in which foreign law contributes to reflection, the ability of such reflection to provide insights into morally justified courses of action, and—most importantly—the authority of moral reflection that is divorced from the idea of universal moral truth.

Here I want to pursue two lines of argument. First, the distinction between the deductive and reflective view should not be neglected. The empirical reality does not lend itself to clear-cut distinctions, and one can often find traces of both views within a single judgment or opinion. This is detrimental to their credibility: a pure deductive view is either implausible (presupposes peculiar metaphysics) or self-defeating (collapses into the reflective view). Second, even though the reflective view is more plausible, it is in need of elucidation. I shall thus explain several ways in which the reflective view can be motivated. I will conclude, however, that the reflective view is quite modest in its ambition to reach universal moral knowledge.

4.3.1 *The deductive view*

We have seen that the deductive view may take different forms: the courts may believe that true moral values will be reflected in global consensus, in convergence between similar jurisdictions, or in the opinions of a single court. But the more we move towards consensus-based arguments the more deductive they are.[135] The reliance on consensus presupposes robust universality and reasonableness: it assumes that convergence in reason-based judgments reflects universally human values. The assumption that supports this model is that if enough people reasoned about a moral problem they would converge on a universal moral truth, irrespectively of their contingent moral outlooks or cultural differences. For example, Cass Sunstein justifies the consensus-based use of foreign law with the assumption that 'each nation is more likely than not to make the right decision'.[136] He believes that consensus can serve as a proxy for adequate moral epistemology: '[i]f we are not skeptics, and if we believe that moral questions do have right answers, then it makes sense to consult the majority's view'.[137] Jeremy Waldron is an exponent of a similar position. The backbone of his explanation of the normativity of consensus is the following claim: '[o]ne might expect that the

[135] Vicki Jackson calls it 'the convergence model', but the deductive model is about the mode of reasoning and not necessarily about consensus. See Vicki C Jackson, 'Constitutional Comparisons: Convergence, Resistance, Engagement' (2005) 119 Harvard Law Review 109, 123–24.

[136] Cass R Sunstein, *A Constitution of Many Minds: Why the Founding Document Doesn't Mean What It Meant Before* (Princeton University Press 2009) 190.

[137] ibid 191.

obviousness of certain moral principles … would be reflected in their ubiquitous adoption as laws in the world'.[138] In this view, consensus is a causal consequence of the perception of moral values.

This view presupposes a two-tier process of deductive infusion of foreign law into domestic constitutional reasoning. First, there are epistemic conditions that must be met by foreign law in order to be considered relevant. Second, if these epistemic conditions are fulfilled we have reason to accept foreign law, for it reveals true values.[139] A crucial epistemic prerequisite is that moral answers are devoid of cultural contingency. For Sunstein, when moral issues are at stake, 'it is necessary to reject any strong form of cultural relativism, according to which the appropriate moral rules are culture-dependent, so that the moral requirements that are suitable for one culture need not be suitable for another culture'.[140] The existence of consensus is a signal that these particularistic experiences have been overcome. Sunstein's model thus relies on unrestricted trust in universality and reasonableness as the elements of value: 'As long as those [foreign] nations allow free and open debate, the very fact that different societies have come to the same conclusion increases one's confidence that the norms are genuinely universal and transcend merely historical or institutional differences'.[141]

But what reason do we have to believe that consensus corresponds to objective moral truths? Not only must this view presuppose a robust moral realism according to which there are moral facts to be discovered in the world, it must also assume that contingent moral attitudes cannot ultimately impede the discovery of such moral facts. Sunstein does not find this problematic. For him, there is an analogy between the authority of foreign law and scientific authority: consulting foreign law is like consulting foreign doctors.[142] Waldron invokes a similar analogy, and contends that there is:

> a body of legal science that stands independently of any particular court … and represents the accumulated wisdom of the law on certain recurrent problems, in much the way that science reflects the accumulated results of experiments in hundreds of different laboratories checking out and building upon each other's work.[143]

Notice that this analogy presupposes that moral-legal and scientific knowledge ('wisdom') are analogous, and that—consequently—moral and scientific truths must be similar. But none of the arguments to support this analogy

[138] See Waldron, *'Partly Laws Common to All Mankind': Foreign Law in American Courts* (n 2) 37.

[139] ibid 73.

[140] Sunstein, *A Constitution of Many Minds* (n 136) 195–96. This view confuses agent and appraiser relativism (see discussion in ch 3).

[141] ibid 197. [142] ibid 190.

[143] Waldron, *'Partly Laws Common to All Mankind': Foreign Law in American Courts* (n 2) 77.

are convincing. Waldron argues that the problems confronted by lawyers are the same, just like the problems scientists face are the same.[144] However, the similarity of questions guarantees nothing in terms of the truth of answers. Sciences answer theoretical questions (what we have reason to believe) while law and ethics answer practical questions (what we have reason to do). It does not follow from the fact that humans ask themselves similar practical questions that there will be convergence on correct answers. It does not even guarantee that there are correct answers. Waldron further argues that there is a common approach to analysing legal problems,[145] but—while this is true—this method can render different results depending on the substantive legal provisions. More importantly, nothing depends on the fact that legal methods are similar to legal methods *and* that scientific methods are similar to scientific methods: the relevant question is whether legal methods are similar *to* scientific methods. There are no such similarities. The truth of a scientific proposition is demonstrated by an application of a methodology that has been successful in discovering what the world is like, whereas the truth of legal propositions is demonstrated by using contingent legal materials. There are space- and time-independent truths about the world, but there are no such legal facts.

The scientific analogy reveals a background assumption of the consensus-based deductive view that moral facts exist in reality and can be traced by reasoning, which is supposed to be analogous to the scientific method. This shows how controversial the thesis actually is. It presupposes that moral judgment is world-guided, much like scientific discovery. It assumes that moral consensus (a causal occurrence in the world) yields moral truth (a normative concept): it thus needs to demonstrate how universal moral truths causally affect culturally embedded moral attitudes. However, while it is meaningful to say that convergence in science is at least partially explained by its ability to track the world-as-it-is,[146] it is doubtful that moral facts are also a part of the world-as-it-is, and it is unclear how these facts would interact with our contingent moral attitudes. Ethical convergence may well be explained by the shared circumstances of human life and our contingent psychological setup. So, even if there is a consensus on the death penalty, slavery, or torture, the best explanation of that fact is not that it tracks the truth of the matter, but that new sensibilities and institutions have developed under contemporary social circumstances. If there is a fact of the matter of what is morally correct, that fact must be quite different from the facts sciences try to discover.

144 ibid 101. 145 ibid 96.

146 Although this is controversial, it is safe to assume it here, for if this is not true for science, then it is certainly not true for moral discourse. For a sceptical view see Richard Rorty, *Philosophy and the Mirror of Nature* (Princeton University Press 1979).

And there is certainly no such moral truth that can acquire authority without implicating our reflection. This is why the deductive view at best boils down to the reflective one and at worst completely fails. Let me explain.

Someone holding the deductive view needs to argue that values are a part of the fabric of the universe. The most famous attempt to do so is Plato's: to explain the existence of values in the world we must presuppose values as non-spatial and non-temporal ideal forms. Moral values are on this model independent of our minds, responses, or experiences. The proponents of the deductive view are accused of presupposing such an odd metaphysics. Justice Scalia, for instance, writes:

> One who believes it falls to the *courts* to update the list of rights guaranteed by the Constitution tends to be one who believes in a Platonic right and wrong in these matters, which wise judges are able to discern when people at large cannot . . . Platonic living constitutionalist must surely consider the views of all intelligent segments of mankind.[147]

This is a serious objection. The deductive view assumes something quite contentious: that values are a part of—as Bernard Williams puts it—'the world that is there *anyway*'[148] and must fit the conception of the world that 'might be arrived at by any investigator'.[149] Why would consensus count in the deductive view if not as a consequence of grasping the realm of values, or arriving at something that is waiting to be discovered?

The assumption that moral reasoning traces the property of wrongness in the world implies a conception of moral truth that presupposes correspondence between value as the feature of the world (truth-maker) and moral belief (truth-bearer). As Mackie points out, for this to be plausible we must populate the universe with entities whose existence we cannot comprehend. The problem is twofold: metaphysically, the view implies the existence of facts which are different from anything else in the world, and epistemologically, to detect these facts we would have to have a faculty different from all the other senses we have.[150] We can neither experience such facts, nor interact with them; yet they seem to be action-guiding in some way and have causal effects on our moral attitudes. The deductive model assumes precisely that: in Waldron's opinion, the 'obviousness' of moral norms will be reflected in global legal

[147] Antonin Scalia, 'Foreign Legal Authority in the Federal Courts' (2004) 98 Proceedings of the Annual Meeting of the American Society of International Law 305, 308. Note that Scalia is not consistent on this matter. In *Thompson*, he wrote: 'The practices of other nations, particularly other democracies, can be relevant to determining whether a practice uniform among our people is not merely a historical accident . . .' (*Thompson v Oklahoma* (n 19) 868 n 4 (Scalia)). If there is no Platonic right and wrong, then all practices *are* just historical accidents.

[148] Bernard Williams, *Ethics and the Limits of Philosophy* (2nd edn, Routledge 2006) 138.

[149] ibid 139.

[150] John L Mackie, *Ethics: Inventing Right and Wrong* (2nd edn, Penguin 1990) ch 1.

consensus.[151] But neither is moral value 'obvious', nor do we have an account of moral perception that would account for this 'obviousness'.

One way to explain the 'obviousness' of moral value is indeed to point to the similar role observations play in moral and scientific theory. This is because in both domains—as Harman argues—there are no 'pure' or pre-theoretical observations:

> ... in both science and ethics, general principles are invoked to explain particular cases and, therefore, in both science and ethics, the general principles you accept can be tested by appealing to particular judgments that certain things are right or wrong, just or unjust, and so forth; and these judgments are analogous to direct perceptual judgments about facts.[152]

This seems to warrant the conclusion that perception in morality and science are the same, but Harman urges us to resist this conclusion.[153] His argument is simple: to support a moral theory that fits our moral observation, we do not need to presuppose anything about the world 'as it is anyway', nor do we have an account of the 'way in which the actual rightness or wrongness of a given situation can have an effect on [our] perceptual apparatus'.[154] In Harman's famous example, the observation that it is wrong for children to set a cat on fire need not presuppose any additional physical properties of the cat being set on fire by children. The observation can be explained by natural facts and psychological sensibility alone. In contrast, for an observation to figure in the best explanation of a scientific theory, we need to presuppose that it does indeed track something in the world. The observation that a siren on a police car sounds higher when the car is approaching than when it is receding from the observer confirms the theory of the Doppler effect about the change in the frequency of a wave relative to the moving source of frequency: for this observation to support the scientific theory, however, we must suppose that it actually discovers the frequency-change in the world. If Harman is right, for the deductive view to hold, there must be something in the world that affects our making of converging moral observations. Harman thinks that this can either be a mind-independent, in-the-world value, or a value that is a consequence of our psychological dispositions and learned behaviour. Since the former is implausible, it must be the latter. And if it is the latter, then consensus cannot claim to represent the universal mind-independent moral truth.

There are two ways to resist Harman's conclusion. They both problematize his understanding of the inference to best explanation. The first accepts

[151] Waldron, *'Partly Laws Common to All Mankind': Foreign Law in American Courts* (n 2) 37.

[152] Gilbert Harman, *The Nature of Morality: An Introduction to Ethics* (Oxford University Press 1977) 5–6.

[153] ibid 6–10. [154] ibid 7–8.

the relevance of scientific explanations for determining the fabric of the universe, but argues that they do not exclude moral facts. The basic idea is that Harman's argument proves nothing unless one is already convinced by his anti-realism. Sturgeon, for example, argues that moral judgments supervene on non-moral facts in a sense that normative observations ought to be the same for each cat-set-on-fire situation in reality. So, if we presume the truth of a background moral theory that makes us perceive the wrongness of setting a cat on fire, then our perception is explained by that true moral theory, just as in the case of science the truth of the observation depends on the truth of the background theory. If we suppose that there are mind-independent moral truths alongside scientific truths, then seeing slavery or setting cats on fire as wrong might well be a consequence of the wrongness of the act.[155]

But if scientific explanations are ontologically determinative, the question is whether the best scientific explanations of moral judgments depend on non-moral natural facts and our contingent moral sensibilities only, or also include true moral facts, which supervene on / are identical to natural facts.[156] Scientific explanations do regularly use concepts that denote groupings of natural facts that cannot be reduced to these facts without losing the explanatory potential; for example, we do not deny the existence of biological or psychological facts, even if they can be reduced to physical or chemical facts. But are true moral facts useful or indispensable in the same sense? The short answer is that there is nothing that is being explained better if we suppose the truth of the background moral theory, as opposed to assuming only a set of contingent moral attitudes together with natural facts.

Let us take the example of the death penalty. There is a growing consensus about its inappropriateness. If the consensus is explained by the immorality of the death penalty, then the deductive view has some purchase. But presupposing the truth of its moral inappropriateness does not add anything to the explanation of its abolition. We need only suppose that our moral attitudes have changed, regardless of their truth. On the one hand, the death penalty has been used ever since there were organized societies. It is reasonable to suppose that an explanation—eg that the moral wrongness of the death penalty will lead to its abolition—will have some predictive value; if it is unable to explain why the perception of moral wrongness of the death penalty has not led to any change for millennia, then it is probably an *ex post facto* rationalization and not an explanation. On the other hand, it is doubtful

[155] See Nicholas L Sturgeon, 'Moral Explanations' in Geoffrey Sayre-McCord (ed), *Essays on Moral Realism* (Cornell University Press 1988).

[156] ibid; Richard N Boyd, 'How to Be a Moral Realist' in Geoffrey Sayre-McCord (ed), *Essays on Moral Realism* (Cornell University Press 1988); David O Brink, *Moral Realism and the Foundations of Ethics* (Cambridge University Press 1989).

that moral truth plays any role in actual social scientific explanations. This is because the abolition or survival of the death penalty, slavery and the like is much better explained by social, economic, and cultural variables than the perception of moral truth.[157] This is not to say that contingent moral attitudes are not accounted for in social processes, but that they themselves have social and psychological causes which explain them better than the convergence towards moral truth.[158]

The second objection is that Harman's understanding of what constitutes the best explanation is too restrictive in another sense. It focuses only on the model of the inference to the best *causal* explanation. This distinction brings the problem to the fore: 'Certain moral principles might help to explain why it was *wrong* of the children to set the cat on fire, but moral principles seem to be of no help in explaining *your thinking* that that is wrong'.[159] In the first case, we make a normative and in the second a causal judgment. The role of moral principles is different from the laws of physics: they help us make normative, not causal inferences. The idea here is that the normative domain enjoys autonomy from the causal world. Moral observations are not causal explanations of the world 'out there', moral facts are not natural facts, and moral arguments are independent from the realm in which causal explanations count.[160]

For the purposes of this chapter it is enough to show the incompatibility of this position with the deductive view. I will thus proceed in two steps. First, let us grant that this conception of ethics is cogent in a sense that it could at least qualify as apt to avoid the pitfalls of robust realism. It makes the claim of the mind-independent objectivity of value *intelligible*, even if not necessarily true.[161] So, I shall assume that this conception could in principle support the deductive view. Second, we then need to see if such a conception of ethics—which is a candidate to account for the universality of objective normative reason and does not rely on false metaphysics—hangs well together with the assumptions implicit in the deductive view. If convergence around moral facts with causal force is an implausible explanation of the convergence of normative responses in foreign law, proponents of the deductive view may still argue that each moral reasoner under idealized conditions

[157] See eg David Garland, *Peculiar Institution: America's Death Penalty in an Age of Abolition* (Oxford University Press 2010).

[158] Brian Leiter, 'Moral Facts and Best Explanations' (2001) 18 Social Philosophy and Policy 79.

[159] Harman, *The Nature of Morality: An Introduction to Ethics* (n 152) 8.

[160] See eg Ronald Dworkin, 'Objectivity and Truth: You'd Better Believe It' (1996) 25 Philosophy and Public Affairs 87.

[161] Bernard Williams, *Making Sense of Humanity* (Cambridge University Press 1995) 174–75.

would reach moral truth starting from normative premises within his evaluative outlook.

Indeed, the stronghold of realism against this sceptical challenge has been to resort to our internal possibility of transcendence of experiences through reflection and reason. If sceptics push hard against moral truth being a matter of correspondence between our responses and moral facts in the world, realists respond that we need not populate the world with spooky stuff to account for the objectivity of moral talk. Kantians, for example, think that the truth of moral propositions is not a matter of their correspondence with something in the world, but a matter of our ability to construct moral laws. The idea is that, in the same way that we can grasp mathematical and logical laws through our capacity to reason theoretically, we can proceed by reflection to impose on ourselves the laws of practical reason.[162] Normativity arises not from the causal force that some moral facts exert on us, standing outside of our psychological apparatus, but from our ability to reflect.[163]

There is much to be said about this conception of value. But if it has any plausibility at all, we must question the soundness of the deductive view. This is so for two closely connected reasons. First, if our ability to reflect is at the foundation of ethics, then giving up on it makes little sense. Can we ever give up on our epistemic authority in morals, if moral laws are a consequence of an ability that we all share as humans? This ability is tied to the conception of a mind capable of reflection, so the very idea that we should give in to moral authority without reflection is incoherent. To the extent that the ontology of value depends on the uniquely human capacity to reflect, moral epistemology must also be appropriated to enable us to reach moral answers on our own. As Hilary Putnam puts it, the idea that we are in principle unable to recognize appropriate moral answers presents 'rampant Platonism'.[164]

To be sure, neither Sunstein nor Waldron are 'rampant Platonists' and they certainly do appreciate the role of foreign law in facilitating moral reflection.[165] They might still argue that convergence among moral reasoners may *give us reasons to question our moral views*. We might—for example—be interested in other people's moral opinions if they spend more time and

[162] I focus here on contemporary Kantians—such as Nagel and Korsgaard—who are more attuned to current philosophical circumstances in which conceptual necessities are distrusted.

[163] Christine M Korsgaard, *The Sources of Normativity* (Cambridge University Press 1996) 93.

[164] Hilary Putnam, *The Collapse of the Fact/Value Dichotomy and Other Essays* (Harvard University Press 2002) 108–109.

[165] For example, this is a mistake in Youngjae Lee, 'International Consensus as Persuasive Authority in the Eighth Amendment' (2007) 156 University of Pennsylvania Law Review 63. Lee is sceptical about the connection between the contingent moral attitudes and universal moral truths, but does not deny the existence of universal moral truths as such. However, if there were such truths, then it would be implausible to think they are beyond our reach and that they would not be reflected in the consensus.

resources on reflection.[166] But this is fundamentally different from arguing that foreign consensus has a claim over our actions just because it says so, or that it has more than a suggestive value to our own moral judgment. If the consensus ought to figure in moral reflection it should then probably form a part of reflection and not preclude it: in other words, it should be the beginning and not the end of reflection. While the reflective view then needs to account for the proper weight of consensus, this certainly renders the deductive view inadequate.

The second reason to retain a critical and reflective stance towards 'truths' expressed in consensus concerns the autonomy of ethics as an evaluative domain. Recall that the proponents of the claim that consensus points to moral truth must show that people who reason about their moral commitments will actually converge on moral truth. This presupposes an empirical thesis about our ability to transcend inherited and culturally embedded moral values through reflection. But if causal and normative domains are separate, then this empirical thesis—to the extent that it has normative consequences—must be further evaluated on moral grounds. If Harman is wrong to confuse the causal and normative explanations, empirical claims cannot simply be taken for granted if they lead to unacceptable moral results. For if we cannot escape the maze of evaluative concerns in reaching moral judgments, we must reserve the right to make a moral call on this issue as well.

Thomas Nagel, for example, argues that 'the only way to answer moral skepticism is to meet it with first-order moral arguments'[167] precisely because the realm of the normative is autonomous in a sense that '[w]e have to have or develop some internal [normative] understanding of the possibility that a belief might be false before any suppositions external to it can bring us to abandon it'.[168] By the same token, the confirmation of the existence of moral truth must also begin with some already existing moral belief and not simply from the fact of convergence in foreign attitudes. This thought is best explained with an example. Consider Justice Daniel's consensus-based deductive view from *Dred Scott v Sandford*:

> ... the following are truths which a knowledge of the history of the world ... compels us to know—that the African negro race never have been acknowledged as belonging to the family of nations; that as amongst them there never has been known or recognized by the inhabitants of other countries anything partaking of the character of nationality, or civil or political polity; that this race has been by all the nations of Europe regarded as subjects of capture or purchase; as subjects of commerce or traffic; and that

[166] Peter Singer, 'Moral Experts' (1972) 32 Analysis 115.

[167] Thomas Nagel, *The Last Word* (Oxford University Press 1997) vii. [168] ibid 58.

> the introduction of that race into every section of this country was not as members of civil or political society, but as slaves, as *property* in the strictest sense of the term.[169]

Even though Justice Daniel thought he had found 'truth and knowledge' in global consensus, no one would today argue that 'obviousness' of moral principles had been reflected in these laws and traditions. Nor would anyone think that he discovered 'wisdom' in foreign law that is comparable to scientific knowledge. Unless one can come up with an account that would with sufficient precision indicate a point in time where the world has reached moral truth, the answer to this type of argument must be normative: treating people unfavourably because of their race collides with our deepest normative commitments. The big question is—on the assumption that our contingent attitudes are inherently connected to moral truth—how can these historical attitudes be so much off track according to today's standards? Examples such as this surely make the conception of a moral truth discernible through reason much less intelligible: they show that we can miserably fail to attain it, even upon reflection and reasoning. Moreover, if there is a variety of moral positions that we may happen to occupy at any given time, then why is *our* position *here* and *now* the relevant one to start the reflection with? I will address these issues in the next chapter. Now let us see if the reflective view is a plausible alternative.

4.3.2 *The reflective view*

The reflective view holds that there is no immediate connection between foreign law and moral truth, but there is a connection between looking at foreign law and becoming aware of appropriate moral answers. The plausibility of the reflective view also depends on its vision of the nature of value. Two questions are relevant. First, is the reflection entailed by the use of foreign law capable of reaching objective and universal moral truths, or always depends on contingent moral attitudes implied by constitutional identity and prevailing moral sentiments? Second, if it is not capable of reaching universal moral truths and depends on contingent attitudes, we need to ask: why are these attitudes normative and why ought they be subject to reflection?

The reflective view is the preferred position in both comparative practice and academic commentary. As we have seen, it is the implicit theory behind the use of foreign law in South Africa and Israel. Moreover, most proponents of the use of foreign law favour the reflective view. Vicki Jackson believes that 'ethical engagement' with foreign law may help 'a judge to distance herself from her own first reactions, testing them for prejudice and subjecting

[169] *Dred Scott v Sandford* (n 13) 475 (Daniel).

them to reasoned interrogation', thus offering 'the hope of more impartiality'.[170] Rosalind Dixon's metaphor of a 'constitutional mirror' captures the same idea: foreign law facilitates detachment from the parochial constitutional experience and enables courts to observe it from distance in a more neutral and unbiased way.[171]

The question is whether such a mirror only makes this local constitutional experience more visible, or if it points to something more objective, universal, or truth-like. The ambition of the reflective view in this regard is unclear. For example—much like Justice Cheshin in *Adalah*—Vicki Jackson talks about the 'supra-positive' and 'universal' dimensions of constitutional rights,[172] but at the same time places weight on particular values and traditions of the constitutional system. How are these 'supra-positive', universal, or transcendental elements of constitutional values supposed to be combined with their contingent and historically embedded elements into a coherent ontology of value? We have seen that the idea that foreign law gives an unbiased and universalistic perspective on local moral commitments is present in practice; for instance, it appears in Justice Barak's notion of 'objective' purpose or Justice Ackermann's idea of the 'universal normative core' of a constitution. Notwithstanding the rhetoric, we have also seen that the reach of reflection conducted with the assistance of foreign law is limited, and ultimately echoes local moral commitments. To the extent that the existence of universal and objective normative reasons cognizable through reflection is the only theory that supports the reflective view, this view may well be under-motivated.

The process of detachment facilitated by foreign law does share some common features with the typical understanding of the moral point of view, which demands that we take an impartial perspective and transcend personal judgments or interests.[173] For example, in Sidgwick's interpretation, the moral point of view asks us to dissolve the distinction between the self and the other, and accept that 'the good of any one individual is of no more importance, from the point of view ... of the Universe, than the good of any

[170] Jackson, 'Constitutional Comparisons: Convergence, Resistance, Engagement' (n 135) 118–19, footnotes omitted. See also Vlad Perju, 'Cosmopolitanism and Constitutional Self-government' (2010) 8 International Journal of Constitutional Law 326.

[171] Dixon, 'A Democratic Theory of Constitutional Comparison' (n 9) 959–60.

[172] Jackson, 'Constitutional Comparisons: Convergence, Resistance, Engagement' (n 135) 18.

[173] Rawls famously captures this idea with his concept of the 'veil of ignorance' (John Rawls, *A Theory of Justice* (rev edn, Belknap Press 1999)). In non-Kantian tradition, Hume and Adam Smith rely on the idea that the moral feeling of sympathy requires us to take the position of a 'judicious' or impartial spectator that can feel other people's experiences as her own. See Adam Smith, *The Theory of Moral Sentiments* (Knud Haakonssen (ed), Cambridge University Press 2002); Marcia Homiak, 'Moral Character' in Edward N Zalta (ed), *The Stanford Encyclopedia of Philosophy* (Spring 2011 edn) http://plato.stanford.edu/archives/spr2011/entries/moral-character/%3E (last accessed 16 July 2014).

other'.[174] Thomas Nagel's account of the moral point of view invites us to think 'from no particular point of view about how to regard a world which contains points of view',[175] and to find 'the best perspectiveless account'[176] of these different perspectives. The thought is that when we occupy an objective perspective ('a view from nowhere') we can abstract from our personal and self-interested standpoint and see moral value not as a consequence of anyone's particular experience, but as an objective thing in the world.[177]

These and similar accounts are in the neighbourhood of the idea of using foreign law to overcome the contingencies of the specific constitutional system which make our value judgments perspectival. We can imagine a court being such a self that reflects on the existing set of values in the constitutional system, by taking into account foreign evaluative frameworks in order to provide the 'best perspectiveless account' of all these experiences. But does it succeed in emulating this process, and does it come close to this ideal of objectivity? While the argument from foreign law goes in the same direction of stripping off the layers of contingency in our value judgments, it falls short of reaching the point of view that would ultimately reveal the objective normative reason. The reflection it entails always goes back to our own values and we cannot completely transcend our constitutional value system through such an exercise. The argument from universal reason is hence neither completely universal nor consumed by reason. It can neither secure Sidgwick's 'point of view of the Universe' nor Nagel's 'view from nowhere', but only a more modest version of this standpoint, which is perhaps more appropriately described as 'a view from everywhere'.

Let me support this claim by looking more closely at the mechanics of the reflection induced by foreign law. There are several *virtues of good moral judgment* that foreign law might facilitate, but they do not guarantee full detachment from the contingent moral experience. The most obvious one is *information*. Moral judgment ought to include sound empirical premises. For example, in *Roe v Wade* the court used foreign experiences to support its claim that mortality rates for abortion are the same or lower than for regular childbirth.[178] The conclusion thus depended on a local value—that higher mortality rates in abortion count against it—and foreign law interfered only with the factual basis of the argument. Similarly, in *Washington v Glucksberg* justices invoked empirical evidence from the Netherlands while discussing the claim that legalizing euthanasia might lead to abuses.[179] This is different

[174] Henry Sidgwick, *The Methods of Ethics* (7th edn, MacMillan 1962) 382. For a critique see Williams, *Making Sense of Humanity* (n 161) ch 13.

[175] Nagel, *The View from Nowhere* (n 1) 161. [176] ibid. [177] ibid 160–61.

[178] *Roe v Wade* (n 16) 149 n 44, mentioning the law of England, Wales, Japan, Czechoslovakia, and Hungary.

[179] *Washington v Glucksberg* (n 17) 732–34 and 785–86 (Souter).

from using foreign law to illuminate the protected value itself. For example, in the *Glucksberg* majority opinion, Justice Rehnquist argued that euthanasia is not practiced in western democracies.[180] He brought up this fact to support an evaluative proposition—that euthanasia is not acceptable—which is not related to the empirical question of whether it is difficult to administer euthanasia in a way that would prevent manipulation. Foreign law can thus be used to support both the evaluative and descriptive premise of the argument even in the same judgment. In the latter case, foreign law serves as a pool of social experiments that contributes to our experience without having to go through the process of trial and error. This kind of use of foreign law does not appeal to universal moral truths, but takes a form of hypothetical imperative: the normative goal is already supplied by the local evaluative outlook and looking at how other legal systems have dealt with similar problems might help us to learn how to achieve that goal.

But sometimes value judgments are imported from foreign law in this way, even if the court claims to be seeking information only. For instance, in *Printz v United States*, Justice Breyer used foreign law—in his words—to 'cast an empirical light on the consequences of different solutions to a common legal problem'; however, the argument was that the balance between 'the practical need for central authority' and the 'democratic virtues of more local control' had been successfully struck in some European states by having the local authorities implement federal laws.[181] While there are obvious similarities between the idea of federalism in Europe and the United States, it also acquires different meanings in national constitutional systems; the balance between central and local government in a constitutional system depends on the local understanding of federalism, unless one believes in federalism as a Platonic ideal-form.[182] Breyer's argument therefore does not cast empirical light only: it aims to readjust the American understanding of federalism by exposing it to different conceptions, such as those applied in Europe.

But this exposure to foreign law might foster another virtue of good moral judgment: *flexibility*. It could be the case that there is a different value that is sub-optimally realized because of an entrenched understanding of federalism. For example, federalism might be motivated by reasons of efficiency, social cohesion, or keeping the government in check. A temperate moral judgment presupposes the ability to re-question one's own position. Looking at foreign law may reveal some of the neglected concerns or might show that the question has been inadequately framed; in such a case, foreign law might prompt the court to overturn its previous judgment.

[180] ibid 710 n 8 and 718 n 16.

[181] *Printz v United States* 521 US 898 (1997) 976–77 (Breyer).

[182] ibid 921 n 11 (Scalia).

For example, in *Bowers v Hardwick*, the Supreme Court upheld Georgia's law, which criminalized consensual sodomy; in so doing it investigated if homosexuals had a constitutionally guaranteed right to engage in sodomy and understood values as being rooted in local traditions.[183] The majority in *Lawrence v Texas* overturned *Bowers* but retained its approach to the nature of value. Justice Kennedy wrote at length about examples from 'Western civilization' that refute the inference in *Bowers* about the traditional ban on homosexual conduct.[184] He thus did not deny that value may be locally constructed, but argued that important aspects of the value of liberty were not taken into account, especially in its implications for privacy and restraint in the state's interference with private life. Kennedy argued that the court ought to understand its previous decisions and the values behind them more flexibly: 'times can blind us to certain truths and later generations can see that laws once thought necessary and proper in fact serve only to oppress. As the Constitution endures, persons in every generation can invoke its principles in their own search for greater freedom'.[185] Kennedy also thought that once the doubts about a precedent become evident, 'criticism from other sources is of greater significance'.[186] One of these sources that enables greater reflective flexibility are the laws of the nations that share similar values and heritage. The best way to understand the use of foreign law in *Lawrence* to elucidate the contours of liberty is not that this concept has a universal meaning to be discovered in the world, but that the core of its meaning is shared with many other countries, and that it includes certain concerns that have been neglected in *Bowers*.[187] The question—according to the *Lawrence* court—was framed wrongly and in so doing it missed important aspects of liberty: it 'demeaned' the claim of the individual as asking for the right to engage in homosexual conduct, while it actually involved their dignity and freedom to be in a personal relationship.[188]

Flexibility usually derives its appeal from yet another virtue of good moral judgment: *coherence*. The *Lawrence* court used foreign law to show that *Bowers* was inconsistent with a set of locally shared values. The aim was not to import universal reasons from foreign law, but to bring local commitments into balance. Yet, coherence is not a guarantor of universal truths, but merely implies that there is a set of evaluative commitments in a community that cannot all be realized at the same time without sacrificing some of them. It requires careful reflection on the consequences of each of the commitments and their relative importance within the local evaluative standpoint.

Reaching coherence is difficult in its own right, and foreign law obviously cannot fully alleviate disagreements. We have seen for example that in Israel

[183] *Bowers v Hardwick* (n 18) (Burger). [184] *Lawrence v Texas* (n 18) 571–73. [185] ibid 579.
[186] ibid 576. [187] ibid 576–77. [188] ibid 567.

there are two sets of values: 'Jewish' and 'democratic', local and cosmopolitan, traditional and modern. These values can sometimes be in tension. In *Adalah*, both Barak and Cheshin used foreign law to address this tension and reached opposing results. But foreign law helped them strike the balance nonetheless. Looking at jurisdictions that share some values with Israel, they both agreed that the commitment to human dignity entails protection of the right to family life. They disagreed about the way the balance between security and dignity plays out under the circumstances of life in Israel. Each opinion reached coherence between the two different sets of values and concerns by sacrificing one over the other; however, looking at the jurisdictions that Israel identifies with helped the justices understand to what extent these cosmopolitan values can be realized in Israel, and where the local factual circumstances or evaluative commitments ought to take precedence.

Attaining stable coherence often demands another virtue: *imagination*. Foreign law can thus serve in overcoming what Justice Ackermann calls 'tunnel vision', which prevents the judge from noticing some aspects of values, less visible connections between them, or fruitful ways in which they can be balanced. Justice Chaskalson described the usefulness of foreign law in *Makwanyane* in the following way: 'foreign authorities are of value because they analyse arguments for and against the death sentence'.[189] He thus understood foreign law as a pool of potential arguments, and not as a source of authoritative solutions: by studying foreign law one makes sure that no argumentative rock stays unturned. Chaskalson's opinion in *Makwanyane* provides a fine example of foreign law being able to expand the imaginative horizons of the court. He used arguments present in foreign law to determine the relevant concerns for his own decision: the arbitrariness and inequality of the death penalty, the consequences for the right to life and dignity, the relevance of public opinion, and the balance between other implicated values.[190] Foreign law can thus point to relevant arguments, possible trade-offs between values, and creative solutions to constitutional problems. Again, this does not mean that foreign solutions are imported because their source points to moral truth, but because judges believe they are appropriate for domestic circumstances.

Imagination is closely connected to another virtue of good moral judgment: *maturity*. It seems sensible to expect that a decision in moral matters will be better balanced if the court is more experienced and aware of possible solutions and pitfalls. But sometimes the courts are not experienced enough. Again, Chaskalson's views on foreign law from *Makwanyane* are illustrative; in his opinion, '[c]omparative "bill of rights" jurisprudence will ... be of importance, particularly in the early stages of the transition

[189] *S v Makwanyane and Another* (n 54) para 34 (Chaskalson).

[190] ibid paras 40–109 (Chaskalson).

when there is no developed indigenous jurisprudence'.[191] Since the South African Constitutional Court did not have enough familiarity with rights-based review of legislation, it looked for inspiration elsewhere; part of the reason why the South African Constitution encompasses the explicit permission to use foreign law lies in the fact that there was no experience or tradition of dealing with constitutional problems from a liberal democratic perspective. This does not mean that conclusions are imported irrespectively of the domestic evaluative commitments. A case in point is Justice Agranat's opinion in *Kol Ha'am*. This opinion starts from a local commitment to democratic government and then tries to discern the appropriate limitations to free speech from the practice of more mature jurisdictions that share this commitment, such as the United States. Similarly, Justice Barak in *Mizrahi Bank* looked at the law of other democratic countries to understand the role of judicial review. In both cases, the democratic orientation of the Israeli constitutional system comes from within the local evaluative outlook, but the system lacks relevant experience and looks for clues from more mature democracies. The use of foreign law rests on a belief that progressive and more experienced legal systems have reached desirable and workable solutions, better adapted to contemporary circumstances.

Does this imply capitulation of moral judgment, making it a deductive view? It seems that as long as epistemic conditions are met, we can rely on the results of the moral inquiry of others. Recall that the objection against the deductive view was precisely that it is implausible that we are able to tell that epistemic conditions are met, while at the same time not being capable of reaching the same conclusion ourselves (but not necessarily in isolation). If we know what it takes to make the same decision, why take the detour via foreign law? The issue is not so straightforward. The process can implicate our moral judgment at different stages of accepting someone as an epistemic authority. If we retain our moral capacities in the process, we can see how the use of foreign law in such a case can be useful but not deductive. Engaging with doctrines from more experienced jurisdictions may be epistemically warranted, as a justification for *choosing* such sources, and not as justification for *surrendering* moral judgment. When acting with limited resources, we sometimes have to make a choice and take into account systems that will—to the best of our knowledge—prove to be useful. A judge would still assess the substantive outcome of the judgment, but the reason to engage with it in the first place may be its origin. This presupposes and does not exclude the capacity to recognize and use moral judgments of others in order to confirm or synthesize beliefs. And that makes such use of foreign law reflective, not deductive.

[191] ibid para 37 (Chaskalson).

A reflective understanding of the argument from universal reason can help us notice that this kind of use of foreign law can work both ways: the court we are looking at may be more experienced, but it may also have a baggage of concerns which younger courts do not face, such as doctrine, intentions of framers, or interpretive techniques. This is why—while new constitutional systems may look at foreign jurisdictions for mature solutions to constitutional problems—the old ones may rely on foreign law to overcome the vice of too much self-containment: good moral judgment thus demands a degree of *openness*. Much of the use of foreign law in the United States can be explained in this way. Even though it has a lot of experience and maturity, the US constitutional system may entrench certain judgments which neither correspond with the current needs of the society nor fit with the overall framework of its values. In most of the cases the US Supreme Court referred to the fact of foreign consensus—across the board or among countries that share its evaluative perspective—as a confirmation of its own conclusions. This could be understood in terms of openness: as a recognition that the maturity of the system, which is responsible for its leadership in the protection of rights, has also ossified specific views which may no longer be acceptable given other evaluative attitudes predominant in the system. This argument may thus be interpreted in light of identity concerns and self-perception, rather than belief that foreign law tracks the truth; for example, the mention of Iran, Pakistan, Saudi Arabia, Yemen, Nigeria, Congo, and China in *Roper* is a reminder that the country cannot remain a frontrunner of human rights protection if these countries have abolished capital punishment for juveniles and the United States has not. However, the value of openness towards global consensus has to be explained by something more substantive than national pride, for pride itself may work both ways, and eventually convince someone of his self-righteousness despite the consensus; furthermore, it is doubtful that the use of consensus is based only on this demeaning sense, in which we see other systems as backwards and realize that even they might be more advanced in certain issues.

Openness to consensus seems like the bulwark of the deductive view. Recall: the argument from consensus may survive even on a non-Platonic deductive view because more people engaged in moral reasoning have better chances to reflectively reach moral truth. The issue directly relates to the understanding of the universality element in the argument from universal reason: we might think that it includes a dilemma between universal human and relativistic or communal values. The question is whether we need to accept this dilemma as categorical. We might have good reasons to retain the choice to reach moral judgments on our own and based on our specific constitutional experience, but to nonetheless appreciate the normative pull of consensus. The question is whether—if we abandon the position that value stems from the standpoint of 'nowhere' or the 'universe' and understand values as contingent and historically embedded—the reliance on consensus makes sense?

The best explanation of the existence of consensus is that similar values have actually been accepted around the world and that they have led the courts to similar normative judgments. We need not presuppose that all judges are engaged in moral reasoning and that as such have better chances to reach moral truth through reason. Rather, a more plausible explanation is that contingent circumstances (evolutionary, sociological, historical, and economic) have produced similar value systems around the world. When relying on consensus, we need only suppose that we share many values with other systems, especially in areas of immense international activity such as human rights. We are both part of the global and our own community's value system. There is nothing mysterious or metaphysical in any of them. Value is again internal to us, only now we are questioning who 'we' are.

Following the assumption that the circumstances of life on this planet have brought about many similarities in the contingent sets of values around the world, it is then plausible to assume that, if there is a global consensus on some issue, we might be missing out on something in our value judgments if we diverge from it. Because of this, the convergence in the world should make us question our value judgments. While it gives us no reason to surrender to consensus, it does carry some weight and invites us to justify our own views again. We may then distinguish our case from the prevailing opinion, or agree with it on substantive moral grounds, and not simply because of the consensus. Thus, the reflective view can explain the normative pull of consensus without renouncing our moral agency: consensus in foreign law ignites reflection instead of foreclosing it. Furthermore, it explains why the argument from consensus is not likely to play an important role in practice: the consensus will often point to well-accepted moral principles that are not a part of controversy, pertain to issues that are long settled, or be too thin to illuminate novel directions for policy in modern societies.

The virtue of openness does not have to imply only the consensus-based use of foreign law. Most cases of the use of foreign law presuppose looking at jurisdictions that share a similar value-framework, so they can clearly contribute to the self-understanding of the system that is making the comparison; if we share values and do different things, there is a good chance that we have probably not fully explored our evaluative outlooks. But openness also entails looking at systems that do not share similar background commitments. We have seen that Aharon Barak denies that there can be fruitful comparison between systems that do not have a 'common ideological basis'.[192] Justice Breyer retreated from his mention of Zimbabwe in *Knight v*

[192] Barak, *The Judge in a Democracy* (n 91) 198.

Florida calling it a 'tactical error'.[193] If we accept the reflective view, there is a way to resist such conclusions. Being exposed to other perspectives could teach us a lot about ourselves. As in *Roper*, we could realize that some of our values are not as progressive as we previously might have thought. But the more important effect goes in the other direction. By distinguishing other systems we learn where the borders of our evaluative outlook are and we test which values are more central to it. Recognizing that a value system is not a real option for us—that accepting it would demand sacrificing a significant part of our identity—can make us rethink some of the moral judgments we share with such a system, and can also confirm our confidence in our own perspective. The benefit of such confrontation is achieving greater self-awareness. It can make us dig deeper into our value system to see whether the moral judgment in question genuinely fits with other judgments we hold important.

These processes are important specifically when the law fails to incite appropriate *sensibility* towards different perspectives. A good moral judgment includes the ability of role-taking and seeing problems from the perspective of the other with whom we may not agree; while this is already psychologically difficult, the law may further entrench a particular perspective that is not shared by all groups within the society. This is particularly problematic if minorities do not have an opportunity to articulate their voice within the dominant legal environment. Foreign law may contribute to a different framing of the issue before the court which better accommodates the needs of minorities. For example, in *Lawrence* the controversy occurred in the context of privacy: the police entered a private residence of the petitioner who was having sex with another man. This fact led the majority to write the opinion in the context of privacy, but the use of foreign law sensitized the court to realize that privacy includes more than the protection of one's home because of its connection with liberty.[194] Unlike *Bowers*, where the court asked if there is a fundamental right to engage in homosexual sodomy,[195] the *Lawrence* court asked whether the state has a legitimate interest to interfere with the liberty of its citizens in the domain of personal relationships. Foreign law served both to draw the attention of the court to this question, and to confirm that a system committed to liberty ought to interpret these kinds of state interventions as unjustified. Kennedy thus concluded that '[t]he right the petitioners seek in this case has been accepted as an integral part of human freedom in many other countries' and that '[t]here has been no showing that in this country the governmental interest in circumscribing

[193] Dorsen, 'The Relevance of Foreign Legal Materials in U.S. Constitutional Cases: A Conversation between Justice Antonin Scalia and Justice Stephen Breyer' (n 28) 528.

[194] *Lawrence v Texas* (n 18) 562.

[195] *Bowers v Hardwick* (n 18) 190.

personal choice is somehow more legitimate or urgent'.[196] Again, the issue is not what privacy means in general, but what are its implications in a system that accepts the values of dignity and liberty.

Finally, another reflective virtue is *clarity*. The first precondition for moral reflection is to understand clearly what relevant concerns are at stake. We have seen that the use of foreign law frequently pertains to proportionality analysis: a set of analytic stages that the courts go through to determine whether a state policy is justified from the perspective of constitutionally protected values. For example, the South African Constitutional Court in *Makwanyane* examined different models of proportionality analysis—from Canada, Germany, and the European Court of Human Rights—to find that such reasoning was 'implicit' in the limitation of the rights clause of the constitution.[197] Similarly, Justice Barak argued in *Mizrahi* and *Adalah* that proportionality analysis was the appropriate framework for exploring the boundaries of justified limitations of human rights and—in so doing—he relied on an extensive examination of foreign approaches to this type of analysis.[198] Again, proportionality analysis as such does not guarantee much in terms of substantive results, and there is no transfer of values from one system to the other; rather, what happens is that one system finds it useful to rely on a procedure that makes explicit the method of analysis that would otherwise stay implicit. It is a matter of importing a reflective technique, not substantive values.

The benefits of the reflective view are twofold. First, it accounts for all the instances of the use of foreign law—including reliance on consensus—without presupposing implausible metaphysical theses. The argument for the use of foreign law is motivated by several reflective virtues that are typically taken to be a staple of good moral judgment. The reflective view describes how we can work our way through the evaluative meaning we impose on the world, and not how we can work our way down from the source of value we discover in the world. Second, it allows us to develop a unified conception of constitutional ethics, one that can combine the argument from constitutional identity and common sentiment together with the argument from universal reason. However, the crucial question then becomes: what gives the descriptive sociological and psychological facts about our normative attitudes their normativity? Why *ought* we reflect on our contingent moral attitudes if this procedure fails to lead us to universal and timeless moral truths?

196 *Lawrence v Texas* (n 18) 577.

197 Section 33(1) of the Interim Constitution of 1993. *S v Makwanyane and Another* (n 54) paras 103–12.

198 *United Mizrahi Bank Ltd v Migdal Cooperative Village* (n 89) paras 83–99 (Barak); *Adalah Legal Centre for Arab Minority Rights in Israel v Minister of Interior* (n 120) 54–75 (Barak). In particular, Barak was influenced by the Canadian law and the proportionality test developed in *R v Oakes* [1986] 1 SCR 103.

Arguments from common sentiment and constitutional identity depend on contingent moral attitudes, and the argument from universal reason enables reflection that is also contingently considered to be beneficial to a good moral judgment. These contingent attitudes are descriptive facts, but—the popular axiom claims—facts are normatively inert. This is why, to motivate the use of these ethical arguments in constitutional reasoning, we need a conception of value that will vindicate our ability to rely on our contingent moral attitudes even if they do not lead to mind-independent moral truths.

4.4 CONCLUSION

This chapter has analysed the use of foreign law in constitutional reasoning, understood as an ethical argument which sees value as universal and based on reason. The purpose was to inquire into the justifications for the use of such an argument and to reveal its metaethical foundations. The constitutive elements of such an argument—universality and reasonableness—can be interpreted in two different ways: deductive and reflective.

According to the deductive view, foreign law acquires the status of objective normative reason once some epistemic conditions are fulfilled. This view should be rejected. It either presupposes an implausible moral ontology which includes moral facts with causal powers, or subscribes to a variant of moral realism which relies on our capability to reason and cannot without contradiction demand from us to fully surrender to a moral authority.

According to the reflective view, foreign law does not point to universal moral truths, but it is helpful in reaching the reflective state in which we can better grasp our own moral commitments and their implications. While in this view the argument from universal reason remains in the neighbourhood of the idea of the view from 'nowhere' or the 'universe'—which should present a point in which we can cognize the value as objective—it falls short of fully recreating it. In the reflective view, we should better think of the use of foreign law as the view from 'everywhere': a useful exercise that can help us develop and clarify our own evaluative framework. The best vocabulary to express this view includes, but is not limited to, several virtues of good moral judgment: information, flexibility, openness, imagination, coherence, clarity, maturity, and sensibility.

The ambition of such reflection as a form of reasoning is limited: it presents a search for reflective equilibrium, and not a deduction from objective reasons. By divorcing the use of foreign law from the strong understanding of universality and reasonableness, we are also dispensing with the idea that it will lead us to universal reasons that are robustly objective. The argument from universal reason cannot thus provide the mind-independent foundation of constitutional ethics. This poses two problems. First, there could still be absolute and mind-independent truths about values attainable through reason. If this is so, then the modest understanding of universality and reasonableness implicit in the reflective view cannot motivate it, and we should be seeking after these mind-independent truths. Second, if there are no such truths discernible through reflection, then why should we reflect upon our values in the first place? Moreover, if we must always go back to our contingent moral intuitions that give substance to our reflective judgment, how are these *facts* about our emotive attitudes *normative*?

All of this makes constitutional ethics metaethically unstable: it needs to explain what makes the sociological fact about contingent intuitions morally relevant, and where the value of reasoning and reflection comes from. These and similar questions are bound to persist unless we have a plausible theory of value that will provide a basis for thinking about the ethical arguments in constitutional reasoning. The task of the next chapter is to develop such a theory. I will argue that the modest idea of practical reasoning is not merely the second-best, but the only one we could possibly hope to have, and that the prospects of overcoming our contingent intuitions and emotional reactions is illusory; moreover, I will try to show that this realization need not lead to a bottomless moral scepticism which renders us unable to make moral judgments at all.

5

Values and Normative Judgment

5.1 INTRODUCTION

Previous chapters have identified a pressing challenge to the judicial use of ethical arguments: common types of ethical arguments in constitutional reasoning suffer from inadequate metaethical foundations. Constitutional courts need a sound theory of value around which their ethical arguments could be constructed. We must therefore ponder the nature of value and normative judgment. In previous chapters, I have already relied on arguments that presupposed specific views about value. The aim of this chapter is to integrate these views into a coherent framework and articulate a philosophical foundation for a theory of constitutional ethics.

Unless a person is unable to act practically, she is asking herself what she ought to do, and is thus experiencing the reality of value. Should I spend the evening with my friends or should I work late? Practical questions like this depend on what I think I have most reason to do, and practical decisions are thus affected by values. To account for the role of values in practical reasoning, it is not enough to explain why I came to think that I ought to work late. Such an explanation can cite a number of causal forces and contingencies in my life, culture, or evolutionary development, which led me to believe that I have most reason to do so. It would certainly be a mistake to neglect such causal explanations, but a full account of value and normative judgment must also address some further features of value-laden practical reasoning. Practical decisions can be subjected to criticism whereby, for example, my friends tell me that I did not have most reason to work late, although I decided to do so. Moreover, some sense must be made of thoughts expressing the normative pull of our values in the form of 'I ought not to feel this'. For example, thinking that I ought not feel guilty for staying late at work signals a gap between what I think I should feel and what I actually feel.[1] The language of criticism and thoughts of mistaken feelings are intelligible and

[1] Allan Gibbard, *Reconciling Our Aims: In Search of Bases for Ethics* (Oxford University Press 2008) ch 1.

need to be accounted for.[2] These experiences seem to justify the notion that I could be in error regarding my practical decision, and that such an error includes the truth of the matter concerning the proper way to decide the dilemma, standing apart from whichever mental state *I* was in while weighing the reasons for and against the decision.

This poses a question of whether there are values which could be true independently of all contingent attitudes about them. Expressed in a more recognizable jargon—the question is whether values are *mind-dependent* or *mind-independent*.[3] If the latter is the case, there is a relatively straightforward way to account for the possibility of error in our moral judgments, while the former is typically understood to be more compatible with the scientific world view and with the reality presupposed by it. The answer to this dilemma, as I will suggest, must not neglect explanations of how we came to occupy a place in the world in which we can experience value. But the answer also depends on the possibility to preserve the reality of our experience of value in the face of such an explanation; it needs to show how we can at the same time be both aware and immersed in the matrix of the human condition, context, contingency, history, identity, language—in other words, the *form of life*—that supplies our values with much of their substance.

In previous chapters I expressed doubt that value is something external to us, found in the world outside our psychological sets.[4] The conclusion followed the idea that there is no evidence of normative properties in the world that could exert causal pressure on our value systems. I shall develop this point at greater length here, and show why our folk normative judgments and values must figure in both theoretical explanations of value and practical normative judgments. The chapter proceeds as follows. First, I will reconstruct the problem about the nature of value in terms of the conflict between the theoretical and practical perspective, and show why some common philosophical approaches to this problem are not satisfactory. Second, I shall examine the nature of value from the theoretical perspective; this perspective tells us that values are contingent and gives us no reason to trust that they are connected to mind-independent truths. Third, I will clarify what are the consequences of the theoretical on the practical perspective; I shall argue that there is no reason to suspend the practical perspective, and that the redemption of our practical confidence emerges once we are reflective enough about it. The aim is to reach a sustainable understanding

[2] Allan Gibbard, *Wise Choices, Apt Feelings: A Theory of Normative Judgment* (Clarendon Press 1990) 12.

[3] Throughout the chapter I will use mind-independent, external, robust, absolute, and universal, as near synonyms that denote a property of values that could be true irrespective of our contingent attitudes.

[4] Bernard Williams, *Moral Luck: Philosophical Papers, 1973–1980* (Cambridge University Press 1981) ch 8.

of value—arising from the dynamics between *confidence* and *reflection*—that is able to preserve both the theoretical and practical perspective.

5.2 THE THEORETICAL AND PRACTICAL PERSPECTIVE

As humans, we are able to occupy two distinct points of view.[5] When deciding what to do *practically*, our values seem to us, and we present them to others, as true. Even the most sceptical among us utter things like 'cruelty is wrong', thereby seemingly describing an occurrence in the world as having a property of wrongness, and having it regardless of contingent attitudes about it here and now. The meaning of the concept 'wrong' seems to be fixed by its reference, the episode in the world that our moral judgment is about. On the other hand, when examining our values *theoretically*, taking the empirical-scientific point of view, we are able to explain our value experiences as causally affected attitudes, contingent on evolution, history, culture, upbringing, or our own choice.[6] This perspective puts in doubt the claim that the property of wrongness exists in the world regardless of our contingent beliefs about it, or suggests that—if there is such a property—our actual beliefs could happen to be completely unrelated to it.[7]

This issue is not mere philosophical hair-splitting. Many feel profound psychological uneasiness arising from the possibility of conflict between these two perspectives. Derek Parfit, for example, thinks that '[i]t would be a tragedy if there was no single true morality'[8] and that '[i]f there are no [irreducibly normative, reason-involving] truths, nothing matters'.[9] We do want our values to matter, and if they matter only if they are true—objectively, once and for all, and independently of what we think about them—then the problem may be daunting. The theoretical perspective could reveal that our values are nothing like that and that we have been deluded. We thus need to see whether there is a conflict between these perspectives, and if

[5] This way of framing the issue owes much to Sharon Street's work. See eg Sharon Street, 'Coming to Terms with Contingency: Humean Constructivism about Practical Reason' in James Lenman and Yonatan Shemmer (eds), *Constructivism in Practical Philosophy* (Oxford University Press 2012); Sharon Street, 'What is Constructivism in Ethics and Metaethics?' (2010) 5 Philosophy Compass 363; Sharon Street, 'Constructivism about Reasons' in Russ Shafer-Landau (ed), *Oxford Studies in Metaethics: Volume 3* (Clarendon Press 2008); Sharon Street, 'Objectivity and Truth: You'd Better Rethink It' unpublished draft https://files.nyu.edu/ss194/public/sharonstreet/Writing_files/Paper%2012%20for%20website%20-%20Objectivity%20and%20Truth%20-%20You%27d%20Better%20Rethink%20It.pdf (last accessed 16 July 2014).

[6] See Gilbert Harman, 'Is There a Single True Morality' in Gilbert Harman, *Explaining Value and Other Essays in Moral Philosophy* (Oxford University Press 2000) ch 5.

[7] Sharon Street, 'A Darwinian Dilemma for Realist Theories of Value' (2006) 127 Philosophical Studies 109. See the analysis later in this chapter.

[8] Derek Parfit, *On What Matters: Volume Two* (Oxford University Press 2011) 155.

[9] ibid 465.

there is, how we can continue with our practical life if there is no 'true' reason to do anything at all and everything is perhaps just an illusion. Even if there is no need to feel excruciated by this thought, how can we go on claiming objectivity and truth for our values without having a bad philosophical conscience[10] There are different ways to respond to the pressure towards the unified world view that would incorporate both the practical and the theoretical perspective. Let us examine some options.

5.2.1 Suppression

One strategy is to *suppress* the compelling character of the theoretical perspective or reduce it to the practical. Typically, the thought is that once the metaethical claims are levelled on the playing field with our deepest moral convictions they will give way, for they will be confronted with the possibility that anything goes. This thought takes diverse forms. Ronald Dworkin, for example, deprives metaethical claims of any self-standing relevance. According to him, the problem is *logical*—if one wishes to allow the effects of metaethical views on substantive values, one is at the same time inferring a normative conclusion from descriptive premises. Such attempts meet a dilemma: either metaethical claims are descriptive and normative inferences from them are guilty of normative fallacy, or alternatively, metaethical claims are normative and cannot without contradiction refute the relevance of all normative claims in general.[11] Dworkin believes that morality is wholly independent of metaethical concerns, that it 'exercises its own sovereignty',[12] but also—more controversially—that 'the question whether moral judgments can be true or false is a substantive moral issue'.[13] The talk of subjectivity of values is an expression of morally relevant attitudes, and is to be abandoned as confused because it claims objectivity for itself.

There is much to be said about the particulars of this argument. Suffice it to note that Hume's law that motivates it applies only to deductive inferences, whereas an argument showing that the best explanation of our values casts doubt on their aptness for truth is perfectly sound.[14] However, the issue is not properly understood as pertaining to the validity of normative arguments, but to the firmness of our belief in the truth of their premises.

[10] Stephen Darwall, Allan Gibbard, and Peter Railton, 'Toward Fin de siècle Ethics: Some Trends' in Stephen L Darwall, Allan Gibbard, and Peter A Railton (eds), *Moral Discourse and Practice: Some Philosophical Approaches* (Oxford University Press 1997) 6.

[11] Ronald Dworkin, 'Objectivity and Truth: You'd Better Believe It' (1996) 25 Philosophy and Public Affairs 87; Ronald Dworkin, *Justice for Hedgehogs* (Belknap Press of Harvard University Press 2011) pt 1.

[12] Dworkin, 'Objectivity and Truth: You'd Better Believe It' (n 11) 128.

[13] Dworkin, *Justice for Hedgehogs* (n 11) 67.

[14] Russ Shafer-Landau, 'The Possibility of Metaethics' (2010) 90 Boston University Law Review 479.

The real question is, why should concerns about the mind-independence of value make us *practically* worried? The answer I want to suggest—and where Dworkin's intuition is right—is that the ability to trust in the absolute truth of our normative judgments does play a role within the internal, ethical perspective. For consider: if there is no logical or any other connection between metaethical statements and normative ethical statements, if they do not correspond in any way that would subject them to the demands of coherence, we could simply continue with our practice as if nothing happened; the attempt to reduce metaethical to normative statements would be superfluous, because they could co-exist within a single perspective without loss to any of them. Yet, the problem seems to be more serious. Bertrand Russell puts it nicely: 'I am not guilty of any logical inconsistency in holding to the [subjectivist] interpretation of ethics and at the same time expressing strong ethical preferences. But in feeling I am not satisfied'.[15] We have to get to the bottom of that feeling and see if it is warranted.

Resistance to the theoretical perspective also comes from the view that it is excessively hegemonic. Thomas Nagel believes that the question about the nature of value is 'about the order of normative explanation'.[16] Evaluative judgments cannot be 'explained' by anything else but 'more general or basic evaluative truths, together with the facts that bring them into play'.[17] The mode of explanation Nagel has in mind is normative and—like Dworkin—he trusts that a causal explanation does not talk to the truth of values: it can be confirmed only by some other irreducibly normative truth. Nonetheless, Nagel argues that the reason to keep these two perspectives separate is not only logical but also *ontological*: our experiences of value as true are real, and thus any conception of reality which aspires to be comprehensive but neglects this must be incomplete.[18] It is not possible to reduce our experience of normative truth and recast it in psychological or some other vocabulary, as it would then be very different to how it appears (peculiarly) to us;[19] such a reduction cannot be made without loss and the world we would be describing would be different from the one in which these experiences exist.

[15] Bertrand Russell cited in John L Mackie, *Ethics: Inventing Right and Wrong* (2nd edn, Penguin 1990) 34.

[16] Thomas Nagel, *Mind and Cosmos: Why the Materialist Neo-Darwinian Conception of Nature is Almost Certainly False* (Oxford University Press 2012) 182; Thomas Nagel, *The Last Word* (Oxford University Press 1997) 141–42.

[17] Nagel, *Mind and Cosmos: Why the Materialist Neo-Darwinian Conception of Nature is Almost Certainly False* (n 16) 182.

[18] See for example ibid ch 5. See also: Hilary Putnam, *Ethics without Ontology* (Harvard University Press 2004); Parfit, *On What Matters: Volume Two* (n 8) ch 31.

[19] Nicholas L Sturgeon, 'Harman on Moral Explanations of Natural Facts' (1986) 24 Southern Journal of Philosophy 69; Nicholas L Sturgeon, 'Moral Explanations' in Geoffrey Sayre-McCord (ed), *Essays on Moral Realism* (Cornell University Press 1988).

This view demands a serious treatment that cannot be fully attempted here. However, we may notice that—as much as the moral anti-realist may need a theory of ethical criticism and error—this view needs a theory of illusion; if subjective experiences are to be allowed into the ontology of the world we may want to distinguish between those that are not true despite their appearance of truth (eg a drug-induced hallucination) and true because they appear to be true (eg value experiences). There must be an epistemological standard that will differentiate truth from illusion. In the case of ordinary perception, we have (at the very least) a robust converging phenomenology that could play such a role, but in the case of moral 'perception' we do not: values may not seem 'glaringly' true to others as much as they seem to Thomas Nagel.[20] Many people recognize that their values are subjective or relative to their culture, but would still express them in a truth-apt language.

The more important question, however, is whether the conflict between these two perspectives is such that it commands the rejection of one or the other. In Nagel's view, if the two perspectives are confronted, the theoretical need not hold sway: 'since moral realism is true, a Darwinian account of the motives underlying moral judgment must be false, in spite of the scientific consensus in its favor'.[21] Again, why should theoretical accounts of morality yield, if the two domains are separate? It seems that we need to start from the other end: while these theories aspire to fend off the possibility for the theoretical to undermine the practical, they fail to appreciate enough the cause of the problem, which lies not in the theoretical domain but in the importance that the absolute truth of normative claims plays within the internal, practical perspective. The key is to resolve the tension within the practical and not to suppress the theoretical.

5.2.2 Denial

In contrast to these views, there are those who acknowledge the pre-eminence of the theoretical perspective and declare the patterns of objectification in the practical perspective bogus, but *deny* that this should be discomforting or drastically influence the way in which we conduct our lives. Let us consider some examples. John Mackie famously believed that moral utterances implicitly claim objectivity for themselves, but that they are all false.[22] To support this claim, Mackie took the theoretical perspective and argued for a set of sceptical claims: the best explanation of the differences between moral codes suggests that our actual values are not perceptions of something external to

[20] Nagel, *Mind and Cosmos: Why the Materialist Neo-Darwinian Conception of Nature is Almost Certainly False* (n 16) 196.

[21] ibid 188. [22] Mackie, *Ethics: Inventing Right and Wrong* (n 15) 35.

us; objective values would be unlike any other feature of the fabric of the world; it is mysterious how we would know such values; it is not specified how values as features of the world would guide our actions; the occurrence of claims of authority and objectivity of values is best (causally) explained without presupposing the existence of objective values; if objective values supervene on natural features of the world we still do not have anything that resembles a full explanation of this relationship.[23] Nonetheless, Mackie also noted that it does not follow that we should or can abandon the practical perspective:

> The denial of objective values can carry with it an extreme emotional reaction, a feeling that nothing matters at all, that life has lost its purpose. Of course this does not follow; the lack of objective values is not a good reason for abandoning subjective concern or for ceasing to want anything. .... the people in whom this reaction occurs have been tending to objectify their concerns and purposes, have been giving them a fictitious external authority.[24]

Mackie thought that morality 'is not to be discovered but to be made'.[25] In his view, this cannot be done from scratch but by building on already existing values;[26] he never explained, however, what exactly gives us the right to go on almost as if nothing happened.[27]

Most of today's relativists also do not refrain from taking the practical perspective. Gilbert Harman, for example, supports a version of moral relativism that holds that the truth of a moral utterance is not absolute but relative to some accepted framework of moral standards. By and large, his views follow from the best theoretical (and causal) explanation of our moral values. But Harman also thinks that: 'Moral relativism denies that we should simply give up on morality in the way that a religious skeptic might give up on religion. There are *practical reasons* to want to retain morality and relative moral judgments'.[28]

Since Harman denies that there are any non-relative practical reasons, the reasons he mentions must also be relative. He sees no problem in such a position; the solution for one who utters something about practical reasons is to specify the framework of values from which one is speaking.[29] This view is coherent, but does not tell us whether the authority with which we speak is undermined. According to Harman, when we judge that what Hitler did

[23] ibid ch 1. [24] ibid 34. [25] ibid 134. [26] ibid ch 5.

[27] Joyce argues that the illusion should be maintained for pragmatic reasons. Richard Joyce, 'Darwinian Ethics and Error' (2000) 15 Biology & Philosophy 713, 730. But it is incredibly difficult to maintain and accept something that one no longer believes in.

[28] Gilbert Harman, 'Moral Relativism' in Gilbert Harman and Judith Jarvis Thomson (eds), *Moral Relativism and Moral Objectivity* (Blackwell 1996) 43 (emphasis added). See also his 'Relativistic Ethic: Morality as Politics' in Harman, *Explaining Value and Other Essays in Moral Philosophy* (n 6).

[29] Harman, 'Moral Relativism' (n 28) 63.

was wrong—further assuming, we may add, that he was a perfectly coherent psychopath and that we cannot find a basis in his moral outlook to show that he was wrong judging from his own set of values—it may be 'more appropriate … to think of Hitler as an *enemy*'.[30] The loss of ability to claim the absolute validity for our own views moves us into the domain of power rather than authority legitimized by the absolute truth. But are shop-lifters, double-parkers or occasional liars also our *enemies*? Can we continue thinking they are wrong without conceiving of them as enemies, as someone who offends the core of our identity to the extent that we need to defend (our) selves? The language of power cannot easily substitute the language of truth, and these are questions for the disenchanted practical perspective, and not for the theoretical.

5.2.3 Rationalization

Finally, there are sophisticated quasi-realist attempts to resolve this problem by interpreting our language of moral objectivity in terms of more complex attitudes of norms-acceptance or contingency plans. For example, thinking of moral attitudes in terms of plans—as Allan Gibbard invites us to do—provides an elegant explanation of how moral reasons can be consumed by our internal motives, but also how we can still feel that we ought to have behaved differently, or that we acted wrongly in acting on our own motives: roughly, our plans may not be fully worked out, or we may neglect some of our own commitments.[31] There is much to be valued about this approach. It allows us to speak as if values were objective and permits our utterances to behave as cognitive and truth-apt in (at least some) logical operations. But quasi-realists also claim that trust in the objectivity of moral reasons itself comes from the practical perspective and cannot be vindicated from the theoretical point of view. Simon Blackburn thinks of objectivity of value as a virtue because—as a matter of internal ethical perspective—it is good to think that, for example, other people's pain is objectively bad.[32] Allan Gibbard translates the claims of objectivity as parts of contingency plans for the future, in which we accept that we would still think of our values as true for any counterfactual that may obtain.[33] This claim—although plausible if we look at it from the practical perspective—needs to be treated

[30] ibid 60.

[31] See eg Gibbard, *Wise Choices, Apt Feelings: A Theory of Normative Judgment* (n 2) and Allan Gibbard, *Thinking How to Live* (Harvard University Press 2003).

[32] See Simon Blackburn, *Ruling Passions: A Theory of Practical Reasoning* (Clarendon Press 1998).

[33] Gibbard's views about the reach of moral objectivity achieved through such expressivist analysis have evolved over time. See Gibbard, *Wise Choices, Apt Feelings: A Theory of Normative Judgment* (n 2) pt 3; Gibbard, *Thinking How to Live* (n 31); and Gibbard, *Reconciling Our Aims: In Search of Bases for Ethics* (n 1).

with caution because it ultimately fails to avoid the conflict with the theoretical. It moves the problem only a little further on, for then these second order attitudes about moral objectivity must also be perspective-dependent and thus relative to a personal framework of values or some kind of social agreement. If for instance, a coherent child-torturer sincerely accepts a contingency plan which specifies that he would believe that torturing children is good under any possible future circumstances, has he earned the right to consider his value system objective? To this, quasi-realists could respond that the question also cannot be answered from the theoretical perspective, and that the response must already presuppose a conception of what it is good for people to think. In other words, it would presumably be bad to think that child-torturers have earned the right to the truth of their value system.

But how can we know who has earned the right to believe in the truth of his particular values? The quasi-realists' answer is satisfying only for those that already believe, because it advises them to continue believing. Let me use an example: the answer to the question whether God exists can appear to be different for a religious person and an atheist, and for the religious person it will certainly depend on his internal religious perspective. But why would the religious perspective apply to the atheist? A religious person would be inclined to think that the atheist is mistaken and would come to think so from the religious perspective. It is crucial to notice that this is done from a *perspective*, even if it is impossible to shake it off. The problem with this view is then: by taking this route, we may earn the right to use cognitive language for our normative judgments, but how do we earn the right to believe in their truth? While Blackburn is right to say that trust in the objectivity of moral talk could be a virtue, this is precisely where the theoretical and practical interact and create uneasiness. Both perspectives claim to answer the same question and command allegiance. To resolve the uneasiness we should perhaps revisit our virtues and realize that this is a problem for the practical and not the theoretical perspective.

Let me now articulate the problem more clearly. We strive towards a unified world view, where the theoretical and practical do not collide. Both perspectives aim to tell us something important about the nature of values, but their answers differ. Both perspectives are inescapable. Common to the several views rehearsed here is that the theoretical does not do damage to the practical: we are advised to abandon the theoretical, ignore it, or subsume it to the practical. But it is hard to resist the feeling that the theoretical perspective affects the conviction with which we can assert our values as absolute and authoritative. As Bernard Williams says, there is 'something blank and unresponsive' in realizing that values may not be objective and that 'it is incredible that this consciousness should just leave everything where it was and not affect the ethical thought itself'.[34] What these views neglect is the fact that the cognitive form of moral language does assume an answer to the theoretical problem and that we tend to assert our moral views as universally true. We thus need to acknowledge that the theoretical perspective has practical consequences, to the extent that the practical advances theoretical claims. The goal is to retain both perspectives: to claim that it is always good to adopt the theoretical perspective would indeed be self-defeating, but to suppose that we need to abandon science in order to have values is equally baffling. The key is to fine-tune the two perspectives until they are compatible. Let us first see where the theoretical perspective leaves us; after that, I shall say what is its proper effect on the practical.

5.3 THE THEORETICAL: VALUES AND CONTINGENCY

There are good theoretical reasons to believe that *values are mind-dependent and contingent*: in other words, that there are no reasons for action independent from valuing attitudes present in our psychological sets.[35] Two clarifications are in order. First, this view does not entail radical subjectivism about value. Even if there are no ahistorical, acontextual, and a priori values, they can be both ubiquitous and profoundly convergent. Given the commonalities in the circumstances of human life—scarcity of resources, necessity of cooperation, and inevitability of death—it would actually be surprising if there were no overlap between the existing moral codes. Talk of mind-dependence, contingency, and relativity does not imply cultural relativism, and can accommodate relativity to the common moral experiences that we share as humans. Second, this view does entail that there are no ethical truths external to our existing attitudes. There are no moral facts as standards fully independent from these attitudes taken as a whole, the facts that could possibly be true even if everyone thought they were not.

However, any single argument trying to demonstrate mind-dependence and the contingent nature of values would be too sweeping. I will thus focus on a claim that is more modest but at the same time captures the nature of our practical predicament: the best causal accounts of the origins of *our* current values show that they are a consequence of contingent circumstances rather than the perception of external and absolute ethical truths. It *does not follow* from this that there cannot be objective values outside our existing value-frameworks and antecedent to our experience (although the argument

[34] Bernard Williams, *Ethics and the Limits of Philosophy* (2 edn, Routledge 2006) 159.

[35] Following Bernard Williams, we can say that the statement 'A has reason to φ' is best understood as saying 'A has some motive which will be served or furthered by his φ-ing' Williams, *Moral Luck: Philosophical Papers, 1973–1980* (n 4) 101.

certainly gives us reason to doubt this), but *it does follow* that our existing value-frameworks are contingent and bear no obvious relation to any realm of value outside them. This creates a gap between the realm of objective values (if there are any) and our existing values, leading to a paralysing practical conclusion: all our actions are most probably morally wrong as they are a consequence of our existing values; even when our actions are not wrong, this is a matter of sheer coincidence; and, finally, even when they happen to be right we cannot know if this is the case.[36]

Notice that causal accounts of the origins of our values need not undermine their truth. Concluding about the truth of a belief from its origins only is a genetic fallacy, for any origin of a belief is logically compatible with its truth. I can, for example, be hallucinating about there being a chocolate on the kitchen shelf while in fact there is a chocolate on the kitchen shelf, so my belief is true regardless of its origin. The same holds for ethics, since my ethical beliefs may be true even if they are a consequence of evolution and socialization. Nonetheless, we can still question whether our moral attitudes satisfy epistemic standards that would permit the assumption that they are grasping a mind-independent truth, external to these attitudes taken as a whole. To the extent to which our ethical beliefs are analogous to the hallucination case they are most probably not true,[37] if the benchmark for their truth is a robust relation of correspondence between our moral attitudes and external normative facts.

To vindicate trust in the truth of our moral beliefs, one would need to offer an account that shows how the causal forces that generated moral beliefs did so in a way that makes them match the external moral facts. The best causal explanations, however, show the opposite: they explain the origins of our beliefs without presupposing a connection with the external facts. Let me focus on evolutionary explanations to demonstrate this, but notice here that if moral attitudes can in principle be a result of causal forces, then *any* causal argument—sociological, cultural, psychological, or historical—delivers the same result; evolutionary explanation simply happens to be general enough and particularly credible so as to serve as a good illustration of a more general point.

[36] Similar arguments have been put forward by Michael Ruse, *Taking Darwin Seriously: A Naturalistic Approach to Philosophy* (Blackwell 1986) ch 6; Gibbard, *Thinking How to Live* (n 31) ch 13; Richard Joyce, *The Evolution of Morality* (MIT Press 2006) ch 6; Philip Kitcher, 'Biology and Ethics' in David Copp (ed), *The Oxford Handbook of Ethical Theory* (Oxford University Press 2006); Philip Kitcher, *The Ethical Project* (Harvard University Press 2011); and Street, 'A Darwinian Dilemma for Realist Theories of Value' (n 7). Sharon Street puts the problem particularly clearly in the form of a dilemma for the realists, and my explanation of the issue is influenced by her formulation. However, I shall articulate the challenge for realists in different terms and focus more on its practical consequences.

[37] See Joyce, *The Evolution of Morality* (n 36) 179–84.

5.3.1 Evolutionary origins of values

Although contemporary accounts of evolutionary origins of our moral sentiments and capacity for normative guidance are at least partly speculative,[38] their insights seem plausible enough to support this conclusion: the best causal explanation of the emergence of normative thinking and ethical concepts does not presuppose the existence of external normative facts.[39] Following Allan Gibbard we can formulate the question as follows: do our normative judgments represent the features of the world?[40] We can easily make evolutionary sense of our perceptual judgments as representing the features of the world. Natural selection benefits those whose sensory system supports reliable descriptive judgments about external reality. The ability to spot the external fact that there is a cliff in front of me or that there is a bear in my cave is beneficial for reproductive success. The best explanation of this ability presupposes that there really are such things as cliffs and bears, because we need to judge these situations accurately in order to survive. In contrast, the best evolutionary explanation of our normative judgments does not presuppose the representation of external features of the world: we do not have the capacity for moral judgment in order to respond to normative facts but—as Gibbard puts it—in order to 'coordinate our activities in mutually beneficial ways'.[41]

This argument must explain how the ability for coordination and norm-governed behaviour would be evolutionarily beneficial for our ancestors. The burden is to show why humans would have engaged in behaviour which is apparently costly for them individually but beneficial for the group. Most theories of the evolutionary development of moral sentiments start from the widely accepted 'kin-selection' hypothesis: psychological altruism in humans—our ability to act on motives the *content* of which is not ultimately derived from our own benefit—develops from altruism towards one's own children and kin; altruistic motives towards kin with whom we share genetic material would be more reliable and thus more adaptive for securing the success of one's genes than egoistic ones.[42] Once we became capable of altruistic behaviour—hence sacrificing some of our immediate desires for the benefit

[38] See: WD Hamilton, 'The Genetical Evolution of Social Behaviour. I' (1964) 7 Journal of Theoretical Biology 1; WD Hamilton, 'The Genetical Evolution of Social Behaviour. II' (1964) 7 Journal of Theoretical Biology 17; Elliott Sober and David Sloan Wilson, *Unto Others: The Evolution and Psychology of Unselfish Behavior* (Harvard University Press 1998); and Walter Sinnott-Armstrong (ed), *Moral Psychology, Volume 1. The Evolution of Morality: Adaptations and Innateness* (MIT Press 2007).

[39] Here I follow Allan Gibbard's early account of the development of our normative capacities, adding some important details to it. See Gibbard, *Wise Choices, Apt Feelings: A Theory of Normative Judgment* (n 2) ch 6.

[40] ibid. [41] ibid 107.

[42] See Hamilton, 'The Genetical Evolution of Social Behaviour. II' (n 38); Hamilton, 'The Genetical Evolution of Social Behaviour. I' (n 38); Sober and Wilson, *Unto Others: The Evolution and Psychology of*

of others—it could spread to non-kin. The emergence of social norms would be fostered by two factors. On the one hand, life in a social group would be favoured by evolution: sharing resources, tasks, and knowledge would be beneficial for our reproductive success. On the other, cooperation would be constantly under threat if there were a possibility of opting out whenever the immediate benefits of pro-social behaviour are outbalanced by the benefits of egoistic behaviour.

Hence, the best way to understand the circumstances of the life of our ancestors is to think of them as reiterations of the prisoner's dilemma—there are mutual benefits for reproductive success to be gained if a system of cooperation is in place, but at the same time each system could always be replaced by another that would make someone better off.[43] In hunter-gatherer societies there were plenty of situations where coordination would enhance the chances of reproductive success for all, and non-cooperation would undermine them. Under these circumstances, the capacity that supports cooperation would be selected, even at some immediate cost for the individual. If our emotional propensities are subject to evolutionary influence at all, it is reasonable to expect that many of them would have a coordinating purpose, including the capacity for normative guidance itself.[44] Charles Darwin's early take on this question reaches a similar conclusion:

> A tribe including many members who, from possessing in high degree the spirit of patriotism, obedience, courage and sympathy, were always ready to aid one another and to sacrifice themselves for the common good would be victorious over most other tribes; and this would be natural selection.[45]

This explanation includes a leap, whereby altruism develops at one's own cost to sustain a system that would only indirectly benefit the individual that incurs the cost. Groups in which non-kin altruism were in place would be more prosperous and thus provide a better environment for passing on genes. To be relatively secure from egoistic impulses, a system of cooperation would have to promote altruistic behaviour towards members of one's own group including non-kin. Contemporary empirical research—although not entirely beyond controversy—shows that differences in genetic material between the groups themselves supported competition between groups that led to group-based altruism, and accounts for the gap between concern

Unselfish Behavior (n 38); Armin W Schulz, 'Sober & Wilson's Evolutionary Arguments for Psychological Altruism: A Reassessment' (2011) 26 Biology and Philosophy 251.

[43] Gibbard, *Wise Choices, Apt Feelings: A Theory of Normative Judgment* (n 2) 62–66; Kitcher, *The Ethical Project* (n 36).

[44] Gibbard, *Wise Choices, Apt Feelings: A Theory of Normative Judgment* (n 2) 67.

[45] Charles Darwin, *The Descent of Man, and Selection in Relation to Sex* (JT Bonner and RM May (eds), Princeton University Press 1981) 162.

for one's own and the group's reproduction.[46] If one's group includes more kin-members than the outside group, one's reproductive success would be directly supported by altruism towards group members as opposed to outsiders; this especially being the case when there was a real threat of lethal intergroup competition.[47]

Thus—while early coordination was probably based on expected direct gains for the individual from cooperation—a stable system of cooperation would demand the development of emotional mechanisms to surpass egoistic motives, such as shame in those that fail to reciprocate and resentment of such behaviour in others. The emergence of reputation and punishment could enable altruistic behaviour towards others, even when the benefactor is ultimately not on the receiving end of the transaction. Those with a good reputation would be chosen for future exchanges of benefits and cooperation, and an individual's past performances would be rewarded or punished by others.[48] Building on the situation in which we shared motivational tendencies for cooperation similar to other animals, we gradually developed a complex system of 'language-infused governance of emotions'[49] that is capable of controlling our feelings and allows for a much more advanced coordination. Having linguistic ability, we are able to be fully informed and aware of other people's past behaviour, to evaluate non-existent situations, and to further develop and accept systems of norms or plans to coordinate our behaviour.[50] We use our normative capacities to manage emotions by engaging in 'normative discussion, actual or imaginative, as we take positions, subject ourselves to the demands of consistency, and undergo mutual influence'.[51] A system of reflective governance of emotions enables modifications of moral feelings and social learning of moral behaviour that we recognize today.

If evolution has generally been able to affect our abilities, powers, and the psychological setup, then there is a very plausible explanation of the emergence and content of normative capacities and moral emotions in terms of their evolutionary function. The explanation comes from the theoretical perspective: the 'function' is defined descriptively, as something that would be favoured by natural selection and it has only an explanatory and not justificatory role. As the first approximation we can draw the following conclusion.

[46] Samuel Bowles, 'Group Competition, Reproductive Leveling, and the Evolution of Human Altruism' (2006) 314 Science 1569.

[47] ibid. [48] See Joyce, *The Evolution of Morality* (n 36) ch 1 and in particular 31–33.

[49] Gibbard, *Reconciling Our Aims: In Search of Bases for Ethics* (n 1) 15.

[50] On the role of language and culture in the development of morality, see Jonathan Haidt, 'The Emotional Dog and its Rational Tail: A Social Intuitionist Approach to Moral Judgment' (2001) 108 Psychological Review 814, 826–28.

[51] Gibbard, *Wise Choices, Apt Feelings: A Theory of Normative Judgment* (n 2) 81.

The best explanation of our perceptual judgments needs to assume some correspondence between these judgments and facts about our surroundings. Their function is to represent the world as it is as accurately as possible. Our normative judgments, however, do not represent anything in the world but serve a coordinating function. They have mostly been perpetuated by the reproductive rewards of coordination and our ability to develop this system further through conscious action.[52] The lesson is that the emergence of the initial ability for normative guidance and many of our actual beliefs have a sound causal explanation that does not presuppose the apprehension of mind-independent moral facts.

Now, evolutionary explanation of moral behaviour is *not complete*. Not all of our current moral attitudes are a direct consequence of evolution, as they sometimes go beyond the simple goal of group coordination and the feelings that sustain it. Other influences have interfered in the meantime, including—importantly—our capacity to govern moral feelings. People feel empathy towards members of much wider groups, and altruism is exhibited towards complete strangers or animals. Hence, the content of moral feelings may not be fully explained as an adaptation but as a consequence of an adaptation: perhaps our capacity for altruism that was necessary for reproductive success in small, partly kin-based hunter-gatherer groups developed beyond its strict evolutionary function. Moreover, as our normative systems become more sophisticated and culturally mature, layers need to be added to the basic evolutionary narrative. Once humans acquired the capacity for normative guidance, the process of ethical change became *socially* embedded and guided: moral values were developed as a reaction to previous failures to secure cooperation and are informed by—as Kitcher puts it—'social apprehension of the ways in which cooperation has broken down'.[53] Existing moral codes and values were socially elaborated in reaction to concrete circumstances in different societies, and thus took different shapes and forms. Moreover, the context in which the capacity for normative guidance operates has changed, not only in terms of the environment that presented our ancestors with different problems to solve, but also in terms of the development of new desires and needs; for example, a desire to develop one's talents could have become more prominent once the desire for food, shelter,

[52] Of course, our normative concepts can pick out a natural property in the world as being the thing to do or resent (Williams, *Ethics and the Limits of Philosophy* (n 34) 140–43). However, even if normative judgments do represent something in the world, they are not normative in virtue of this representation. The descriptive component of a thick judgment that represents something in the world could be replaced by a descriptive judgment without loss to this representation, but without capturing the prescriptive part of the judgment. Gibbard, *Wise Choices, Apt Feelings: A Theory of Normative Judgment* (n 2) 110–20; and Gibbard, *Thinking How to Live* (n 31) chs 1 and 2.

[53] Kitcher, *The Ethical Project* (n 36) 98.

and health had been secured.[54] Finally, the evolutionary explanation does not presuppose that we are genetically determined to make specific moral judgments. Instead, a more plausible picture is this: our unreflective behavioural dispositions are affected by evolution and are likely to be fitness-enhancing as they are in other animals; as a consequence of evolution, we also acquired the ability to reflect on moral motives and be normatively guided; using this ability, we further moulded our unreflective dispositions through culture and social learning.[55] We should thus be careful not to subscribe to genetic determinism and assume that evolutionary biology can completely illuminate the content of our present moral sentiments. But if evolution has played a role in the development of our moral attitudes, it should be able to explain at least some of our contemporary values. Let me use some examples.[56]

First, take one of the simplest and most universal reasons that people recognize: the reason to, *ceteris paribus,* avoid life-threatening dangers. This value makes perfect sense in evolutionary terms—clearly, staying alive is helpful if one wishes to reproduce, while dying is not. Compare this to an account that would claim that we were selected to recognize the true fact that we have reasons to, *ceteris paribus*, avoid life-threatening dangers, and that it just so happens that this is also beneficial for our reproductive success. At best, such an explanation introduces one step too many and at worst it is not an explanation at all. Second, we have seen that in the evolutionary explanation altruism spreads in circles, from closer kin-based to wider groups. This is again confirmed by our actual attitudes: most people think that they should care more about their children than distant relatives, about relatives than compatriots, about compatriots than foreigners, and about humans than animals.[57] People believe, for example, that their children should inherit their houses, that their tax contributions should be used to support the welfare of their countrymen rather than distant others, and that eating human flesh is much worse than enjoying a beef burger. Although we are able to change and govern our emotions—and we witness important transformations in all these areas—it is remarkable that the amount of actual care for different groups still corresponds to their significance for spreading our genes. Moreover, even if the emotions of care spread beyond our immediate group, this is not detached from the evolutionary template: because evolution favoured seeing in-group members as deserving receivers of our care, moral change

[54] ibid 137. Sociology documents similar processes; see eg Ronald Inglehart, *The Silent Revolution: Changing Values and Political Styles among Western Publics* (Princeton University Press 1977).

[55] Street, 'A Darwinian Dilemma for Realist Theories of Value' (n 7) 118–19.

[56] The discussion here builds on Sharon Street's examples from ibid 114–17.

[57] The requirement of rigid moral impartiality does not correspond to our contingent moral intuitions. See eg Susan Wolf, 'Moral Saints' (1982) 79 Journal of Philosophy 419; and Bernard Williams, *Making Sense of Humanity* (Cambridge University Press 1995) ch 13.

proceeds precisely through an extension of the notion of an in-group member. So, for example, what we see as moral progress usually presupposes a realization that other creatures are similar to ourselves, and what we see as moral regress typically presupposes dehumanizing other beings to conceive of them as less similar to us.[58] Third, if we look at emotions that would be necessary to support the rudimentary systems of cooperation, we still find them today: for example, we respect and praise those that reciprocate or act altruistically, and resent those that do not reciprocate or are egoistic.[59] Fourth, evolution can even explain why we would believe that our values are objective, universal, and absolute. If a system of values is beneficial for reproductive success, it would be much more efficient and adaptive if people thought about it in these terms.

Evolution gives us an explanation of why we do not have these and countless other possible values, and does so without presupposing that our values track any mind-independent—transcendent or natural—moral facts.[60] The force of explanation is astonishing if we understand it against the background possibility that we could have in fact thought of values as purely optional, valued breaking promises, praised torturing one's own children, or admired suicidal behaviour. As Sharon Street observes, the scope of possible evaluative judgments is potentially enormous and evolutionary explanation derives its force from an outstanding overlap between our actual moral judgments and those that would be favoured by natural selection.[61] The alternative explanation—one that would suggest that our values do reflect mind-independent moral facts—carries the burden of showing how exactly we have evolved to track these facts.

Let us now look at the problem more analytically. There are three pieces of the puzzle we need to connect in a way that would make sense. First, there is an attitude-independent moral truth (T); second, there are our contingent moral attitudes (C); third, there are attitudes that are favoured by evolution (E).[62] There is an important correlation between C and E: if the evolutionary explanation above is correct, then we can see why our contingent moral attitudes correspond to the attitudes that would be favoured by evolution. The connection to be ultimately explained is between our contingent moral attitudes C and attitude-independent truth T; however—and this is the crucial point—if C is strongly influenced and importantly corresponds to E, then we also need an explanation of the correlation between E and T. In other

[58] See eg Peter Singer, 'Morality, Reason, and the Rights of Animals' in Frans de Waal (ed), *Primates and Philosophers: How Morality Evolved* (Princeton University Press 2006).

[59] Kitcher, 'Biology and Ethics' (n 36) 172.

[60] Street, 'A Darwinian Dilemma for Realist Theories of Value' (n 7) 113–21.

[61] ibid 113–21.

[62] See Gibbard, *Thinking How to Live* (n 31) 264–67.

words, we need to see why tracking mind-independent moral truth would be favoured by evolution. Moreover, until the relationship between C and T is spelled out, we cannot help ourselves with C to prove that something is T, for that would beg the question: one cannot assume the connection between C to T while at the same time trying to account for it. Finally, it will not work to show that whatever E is also T, for that would again need to be assessed (if it is plausible at all) starting from C, and we need an independent and non-question begging reason to think that C tracks T. The conundrum boils down to an old epistemological challenge to moral realism with an evolutionary twist: on the one hand, to access moral truth we always start from our contingent attitudes about it, but it is not clear what would make us reliable trackers of mind-independent moral truth; on the other hand, numerous causal forces affect our contingent moral attitudes, and these causal forces are not connected in any way with independent moral truths. The realist model cannot work unless all these relationships are intelligible. Notice that the realist answer to the problem could roughly take two routes: one would deny or relax the relationship between E and C, and then show that C somehow tracks T, the other would accept the correlation between E and C, and then show that E favours T.[63] Let me explain why both routes fail.

5.3.2 Diminishing evolutionary influence

In setting out the argument in a similar form, Sharon Street, for example, supposes that our contingent moral attitudes are 'thoroughly saturated with evolutionary influence'.[64] One objection could claim that this assumes too much in terms of science, and deny that C importantly corresponds to E. But this is not crucial for the argument. We can grant that the evolutionary explanation of our values is plausible but limited. A modest thesis following from the evolutionary account given above could be this: on the one hand, the emergence of our capacity for normative guidance—as other capacities in humans—has been a consequence of evolution; on the other, our values—as other psychological traits—have generally been under the influence of evolutionary forces and a portion of their content is a consequence of their fitness-enhancing propensity. To refute this modest connection between E and C and pursue the objection, the realist would need an alternative explanation that would reject the evolutionary influence and at the same time offer a more plausible genealogy of our values (coupled, of course, in the second step with a claim that such development is oriented towards the apprehension of independent moral truths T).

[63] Street, 'A Darwinian Dilemma for Realist Theories of Value' (n 7) 109. [64] ibid 114.

The existing causal explanations of moral attitudes do not include such claims. It is easy to see why. Although evolution does not provide a complete causal explanation of values, the alternatives that would replace it do not seem to be better candidates to demonstrate that they match external normative truths. While evolution is at least a universal phenomenon, other explanations show the contingency in even starker terms because they must account for the enculturation of values. For example, we could look at the ways in which the major religions shaped our values,[65] but then we would have to ask which one managed to grasp them correctly and *why*. Thus, any other causal explanation would take us even further away from the desired fit, for it would soon be clear that the convergence in our moral attitudes decreases once other causal factors are taken into consideration.[66] To sidestep the problem, the realist must either deny that our contingent attitudes C are subject to causal influences, or show that the external moral truth T is a stronger causal force than evolution E and other factors that affect our attitudes.

A more sophisticated argumentative path would be to grant the evolutionary influence on our normative capacities and the content of our values, but argue that our ability for normative guidance over time becomes detached from evolutionary influences and starts to track normative truths. This explanation would both accept the limited connection between E and C, and argue for a correlation between C and T, without presupposing anything from E to T directly. It would hence have to demonstrate the possibility that our value-judgments took off and became—even if gradually—discontinuous with the contingent moral attitudes, and—moreover—that once they took off they also started to fit the external normative facts. Let us then focus on the possibility of the transformation of our contingent attitudes C and once more put aside the problem of C tracking T. The appealing intuition behind this objection builds on the limited reach of evolutionary explanations of our abilities, and hence attempts to account for the role of human invention, choice, and social learning. For example, the ability to read English or do microbiology has grown out of the linguistic and cognitive capacities we have as humans, but the skills we have on the basis of these capacities are not innate but have to be learned and have undergone substantial refinement that need not have a full evolutionary explanation.[67] Perhaps something similar happened with

[65] For the classical example of a sociological causal explanation of moral values see Max Weber, *The Protestant Ethic and the Spirit of Capitalism* (Routledge 2001).

[66] This is why the pressure to reject the relevance of causal explanations *as such* is strong. Thomas Nagel bites the bullet and denies the truth of evolutionary theory because it undermines moral realism, and this is possibly the most honest realist answer to the problem.

[67] Gibbard, *Thinking How to Live* (n 31) 265–66; Street, 'A Darwinian Dilemma for Realist Theories of Value' (n 7) 142.

our capacity for normative guidance: through reflection we were able to overcome the evolutionary influence on our moral attitudes.

While reflection undoubtedly plays a role in shaping our attitudes, the question is whether there is autonomous or 'pure' moral reflection that is able to counterbalance evolutionary and social causal forces. The classical Kantian picture of reflection presupposes examination of a moral attitude as an object of impartial attention while being unaware of other moral dispositions and one's identity.[68] The theoretical and the practical perspective are here analogous: both presuppose disconnection from contingent experiences and our ability to call them into view in the quest for truth. But, this picture implausibly equates—as Bernard Williams notices—reflection with detachment.[69] The mistake in this view is that it must presuppose some contingent motivation to engage in reflection in the first place and to accept its outcome.[70] In the case of theoretical reflection, the pre-reflective and reflective self both search for truth, and that provides the unity of motivation; in the case of practical reflection, if we leave all of our contingent desires and motivations before we enter reflection, we then also have no reason to care about the result of the reflective exercise at all. Reflection cannot supply us with the complete practical motivation, as it is supposed to do in this picture: evaluative attitudes must enter the equation if we expect to see them at the other end, and these attitudes come from a place that is causally affected.

The question—whether a fully detached reflection can create discontinuity between E and C—is, however, best understood as an empirical one. Research shows that a completely detached moral reflection is an illusion; at best, we reason about moral attitudes from the perspective of other attitudes, adjusting them to the ones we find more important, or trying to achieve a higher level of coherence in our moral outlook.[71] But once we reach the bedrock of firmly established moral intuitions—emotionally laden evaluative attitudes—or a reflective coherence of these intuitions, there is nothing to support them further. Jonathan Haidt has demonstrated that our immediate reactions to moral problems are automatic and emotional, and reasoning mostly provides *post hoc* rationalization or attempts to change the opinion

[68] See eg Immanuel Kant, *Groundwork for the Metaphysics of Morals* (Allen W Wood tr, Yale University Press 2002); Thomas Nagel, *The View from Nowhere* (Oxford University Press 1986). In contrast, Korsgaard argues that those who do not care about anything at all would have no categorical moral reasons to act. See Christine M Korsgaard, *The Sources of Normativity* (Cambridge University Press 1996).

[69] Williams, *Ethics and the Limits of Philosophy* (n 34) 69 and 110–19.

[70] ibid ch 4 and especially 66—69.

[71] See: Haidt, 'The Emotional Dog and its Rational Tail: A Social Intuitionist Approach to Moral Judgment' (n 50); Gilbert Harman, Kelby Mason, and Walter Sinnott-Armstrong, 'Moral Reasoning' in John M Doris and Moral Psychology Research Group (eds), *The Moral Psychology Handbook* (Oxford University Press 2010).

of other people.[72] Multiple mechanisms that prevent a completely detached reflection are at work when we reason morally: we tend to side with our own group and with the people we like, we stick to the existing moral views, we aim to bring our beliefs into coherence with attitudes which are crucial for our identity and self-perception, and we seek to confirm and justify our immediate intuitions rather than truly to question them.[73] This is not to say that we cannot trigger new intuitions or change attitudes through reflection and persuasion, but most of the people most of the time do not engage in or are not capable of such reflection, and so the transformative potential of reflection is limited.[74] There are thus serious doubts about the ability of reflection to generate a radical disconnect with evolutionarily affected moral attitudes. If we are able to overcome the evolutionary influence on our attitudes and discover the true way to live T, we should be able to do so as 'normal human beings in normal conditions'.[75]

To surpass this problem, one could turn to the role of extraordinary individuals that spur revolutionary ethical changes. Compare: in the same way that scientists have been able to improve our common theoretical sense, progressive individuals—philosophers included—could have managed to ignite progress within our common ethical sense. The analogy, however, needs more detail. Much of scientific progress proceeds in a way similar to the method of 'reflective equilibrium', familiar from ethics: taking some beliefs and theories to be true and questioning others.[76] In both science and ethics, we are repairing the ship while at sea,[77] and there is always some continuity with previous beliefs and intuitions.[78] To the extent that there is gradualness in ethical thinking, we should not expect the E to C connection to be lost by any amount of reflection, and all of our subsequent ethical attitudes would still be continuous with the initial ones, affected by evolution. Yet, there is a crucial difference: we have an evolutionary explanation of why our theoretical beliefs represent the world as it is, and why ethical attitudes do not.

If a radical ethical change by reflection were possible, it would occur in episodes of revelation, perhaps similar to those of scientists making paradigm-changing discoveries, where new observations play a crucial role. It is indeed tempting to make this parallel and describe ethical intuitions about certain

[72] Haidt, 'The Emotional Dog and its Rational Tail: A Social Intuitionist Approach to Moral Judgment' (n 50) 816.

[73] ibid 820–22. [74] ibid 819–24. [75] Gibbard, *Thinking How to Live* (n 31) 267.

[76] Naturalist realists use this observation to argue that ethics and science are in fact analogous. See: Sturgeon, 'Moral Explanations' (n 19); Richard N Boyd, 'How to Be a Moral Realist' in Geoffrey Sayre-McCord (ed), *Essays on Moral Realism* (Cornell University Press 1988); and David O Brink, *Moral Realism and the Foundations of Ethics* (Cambridge University Press 1989).

[77] The metaphor is from Williams, *Ethics and the Limits of Philosophy* (n 34) 113.

[78] Harman, Mason, and Sinnott-Armstrong, 'Moral Reasoning' (n 71).

events as 'perceptions', as we often make our judgments instantly and with an immediate emotional reaction.[79] However, it is impossible to make these judgments without having an already acquired propensity to react in a certain way. We are only able to make sense of moral problems starting from socially embedded concepts; otherwise we would not think of them as *problems* in the first place. Some people may be capable of a more reflective approach to moral issues that generates significant changes in their and other people's attitudes, but the process through which this happens is also not accurately described as revelation or perception but as—particularly imaginative, sensitive, and reflective—endorsement of moral emotions that are not too far from the already existing ones taken as a whole.

History also does not mention moments of eye-opening ethical revelations.[80] After studying actual historical records on the role of reformers in ethical changes, Kitcher for example concludes that there is no reference to sudden discoveries of an external ethical reality or of unexpected forces that revealed themselves upon observers: '[t]he historical figures who figure in ethical transitions . . . do not start from some situation in which they lack ethical convictions, follow a process of reasoning or observe some facet of reality, and thereby arrive at a well-grounded belief in an ethical judgment',[81] but they approach the issue in the vocabulary of their culture and make 'proposals on the basis of information they find salient'.[82] Typically, ethical changes include a realization that current attitudes are based on a factual mistake (eg discovering that women are not less capable than men) coupled with a steadily growing emotional reaction that this insight does not cohere with the prevailing attitudes. The process ends with a new emotional stability that is found by adjustments in other incoherent attitudes.[83] Moreover, to be truly inspiring, these changes initiated by remarkable individuals need to build on actual social attitudes and prevailing sentiments, and are best described—if we are to use scientific metaphors—not as discoveries but as successful and possibly useful inventions. A realistic understanding of moral reflection thus confirms the continuity between E and C. The fact that changes are always more gradual than they may seem does not of course prove that over time change will not be comprehensive or even complete; however, since there is a significant overlap between the moral attitudes favoured by evolution and actual contingent attitudes today (E⇒C), we have all the reason we need to

[79] John McDowell, *Mind, Value, and Reality* (Harvard University Press 1998) chs 7 and 8; David Wiggins, *Needs, Values, Truth: Essays in the Philosophy of Value* (Blackwell 1987) ch 5.

[80] See generally Kitcher, *The Ethical Project* (n 36) chs 4 and 5; Jerome B Schneewind, *The Invention of Autonomy: A History of Modern Moral Philosophy* (Cambridge University Press 1998) ch 23.

[81] Kitcher, *The Ethical Project* (n 36) 179. [82] ibid. [83] ibid 178–86.

doubt this. Finally, even if the change did happen, we still do not have an explanation why more reflection would lead to moral truth (C⇒T).

5.3.3 Expanding evolutionary influence

The second strategy a realist could adopt would be to accept the influence of evolution on our contingent moral attitudes (E⇒C), but argue that there is a correlation between evolutionarily favoured attitudes and morally correct ones (E=T). As this explanation needs to account for the relationship between E and T it must at a minimum start with a claim that there is an overlap between the two. But it must also offer an argument *why* this is so, for it would otherwise restate the problem: it would simply accept a correlation between E and C and assert that it just so happens that E and T are connected. This is, of course, not enough to defend moral realism because the question is precisely how to account for the relationship between E and T, which would then support C=T, the connection we are ultimately after. We may think of two ways in which the argument could be provided.

The first does not claim any independent causal link between E and T, but merely tries to establish correspondence between the two. In such a case, evolution may or may not have made C track the truth T, but we have an independent confirmation that E and T are identical. The form of the argument is indeed correct, as establishing a causal connection between E and T is not necessary—if E=C and E=T then it follows that C=T. But such an argument suffers from the structural problem identified above: it cannot offer an account of moral truth T that will hold independently of our contingent moral attitudes C, and that is exactly the relationship that needs to be specified (C=T). Independent confirmation that E correlates to T can come from the theoretical or practical perspective, and David Copp's treatment of this issue can illustrate the problems with both approaches.[84]

Copp agrees that evolutionary forces have significantly affected our actual moral attitudes, but wants to refute the evolutionary challenge by providing an account of the 'truth conditions for moral propositions'[85] that aims to shed attitude-independent light on T. In his view, moral standards are true if they are 'included in or implied by the moral code the currency of which in the relevant society would enable the society better to serve its basic needs than would the currency of other sets of norms'.[86] Let us assume that this desideratum can be sufficiently specified and that his theory is able to discriminate between true and untrue standards. We can see that Copp's theory

[84] David Copp, 'Darwinian Skepticism about Moral Realism' (2008) 18 Philosophical Issues 186. See also Sharon Street, 'Reply to Copp: Naturalism, Normativity, and the Varieties of Realism Worth Worrying About' (2008) 18 Philosophical Issues 207.

[85] Copp, 'Darwinian Skepticism about Moral Realism' (n 84) 198, 199.

[86] ibid 200.

presupposes a significant overlap between E and T (E≈T) and—because evolution does favour norms that better satisfy the needs of societies such as cooperation and cohesion—we can further assume that he succeeds in establishing this.

But how does it fare as a theory of 'truth conditions of normative propositions'? Such a theory must hold true without recourse to contingent attitudes C for it would otherwise not settle the issue. This depends on whether Copp's theory includes substantive views about T; in other words, whether the ideas that it relies on—such as that each society has 'needs' and that a moral code has a 'function'—are evaluative or not. Copp is ambivalent on whether his theory takes the theoretical or practical perspective and does not clearly delineate between the two:

> My argument for the society-centered theory rests ... on second-order philosophical intuitions, including the idea that morality has the function of making society possible, and on the standard-based account of the semantics of normative judgment. To be sure, we would not find the society-centered view to be plausible if its implications conflicted dramatically with our moral views ... Yet my argument does not rest on our moral intuitions. Indeed, I think we can imagine a Martian philosopher, with different substantive moral intuitions than we have, nevertheless coming to accept the society-centered theory for the very reasons that led me to the society-centered view.[87]

The problem in this passage is that Copp makes his theory both dependent and independent from contingent moral views: it would be implausible if it did not match our moral views but it supposedly does not depend on such views. Where does the confusion come from? Let us see how the Martian philosopher (call him Marty) would understand the problem.

Suppose Marty is approaching our planet as an anthropologist and takes the *theoretical perspective*. He examines our moral codes and, indeed, concludes that Copp's account accurately represents important truths about our practices. Has Marty found the absolute moral truth T? No, because Marty needs to examine our actual moral practices and attitudes C to generalize to his conclusion, and if our contingent attitudes C were very different, then his account of T would be different as well. Now, to this Copp could object that his theory gives us only the 'truth conditions' for moral propositions, a metaethical framework fully independent from contingent moral attitudes C. This would mean that Copp's theory is defined in a sufficiently formal way to accommodate the differences between sets of contingent attitudes C and Cm, valid on Earth and Mars respectively.[88] Martians could define the

[87] ibid 203.

[88] Russ Shafer-Landau argues that someone who thinks that torturing children for fun is moral simply fails to understand what morality is. The concept of morality has semantic boundaries which allow us

needs of their society in a morally repugnant way judging from our perspective C: they may, for example, favour mass rape as the best way in which their society can reproduce, or they may think that the basic 'need' of their society is not reproduction and coordination but complete annihilation of its own members. Would Cm then qualify as a true moral code on Copp's test? If yes, then Copp's theory does not include any normative assumptions and can accommodate both C and Cm as true sets of beliefs. However, it cannot then separate between C and T. This is because T would then only restate the set of contingent evaluative attitudes in any given society (C, Cm). Moral truth T is then equivalent to whatever the society contingently believes is the case C: it tells us to do whatever we think we should do. But notice that the notion of mind-independent truth T presupposes at least the possibility that some of the contingent attitudes C may not be true, and that it needs to hold true independently of actual moral attitudes. To say that T is always depends on C gives up on the notion of T as mind-independent, and is something that anti-realists would gladly accept.

Suppose on the other hand that Marty takes the *practical perspective* and wants to find out how to live. Would Marty be convinced that David Copp from planet Earth has found the true way of living T? No, if the contingent attitudes C and Cm are not similar. To answer the internal moral question about the best way of living that would also retain the critical distinction between C and T, Copp's theory would need to do some independent normative work and help us tell true from false moral judgments. But if it allows us to say that C is true and Cm is not, it already contains normative assumptions that are dependent on the set of contingent beliefs (in this case C) and cannot thus show, but can only presuppose, that C=T. Recall that Marty could hold a set of beliefs that is completely different from Copp's theory: perhaps Martians never depended on living in groups and never experienced competition for resources, and the struggle for reproduction under the conditions of life on Mars has led them to hold a completely different set of moral attitudes. Copp's theory, based on C, would be very different from Marty's contingent attitudes Cm, and he would reject it as a true way of living judging from his own world view.[89]

to define morality in non-moral terms, so the Martian morality does not count as true morality. This is supposed to hold without any moral assumptions feeding into the conception of absolute moral truth T. However, evolutionary explanations aim to account for the *evaluative* rather than narrowly defined *moral* attitudes, so we cannot sneak in evaluative assumptions on the basis of semantics, because that would still beg the question (C would be equalized with T). See Russ Shafer-Landau, 'Evolutionary Debunking, Moral Realism and Moral Knowledge' (2012) 7 Journal of Ethics & Social Philosophy 1, 11–12.

[89] Many other objections to evolutionary scepticism about absolute ethical truths take a similar form and suffer from the same inadequacies. See eg David Enoch, 'The Epistemological Challenge to Metanormative Realism: How Best to Understand It, and how to Cope With It' (2010) 148 Philosophical Studies 413. Enoch assumes that survival is roughly good independently of our attitudes (T) and then shows how it is plausible that E matches T because our evolutionarily induced attitudes fit the truth that he presupposed (ibid

To conclude, the theory is thus either too thin or too thick to be independent from contingent attitudes about morality: an account of moral truth T would need to point to things that are worth pursuing in life independently of our own views about them. The problem is that there are no normative theories of moral truth T that would strike every imaginable observer as correct. Even if most people find them plausible, they do so because they already occupy a particular spot in the universe with a set of contingent attitudes. Therefore, either Copp's second order philosophical intuitions are theoretical, in which case he has offered a theory of moral truth that generalizes and makes best sense of the existing social practices and contingent attitudes C, or he has given us a moralized account of T from the practical perspective that also presupposes C. In each case, he has not accessed to T without recourse to C, which is something that the successful rebuttal of the objection would need.[90]

The only way to surpass the problem is to take the other route identified above: to try to establish a causal link between E and T. This path would affirm E⇒C, but also argue that E⇒T holds. It would show that it is no coincidence that our moral attitudes are true and would—as Gibbard puts it—offer a 'deep vindication' of our ability to make true moral judgments.[91] For the reasons already mentioned it does not suffice to assert that whatever is evolutionarily beneficial is good, as this claim would have to be supported by an argument that starts from our contingent attitudes (C=E and C=T). Moreover, the claim is implausible if one actually starts from C. From the fact that doing φ fulfils our evolutionary function, it does not follow that there is a moral requirement to φ: for example, if my biological function were to reproduce it would not follow that I have a moral duty to reproduce or donate to the sperm bank as much as I can.[92] There is a difference between biological functions and moral oughts. This illustrates our inability to surpass the contingent evaluative attitudes in our moral judgments C and

430–35). He thus asserts T starting from C, and assumes the relationship between C and T that he needs to explain. A similar argument is put forward by Erik J Wielenberg, 'On the Evolutionary Debunking of Morality' (2010) 120 Ethics 441. In his view, cognitive capacities 'entail' moral facts about rights (T) and lead us to believe that we have those rights (C), so we supposedly have an explanation that connects C and T (the same capacity that is constitutive of T makes us believe C, and C=T holds). However, it is not at all clear why would cognitive capacities 'entail' certain facts about rights if we do not show this starting from C. Perhaps this is why Wielenberg—similarly to Enoch—supposes that the relationship of supervenience of moral facts on natural facts is a relationship which has 'no further explanation' (ibid 460), just like laws of nature have no such explanation or vindication. But to say that there is no need for or possibility of explanation is not the same as to offer one and hence does not answer the problem.

[90] Copp could argue that we are able to grasp moral truths T by pure theoretical reflection or some transcendental process but that is implausible for the reasons already mentioned.

[91] Gibbard, *Thinking How to Live* (n 31) ch 13.

[92] The example is from Robert Nozick, *The Nature of Rationality* (Princeton University Press 1993) 30.

reach directly absolute moral truths T. If we assume that E really does determine T, then it would follow that discovering biological facts about evolution could settle moral problems: for instance, the discovery about the most evolutionarily beneficial norms for conducting abortion would determine the outcome of the abortion debate.[93] But this is manifestly not plausible—this debate can be settled only by engaging in moral persuasion within the contingent moral practice C—and facts about evolution would rarely if ever count for something in our evaluative judgments.

The final way for a realist to get out of the conundrum is thus to suppose that evolution would make us track T. This explanation would have to show that there is some evolutionary benefit to grasping an independent moral truth T, in addition to accepting contingent norms beneficial for reproductive success. However, presupposing moral truth is superfluous in the best explanation of the origins of our moral attitudes. Consider an example: contingent attitudes C are such that we provide more care for those that we consider our in-group members. This is the explanandum. The anti-realist evolutionary explanans is that this attitude—for all the reasons mentioned—promoted reproductive success of the members of the group. The alternative realist explanans is that grasping moral truth (T) of favouring in-group members promoted reproductive success. There are two problems the latter explanation needs to face, coming both from the theoretical and practical perspective. First, it is not clear how its explanans sheds light on the explanandum it sets out to explain: it adds an unnecessary element to the story and does not show *why* we happened to have the attitudes we have. It tells us that we ended up having these attitudes because they are true, which is not better than simply asserting the belief in C=T.[94] Second, moving to the practical perspective, this explanation commits itself to the view that C (such as caring more for the in-group members) is always in the neighbourhood of T. This is because on this account evolution brings contingent attitudes to match T. But the thought that C=T would make many feel uncomfortable, for if we believe in absolute moral truth we may want to leave the possibility that we could all be wrong in our current moral attitudes towards the members of outside groups. So how can we tell whether valuing the members of our group more than outsiders is morally correct? This brings us to the next problem.

The E⇒T explanation faces problems when the dimension of temporal change in contingent moral attitudes C is introduced. Evolution is an indefinite process and if T is by definition absolute and static, then it follows that we can never reach it. This gap between E and T thus defeats the possibility that

[93] Joyce, *The Evolution of Morality* (n 36) 176–77.

[94] Street, 'A Darwinian Dilemma for Realist Theories of Value' (n 7) 129–34.

C could match T. Our contingent attitudes C are undoubtedly in a constant state of flux, changing over time, and if E⇒C is true then the process will continue endlessly into the future. If—at the same time—we are approximating to moral truth (E⇒T) then the question is: has that already happened or is it about to happen? Again, the temptation is to assess the proximity of C to T at any given point in time starting from our current contingent attitudes. This is where the realist explanation may face a morally unacceptable consequence, because it is forced to argue that any prevailing attitudes C must approximately be true, because evolution has brought us in the ballpark of normative truths T. But the moral plausibility of this claim depends on the time at which the argument is made: for example, we would get different answers from ancient Egyptians, the founding fathers of the US, or hipsters living in Brooklyn. We can always find out tomorrow that our attitudes of today are morally repugnant. Or—even more problematic—we could feel that things have changed for the worse. It does not help to argue that T also changes over time to fit the factual circumstances: if we believe in T then we surely want to say that slavery was wrong *period*, not that slavery is wrong under present circumstances. The same argument from E⇒T could have been made when slavery was widely accepted. We are not warranted to assume that we have reached the end of evolution at any particular moment. How can we ever know if we have reached the truth T? We cannot, except by judging from our contingent attitudes. But for all we know we may be very far from T, and—in fact—it is most probably beyond our reach as we indefinitely evolve in our attitudes. So, we constantly search but never find T, and we need to face the consequences of this thought.

5.3.4 Defying evolution

Finally, let me address the main objection to this view. Most counter-arguments are defensive: they neither show the existence of mind-independent moral truths (T) with causal powers, nor offer convincing alternative accounts that show how we would reliably track them; rather, they typically draw the analogy between our knowledge of moral facts and mathematical or philosophical facts, pointing to the 'companions in innocence'.[95] However, these could well be the 'companions in guilt'—for example, one could reject the view that there are distinct 'philosophical facts';[96] or they may not be 'companions' at all—for instance, one could indicate that a significant portion of

[95] ibid 129–34.

[96] The example of 'philosophical facts' is from Wielenberg, 'On the Evolutionary Debunking of Morality' (n 89) 28–29.

mathematical knowledge figures in scientific explanations.[97] But there is a potentially more threatening objection of this sort which concerns the benefit of the doubt that we grant to perceptual and moral judgments respectively. The objection is well captured by Russ Shafer-Landau:

> If we are required to suspend judgment about all perceptual beliefs—as we must, if required to do so in the moral case—then we will most likely not be in a position to confirm the reliability of our perceptual faculties. We must presuppose the truth of at least some central, widely uncontroversial perceptual beliefs in order to get the confirmation of our perceptual faculties off the ground. But if we are allowed such liberties in the perceptual realm, we should be given similar license for morality. And then the debunking game is up.[98]

Shafer-Landau here relies on the notion of parity in reasoning between perceptual and moral judgments. If we are not able to resort to C in order to vindicate the existence of T, then equally we cannot presuppose the truth of contingent perceptual judgments to vindicate the facts about the objects of our perception. We must grant the same initial plausibility to both.

The objection does not do much damage to the argument in this form. To show this we need not rely on the differences between the phenomenology of our perceptual and moral judgments: in other words, on the fact that we tend to agree about the things we see, while we disagree about the things we ought to do. Instead, recall that the evolutionary test shows *why* our perceptual judgments are true—their accuracy in tracking mind-independent truth is beneficial for reproductive success, but the same case cannot be made for moral judgments. The objection thus must raise the stakes higher, for it must deny that the evolutionary test is valid. It could then take the following route: the belief in evolution itself must presuppose the truth of some of our perceptual judgments that are at the foundation of our ability to do

[97] The analogy with mathematics is roughly this: in both ethics and mathematics, there is no object that our judgments are about, and we are able to reach judgments simply by reasoning about them. (See Thomas Scanlon, 'The Appeal and Limits of Constructivism' in James Lenman and Yonathan Shemmer (eds), *Constructivism in Practical Philosophy* (Oxford University Press 2012) 226–27). Yet, most of us do not doubt that mathematical judgments can be true in a robust sense. However, the evolutionary explanation of our mathematical ability presupposes that it would help us judge reality accurately. Further, many true mathematical facts figure in scientific explanations, while true moral facts play no such role. As Gibbard puts it 'at least for arithmetic and geometry, mathematics is part and parcel of empirical knowledge', the fact that we have knowledge of mathematics is one 'aspect' of our empirical abilities (Gibbard, *Reconciling Our Aims: In Search of Bases for Ethics* (n 1) 21). Even those mathematical facts that do not figure in scientific explanations presuppose the truth of and are continuous with mathematical facts that do figure in scientific explanations, and—moreover—they may come to be scientifically useful in future. See more generally: WVO Quine, 'Two Dogmas of Empiricism' (1951) 60 The Philosophical Review 20; Hilary Putnam, *Philosophy of Logic* (Harper & Row 1971) chs 7 and 8. A recent counter-argument to the view expressed here is Justin Clarke-Doane, 'Morality and Mathematics: The Evolutionary Challenge' (2012) 122 Ethics 313.

[98] Shafer-Landau, 'Evolutionary Debunking, Moral Realism and Moral Knowledge' (n 88) 28.

science. If so, then the argument is circular, as the very test that is supposed to vindicate our perceptual judgments must presuppose the truth of some of them. If we cannot assume that C=T is true in the moral case, then we equally cannot presuppose the contingent truth of evolutionary beliefs (Cevolution) to show the truth of evolution (Tevolution). Therefore, evolutionary discrediting of moral attitudes analogously discredits beliefs about evolution. More fundamentally, the idea would be that just like the 'one thing physics cannot do is account for its own possibility',[99] evolution cannot stand on its own feet to explain itself. The dilemma is this: either moral truth enjoys the same benefit of the doubt as the truth of evolution, and values are as well among the fundamental features of the universe;[100] or evolutionary explanation 'hammers itself into the same ground into which it had previously pounded morality'.[101] If we do not want to end up with a sceptical view about evolution itself, we need to give up on the evolutionary test for truth and knowledge.

Notice, however, that the objection misinterprets the target of the evolutionary test of our epistemic abilities in the moral domain. The evolutionary test does not aim to offer an all–encompassing account of knowledge, but—much more modestly—to point out that if evolutionary theory is right we have reasons to doubt our ability to track mind-independent moral truths. It is notoriously difficult to show that there is no evil demon that controls our senses, that the world around us exists, or that it functions according to scientific laws. So, the argument does not aspire to do that. It does not offer an epistemic foundation from which we could derive all our justified beliefs. It argues—instead—that the belief in the possibility that our moral attitudes match the external normative truths does not sit well with the web of beliefs that we are quite confident about. Now, it is then equally open to anyone to argue that unless we show why our perception and scientific theories are true we cannot rely on them to cast doubt on our knowledge of mind-independent moral truths. The flipside of this objection is that among its premises it must question the truth of evolution and the validity of scientific forms of explanation. The counter-argument to the objection is thus a *reductio ad absurdum*. While evolutionary theory and the perceptual judgments that are at its basis may not enjoy an epistemically privileged status, the realist *modus tollens* is hard to swallow: evolutionary theory implies that we cannot be certain about the truth of our moral judgments, we are certain

[99] Hilary Putnam, *The Collapse of the Fact/Value Dichotomy and Other Essays* (Harvard University Press 2002) 106.

[100] Nagel, *The Last Word* (n 16) 140.

[101] Peter Railton, 'Darwinian Building Blocks' in Leonard D Katz (ed), *Evolutionary Origins of Morality: Cross-Disciplinary Perspectives* (Imprint Academic 2000) 57, cited in Joyce, *The Evolution of Morality* (n 36) 183.

about the truth of our moral judgments, therefore evolutionary theory is false.[102]

We are in a way back at the beginning. The commitment to the possibility of knowledge of mind-independent moral truths puts us in an uneasy position between the theoretical and the practical perspective. There are good theoretical reasons to doubt that our attitudes track mind-independent moral truths. The reason why some find the realist *modus tollens* against evolution convincing is because they think that the theoretical is intrusive on the practical. It seems as if they must give up on their moral attitudes and suspend all moral judgments until the theory is demonstrated to be false. So, they choose differently: to retain the practical at the expense of the theoretical. But practical consequences are different.

5.4 THE PRACTICAL: CONFIDENCE AND REFLECTION

Our inability to reach the realm of mind-independent values ends in a paradox: the practical perspective is inescapable and includes value-judgments; we can only make these judgments on the basis of our contingent values which are disconnected from the presupposed realm of robustly true values; what we *ought* to do (reason from robustly true values) bears no systematic connection to what we *can* do (reason from our own values), hence the ought-talk is completely confused as we have no hope of ever willingly doing what we ought to do. How should we treat our moral judgments upon this realization? The problem could lead to a stalemate. It could seem that—when it comes to living our lives—we are deeply misguided. Performing the right action becomes unavoidably a matter of luck and coincidence. Blackburn describes the problem lucidly: 'the nightmare is one of being left no basis for trust in [one's own] judgment. It is the fear of being left unable to judge at all and so, in an entirely literal sense, the fear of losing [one's] mind'.[103] It is not surprising that the theoretical perspective faces opposition. We want to think of ourselves as reliable in deciding how to live.

I want to argue that there are two consequences of this predicament for the practical perspective. They both pertain to the second order evaluative attitudes that determine how we treat our first-order normative judgments. The first is liberating and reassuring: instead of hopelessly trying to reach the values that are completely beyond us, we need *confidence* in our existing values, and—in fact—confidence is inescapable because the only thing

[102] See Nagel, *Mind and Cosmos: Why the Materialist Neo-Darwinian Conception of Nature is Almost Certainly False* (n 16) 188.

[103] Blackburn, *Ruling Passions: A Theory of Practical Reasoning* (n 32) 294.

we can do is practically reason from our own values.[104] If we cannot close the gap between the independent realm of values and our current values, the only path we have is to stop worrying about absolute moral truths and reaffirm our practical identity that includes a set of contingent evaluative attitudes. The second consequence pulls in the opposite direction: we need to incorporate insights about the inevitability of contingency in practical thinking into the *reflection* about existing values. The realization that our ethical attitudes are contingent and that the only thing we can do is reason from the existing value-frameworks should promote a thoughtful, self-aware and flexible approach to practical questions.[105] Reflection, as a counterbalance to confidence, thus incorporates a number of normative ideas about the virtues of good moral judgment. The need for reflection emanates from the non-absolute and non-eternal character of (our) moral values, but does not claim to be a universally valid requirement itself: on the one hand, it is a moral sensitivity that seems appropriate for a moral framework that placed high hopes in externally validated normative truth, and on the other, it emphasizes the values that are already part of our moral framework but now gain more prominence given the change of balance against the value of believing in absolute moral truth. Moral judgments, in this model, ought to include a more modest attitude towards our own moral position, and rely on persuasion and imagination, rather than authority and truth. Ethical choices are then to be made in the process of interaction between confidence and reflection, immersion and detachment, action from and deliberation upon our own values.

5.4.1 Confidence

Where does this practical confidence come from? We have seen that many believe that the contingent character of values is not a problem at all, or—if it is—that it affects only those that afforded our values more authority than they could actually have.[106] To an extent this is correct. Notice that the problem arises only if we suppose that values are mind-independent. The practical perspective that does not subscribe to this premise is not damaged if it turns out that values are mind-dependent: there is no need for deep

[104] The term 'confidence' or 'practical confidence' is mentioned in Bernard Williams' and Allan Gibbard's work (Williams, *Ethics and the Limits of Philosophy* (n 34) 171–72 and Gibbard, *Thinking How to Live* (n 31) ch 13). Although the term is the same, I do not borrow the notion behind it. In my parlance, confidence includes the feeling that one can rely on one's own values that comes from the realization that there is nothing to support them further and that the practical perspective is inescapable.

[105] Rorty described a person having a similar reflective attitude as a 'liberal ironist'. My approach here is similar in sentiment but very different in the details and doctrines that support it. See Richard Rorty, *Contingency, Irony, and Solidarity* (Cambridge University Press 1989) ch 4.

[106] See the discussion of Mackie's and Harman's views in this chapter.

vindication, because there is nothing to be vindicated. But this view thrives on a too sharp distinction between the theoretical and the practical and fails to appreciate some important aspects of the problem.

Let me use an example. There are causal—evolutionary, sociological, or psychological—explanations of our propensity to laugh. But there is also an important difference between causally explaining why something is funny and laughing at someone's joke or experiencing humour internally; there is also a difference between external statements about humour and internal humorous statements, and one could comprehend one kind of statement without understanding the other. Imagine a scientist who understands humour perfectly well from the external perspective, but, at the same time, never laughs, finds nothing funny, and is unable to experience humour properly from the internal perspective. He would still be able to study humour as a phenomenon, describe it, and point to its causes. Similarly, one could be witty without understanding or being able to explain why we laugh.

There is an analogy with the evaluative domain. We are able to explain normativity scientifically and experience it internally, and these two enterprises seem very different. For example, Dworkin's claim that metaethical statements are normative statements is analogous to saying that, by explaining humour from the external perspective, one is actually joking.[107] Moreover, the explanation of the cause of our propensity to laugh would not have any lasting effect on what we find funny. Suppose you went with our scientist to a comedy show, and he explains to you that you will be laughing only because by so doing you increase your reproductive prospects or because the jokes are incongruent with your cultural world view. It would neither spoil the fun nor have a chilling effect (besides the fact that you went out with a very boring person). Likewise, learning about the contingency of values need not practically affect us.

There is an important difference, however. It is easy for us not to take humour seriously. Although the grammar of humour reveals a similar pattern to moral grammar—seemingly ascribing a property of 'being funny' to natural facts—it is not difficult to accept disagreement about humour and say things like 'he lacks a sense of humour' or 'I find it funny but she doesn't'. Not so with morality. In the moral case, it is hard to keep the external and internal point of view separate: there is nothing funny about injustice or evil, and we do tend to think that one can be robustly right or wrong in practical matters. The argument that aspires to retain confidence in our values cannot thus merely rely on the distinction between the theoretical and practical. We

[107] Perhaps closer to Dworkin's position would be to say that metaethical statements are analogous to *bad* jokes.

want our values to be true to be confident in them, and the commitment to the truth of values is inherent to the moral practice and discourse.[108]

A more plausible argument for practical confidence builds on the commitment of moral practice and discourse to the mind-independent truths of values, but realizes that this is a *normative* commitment. It treats the requirement of believing in mind-independent normative truths as one of the normative premises within our practical outlook. The idea is this: the practical perspective—once conscious of the paradox that renders us incapable of knowing how to live our lives—ought to reject the commitment to absolute moral truths as a parasite that threatens its existence. Judging from the practical perspective, we should choose to renounce one of the evaluative assumptions we find untenable, for it is incoherent with the very possibility of occupying the practical perspective. As long as we believe in the correspondence of our moral attitudes with mind-independent truths we are bound to lose confidence in our values; but if we abandon this assumption, the practical perspective is not in peril. The practical perspective is thus vindicated from within.

The reasoning does not deduce anything from 'is' to 'ought' and takes the following form. The normative premise is: (P1) to know how to live or what to do, one should grasp mind-independent normative truths. P1 is then combined with a descriptive premise supplied by the theoretical perspective: (P2) we cannot grasp mind-independent normative truths. This leads to a normatively unacceptable conclusion: (C) we do not know how to live or what to do. Since the conclusion is unacceptable, we drop the first premise. The structure of the reasoning follows the pattern that we regularly observe in moral practice: if a general principle leads to highly counter-intuitive conclusions in the factual context to which it applies, we abandon the principle.[109] The thesis we should then accept is that one need not know mind-independent truths to know how to live or what to do.

The intuition behind this argument is right, but some clarifications are in order. There are two main reasons why the argument may not quite succeed in redeeming our confidence. First, it may appear that the valueless perspective is a real option. On the one hand, we may well embrace the conclusion

[108] This point, however, should not be overstated. Commitment to the robust truth of moral beliefs is often a matter of degree. For example, we may think that torturing children for fun is robustly and come-what-may wrong, but that whether we ought to have a welfare state is a matter of opinion. A more precise formulation is then: we consider some of our contingent moral attitudes robustly true.

[109] See Sharon Street, 'Does Anything Really Matter or Did We Just Evolve to Think So?' in Gideon Rosen and others (eds), *The Norton Introduction to Philosophy* (Norton 2015); Street, 'Coming to Terms with Contingency: Humean Constructivism about Practical Reason' (n 5) 55–57; and Street, 'A Darwinian Dilemma for Realist Theories of Value' (n 7) 109. For a more sceptical view see Elliott Sober, *From a Biological Point of View: Essays in Evolutionary Philosophy* (Cambridge University Press 1994) 102–104 and 109–11.

that we do not know what to do or how to live. On the other, the question of what to do or how to live may be different from the questions of what do we *ought* to do or how we *ought* to live. We could then abandon the latter, moralized version of the practical perspective, and proceed on the basis of the former, starting from some other motivation; for example, instead of asking what ought we to do, we could ask what do we really want. Thus—to retain practical confidence—we need to realize that there is no valueless practical perspective and that these questions cannot be completely separate. Second, and connected to this, confidence could be lost in interaction with others who hold a different set of values. The problem is clearest when we confront the amoralist, a person that does not care about moral values at all. If the amoralist is not inherently irrational or acting against his own happiness, he does not have any reason to be moral; and if the amoralist need not be committed to absolute moral truths, how do we have the authority (and hence confidence) to impose our values on him? Thus, we need some other source of confidence that would replace the belief in mind-independent truths.

To answer the first problem, it is enough to understand that even if we could choose to abandon our current values, this would be an ethical choice nonetheless. The practical perspective is inescapable and such choice would follow from whatever we think we have most reasons to do. Even deciding to do *nothing* is deciding to do *something*. For example: deciding not to blame someone for stealing is to allow the thief to get away with stealing without being blamed. This may be justified for a number of reasons—he may, for instance, be stealing because this is the only way for him to survive—but the judgment is still to be made from the practical perspective. When confronted with situations like that we have a *practical* choice: how do we act? Every decision will necessarily be answerable to our set of values. It is then highly improbable that the fact that values are contingent would prevail over the strong moral reasons we have to punish murderers, praise altruism, or help those in need. Even if we could decide not to act upon our moral motives and follow our intuitions, this would at the same time mean that we allow the actions that we resent.[110] Why *should* we do this? Suspending moral judgments is an option only 'for those who can afford to think of their lives as play'.[111] The fact that values are contingent is practically insignificant in comparison to the amount and gravity of evil in the world. To conclude: because suspending moral judgment is also a moral judgment, and because the practical perspective is inescapable, we have no reason to prefer the seemingly valueless perspective to our own moral attitudes.

This leads to the second challenge. For if this is true, we can only follow *our* own contingent set of values. The others may have different values;

[110] See Blackburn, *Ruling Passions: A Theory of Practical Reasoning* (n 32) 294.

[111] ibid.

worse still, they may not have moral values at all or may not care about them. If the first problem asks 'why values?' the second asks 'why *your* values?' What then gives us the right—or confidence—to impose our views? The problem is typically framed in terms of disagreement, but this is not the most helpful way of approaching it. If we are to retain confidence in our values, then even agreement cannot help us: it is far from clear why *anyone's* contingent agreement would matter at all. Its normativity would be in doubt as much as the normativity of any other contingent attitude.[112]

To answer what we need, we must realize what we have lost. Belief in the mind-independent character of our values served to justify our own identity rather than to show to the amoralist that he should comply with our values. If the failure to confirm their mind-independent character causes a loss of confidence in our practical identity, it is probable that the confidence can be reaffirmed with reference to identity. It will, in other words, find its source not in *truth* but in the *self*. As Williams puts it, 'the point is not that the intuitions should be in some ultimate sense correct, but that they should be ours'; but—he continues—'The problem is who *we* are'.[113] The source of confidence is then to be found in the process of answering both what does *we* stand for and what do we stand *for*. Such confidence rejects the assumption that we must make the amoralist care and asks instead whether *we* care enough. It then reveals the core of moral attitudes which we cannot give up on, and which—even on reflection—do not yield to competing concerns about their lost authority. It also includes the awareness of other experienced forms of life and takes into account the fact that ours may be one among many; it situates, understands, and embraces our position in the world together with our evaluative perspective.

This challenge will, however, inevitably affect confidence. Compared to truth, identity seems too weak a foundation. The next section will thus say more about this and contrast confidence with the idea of reflection. But it is important to recognize that the effects are not sweeping. The problem must again be addressed from one's practical perspective. We are bound to become uncertain about some moral judgments if we reflect enough.[114] Yet, some things we will resent so much that we can think of our action against

[112] This is not to downplay the problem of disagreement but to understand what the question is really about. But disagreement is also always a matter of degree, for there must be something to disagree about, something recognized as a problem. The theoretical understanding of the normative domain suggests that there will be a significant overlap between human cultures and that there is a lot of convergence between existing moral codes, at least in their central features. There could be a disagreement about the substantive moral judgment but no disagreement about the best way to tackle it or reach agreement, so we can still often rely on this second-order agreement: norms become pervasive wherever humans get in touch with each other. In my model, disagreement is addressed within the idea of reflection.

[113] Williams, *Ethics and the Limits of Philosophy* (n 34) 102.

[114] It may seem—as it seems to Williams—that the reflection may destroy the moral knowledge we had pre-reflectively. I am not sure if this is the best formulation of the idea, but reflection can certainly make us less or more confident in our judgments and intuitions. See ibid ch 8.

them as a self-defence or—better to say—defence of the self: they will disturb our world view to the extent that the loss of confidence will seem insignificant. Philippa Foot coveys this thought with particular elegance:

> We are apt to panic at the thought that we ourselves, or other people, might stop caring about the things we do care about, and we feel that the categorical imperative gives us some control over the situation. But it is interesting that the people of Leningrad were not struck by the thought that only the *contingent* fact that other citizens shared their loyalty and devotion to the city stood between them and the Germans during the terrible years of the siege. Perhaps we should be less troubled than we are by fear of defection from the moral cause; perhaps we should even have less reason to fear it if people thought of themselves as volunteers banded together to fight for liberty and justice and against inhumanity and oppression.[115]

The thought is that to the extent it is possible to think of some parts of our practical perspective in these terms, there is hope that confidence can be restored. Once we realize that the role of truth was to give us confidence, we are faced with a dilemma: should we care about the fact that—for example—a perfectly coherent psychopath who values torturing children for fun does not in so doing fail to be rational, or about the fact that *we* do not want to allow torturing children. It is absurd, judging from the practical perspective, to conclude that we ought not to react to prevent that, even if our judgment does not have the absolute or timeless character we thought it did have.

The question is then whether the argument can justify the confidence on the part of those that do, for example, value torturing children for fun. The fact that values are contingent leaves us without an argument that would prove the absolute irrationality of an immoral set of beliefs. There are two responses to this. First, the obsession of moral theory with the amoralist and with the challenge he poses to the reasons to be moral should be somewhat softened by the approach that is aware of the causal origins of our contingent moral attitudes. Instead of showing the inherent irrationality of the amoralist (for why should he care about being rational?) or demonstrating that his position is conceptually impossible, such an approach notes that his position will be empirically exceptional because we share very similar propensities and conditions of life.[116] The amoralist, on this reading, has been a bit of a red herring in the debate: prejudice is much more a consequence of not taking into account the full implications of one's moral outlook through reflection than of being consistently prejudiced.[117] Second, once we do face

[115] Philippa Foot, 'Morality as a System of Hypothetical Imperatives' (1972) 81 The Philosophical Review 305, 315–16.

[116] See Bernard Williams, *Morality: An Introduction to Ethics* (Harper & Row 1972) ch 1.

[117] Williams, *Ethics and the Limits of Philosophy* (n 34) 115–17.

a consistent amoralist, the judgment of whether he has earned the right to have confidence in his values would still have to be assessed from our practical perspective, just as our confidence has been restored from within. As we have seen, care for our own values will simply outweigh care for the amoralist.

There is an element of faith in this conception of confidence. Whereas confidence based on mind-independent moral truths stems from faith in God or universal and absolute moral standards, the disenchanted practical perspective builds confidence on its faith in humanity. This is a leap of faith nonetheless; it is possible—regardless of the evolutionary explanation of the convergence of human values—that we will one day wake up in a world completely unknown to us, ruled by the amoral. Unlike the confidence given by the absolute belief in the righteousness of our own practical perspective, such confidence will have nothing non-contingent and universally valid to cling to. However, confidence would not be what matters if it somehow turns out that humans are inherently evil: the loss of hope would be a luxury that we cannot afford. In the meantime, we have all the moral reasons we need to prefer a confidence that is based on trust in humanity. Such confidence is profoundly humane, for it celebrates our capacities instead of suppressing them: instead of thinking of practical perspective as a set of unchangeable principles written in stone, we now realize that values can change, and that we can even choose them; instead of externally imposed values, we see their deep connection with our identity and all other concepts through which we experience and make sense of life; instead of thinking about our contingent values as misguided because they are causally affected, we are now free to embrace them. At the bottom of our moral judgments—we now realize—there can be nothing else than our deep intuitions about how to live.

5.4.2 Reflection

The notion of confidence leaves us with the picture of values as deeply held but nonetheless contingent; they are probably best understood as intuitions—states of mind the content of which is an emotional attitude towards actions, situations or events that are evaluated as positive or negative, good or bad, right or wrong. Judging from the practical perspective we ought to place trust—indeed have confidence—in these intuitions: there can be nothing better to replace them, for the very idea that something could be better must start from these intuitions. [118] Yet, such confidence is both defeasible and a matter of degree. Contingent intuitions are the foundation of moral

[118] Some philosophers argue that a part of our intuitions should be dropped because they are imposed on us by evolutionary or other causal forces. (See Peter Singer, 'Ethics and Intuitions' (2005) 9 The Journal of Ethics 331, 351.) What they fail to see is that it is impossible to make this argument without relying on

judgments, but they are at the same time their foundation *only*. Once their ability to track mind-independent truths is demystified, we need some other approach to judging these intuitions as warranted or trustworthy.

One option would be to consider all the intuitions we have as justified. Such a response, however, would be insensitive to the fact that the warrant that has supported our intuitions so far—the mind-independent truth—is beyond our reach; the quality and force of confidence cannot simply be the same. Nietzsche motivates this idea convincingly:

> But why do you *listen* to the voice of your conscience? And what gives you the right to consider such a judgment true and infallible? For this *faith*—is there no conscience for that? Have you never heard of an intellectual conscience? A conscience behind your 'conscience'? Your judgment 'this is right' has a pre-history in your instincts, likes, dislikes, experiences, and lack of experiences. 'How did it originate there?' you must ask, and then also: 'What is it that impels me to listen to it?' ... the *firmness* of your moral judgment could be evidence of your personal abjectness, of impersonality; your 'moral strength' might have its source in your stubbornness—or in your inability to envisage new ideals. ... if you had thought more subtly, observed better, and learned more, you certainly would not go on calling this 'duty' of yours and this 'conscience' of yours duty and conscience. Your understanding of the *manner in which moral judgments have originated* would spoil these grand words for you, just as other grand words like 'sin' and 'salvation of the soul' and 'redemption' have been spoiled for you.[119]

Nietzsche argues that learning about the origins of moral attitudes ('intellectual conscience') ought to destabilize their 'firmness', 'strength', or 'grandness' so that it becomes unclear why we need to 'listen' to them anymore. In other words, the theoretical perspective exposes the contingent nature of values, so they lose their authority over us and we lose our confidence in them.[120] The message, however, is not one of despair but of caution; Nietzsche warns us that we have these values because we might have lacked character, or been inflexible, fearful, and unimaginative in our moral judgments. Our confidence cannot be based on the self-righteous conception of values:

intuitions, and that the theoretical perspective tells us that our practical perspective in fact consists of these causally affected intuitions.

[119] Friedrich Nietzsche, *The Gay Science; With a Prelude in Rhymes and an Appendix of Songs* (Walter Kaufmann (tr), Vintage Books 1974) 263–64, footnotes ommitted.

[120] It could seem as if the theoretical perspective is not 'behind' but 'above' the practical in this picture, as Nietzsche starts this section with an exclamation: 'Long live physics!' (ibid 263). But this would be to move too quickly. In a beautifully paradoxical ending to the section, Nietzsche says that what moves us towards the theoretical is one of our values: 'long live physics! And even more so that which compels us to turn to physics—our honesty!' (ibid 266). The connection and interaction between the two perspectives is thus more nuanced. See also ibid 283–85 where he openly admits the fundamental difference between the two perspectives.

> You admire the categorical imperative within you? This 'firmness' of your so-called moral judgment? This 'unconditional' feeling that 'here everyone must judge as I do'? Rather admire your *selfishness* at this point. And the blindness, pettiness, and frugality of your selfishness. For it is selfish to experience one's own judgment as a universal law . . . [121]

The point here is not to abandon the practical altogether—which as we have seen is impossible—but to approach our judgments in a self-conscious way. Notice the subtlety of the argument: Nietzsche does not argue that we ought to abandon the values simply because they have a causal pedigree, but because they may be a result of attitudes that we find normatively unacceptable. Instead of reasserting the absolute value of our practical outlook, Nietzsche's idea is both to look at our own values more critically and to overcome them to the extent they are constraining and unimaginative: 'Let us therefore *limit* ourselves to the purification of our opinions and valuations and to the *creation of our own new tables of what is good* . . .'.[122] Confidence thus needs to be counterbalanced with an attitude to our moral intuitions that is aware of their contingent character and that is creative enough to overcome them. We might have taken our values for granted without being reflective enough.

Now, overcoming, counterbalancing, or revaluating values is puzzling to say the least: each such attempt must specify the evaluative perspective from which it departs and explain why some values enjoy a privileged status. For example, Nietzsche thought that we need a revaluation of all values or at least the ones predominant at his time, that impeded the development of what he considered to be valuable and strong character;[123] in so doing, he departed from a substantive idea about the life worth living, had quite a bit of confidence in his own intuitions, and was sceptical of any convergent practical perspective.[124] But even without subscribing to Nietzsche's concrete proposals or to the perplexing idea of revaluation of *all* values, we can see that his diagnosis of the problem is apt. The loss of the ability to claim the absolute truth for our values does challenge the way we ought to treat them, unless we wish to engage in self-deception.

[121] ibid 265. [122] ibid 265–66.

[123] Friedrich Wilhelm Nietzsche, *On the Genealogy of Morals and Ecce Homo* (Walter Kaufmann (ed), Walter Arnold Kaufmann and RJ Hollingdale (trs), 2nd edn, Vintage Books 1989) 20.

[124] Foot argues that Nietzsche is appealing to a set of intuitions about good character and good life that has some purchase within our own evaluative outlook (see Philippa Foot, *Virtues and Vices and Other Essays in Moral Philosophy* (Clarendon Press 2002) ch 6 esp 88–89). This may not be the best exegesis of Nietzsche's views (see eg Brian Leiter, 'Nietzsche's Metaethics: Against the Privilege Readings' (2000) 8 European Journal of Philosophy 277, 287–90) but it certainly makes sense as an independent position. It fits with my notion of confidence and with the view that we cannot escape the practical perspective, while at the same time avoids Nietzsche's scepticism about common morality or lack of interest in those that do not share his evaluative standpoints.

So how to approach this problem? Instead of starting from first-order intuitions about the good life, a more promising route is to adjust the second-order evaluative attitudes *about* these first-order intuitions, for this is where the problem has arisen. The exercise then does not remain at the level of deciding *what to do*, but takes place at the level of planning or deciding *what to value*.[125] The question is which of the intuitions and judgments deserve our confidence, which ones are worth our trust even after reflection. The goal is not to cede to the theoretical as the 'conscience behind conscience', but to be able to think of the theoretical and the practical as a single coherent conscience. What we need then is to outline the fundamentals of the process of reflection through which we could curb the excessive confidence.

Before I explain this in more detail let me clarify the fundamentals of the approach. First, I argued in previous chapters that the move from agent to appraiser relativism is baffling: the ideal of universal tolerance cannot follow straight from the fact that contingent sets of evaluative beliefs are different. The approach here is fundamentally different. The normative allure of reflection and respect for other points of view comes from within our contingent set of evaluative beliefs that has lost the absolute confidence in its rightfulness; we are moving, in other words, completely within the practical realm once the encounter with the theoretical is resolved. Second, I also argued that reflection could not get us to mind-independent truths in the practical domain, and that the authority of reflection could not be based on the analogy between theoretical and practical reason. In the model I now propose, we are moved to reflect, but for a different reason: although confidence is inescapable, reflectiveness refines a disproportionate confidence based on a belief in the mind-independent truth of our values. Third, although I will clarify which attitudes should gain more prominence under this model, it is doubtful that any approach of this kind could arrive at a clear-cut measurement for the trustworthiness of intuitions, let alone a quantitative measurement. The outcome of such an exercise will always depend on untidy intuitions, experiences, contexts, and the types of interactions we engage in. The hope is only to outline a vocabulary in which we can cogently express these reflective concerns.

What are then the elements of reflection? Roughly, a reflective attitude will be critical towards dogmatism and self-deception, mindful of other forms of life, thoughtful, flexible, and capable of taking different perspectives. It is perhaps best to think of reflection along two interdependent dimensions: internal and external. The internal dimension of reflection concerns

[125] I think here of higher order volitions or the ability of 'reflective self-evaluation' that is often thought of as being constitutive of personhood. See Harry G Frankfurt, 'Freedom of the Will and the Concept of a Person' (1971) 68 The Journal of Philosophy 5, 7.

finding out what one really values and how firm these values are even upon recognizing their contingency. The external dimension relates to the treatment of other value systems—which we now realize are as contingent as ours—and asks how they affect our values, how much respect, leeway, or tolerance we are ready to grant them, and how we deal with unavoidable disagreements.

Turning to the *internal* dimension of reflection, the question is, where to start? We need to ascertain which attitudes we can initially be more confident about. One cannot start the reflection from nothing, and the talk of choice or planning what to value can in this sense be slightly misleading. Reflection can neither begin from a normatively blank, non-evaluative standpoint; nor can it entail a radical choice of values, independent from any contingent attitude.[126] As I suggested before, confidence can find refuge in identity. Identity is here understood in a thin sense: it comprises a set of values that are a precondition for occupying the evaluative perspective.[127] Thus it is not that identity is valuable in and of itself; rather, the idea is that it is inescapable. As Charles Taylor puts it, 'identity refers us to certain evaluations which are essential because they are the indispensable horizon or foundation out of which we evaluate or reflect'; to be without them is be to be 'a kind of extensionless point, a pure leap into the void'.[128] The turn to identity is therefore a consequence of the fact that a revaluation of values must proceed from one's own standpoint, incrementally and by holding some of values constant, while changing others. It is impossible to overcome oneself in one go, and evaluative judgments that are part of our identity are unavoidable.

There is also another slightly more robust sense in which the core of our values is inescapable: we cannot stop having them and continue being ourselves. The thought here is that if I choose to abandon these values, I seize to be the *I* that made this choice. It is practically impossible to renounce this core of self-constituting values without losing integrity, and it is normatively perplexing to demand such a deep psychological alienation from the attitudes through which one makes sense of life. Quite literally, it would isolate the agent 'from his actions and the source of his action in his own

[126] Charles Taylor, *Human Agency and Language: Philosophical Papers I* (Cambridge University Press 1985) 29.

[127] Korsgaard also starts from having a practical identity as a precondition for finding anything else valuable, but argues that this fact forces us to value the ability of having a practical identity as such, and thus also the humans who have this ability. There is a typically Kantian leap in conclusion here: from valuing *my* ability to valuing the ability *as such*, and valuing *other people* for having it (see Korsgaard, *The Sources of Normativity* (n 68)). For criticism along those lines see R Jay Wallace, 'Constructivism about Normativity: Some Pitfalls' in James Lenman and Yonathan Shemmer (eds), *Constructivism in Practical Philosophy* (Oxford University Press 2012). In my conception, no concrete normative consequence follows from valuing one's identity, and the whole model depends on its intuitiveness within our contingent evaluative outlook.

[128] Taylor, *Human Agency and Language: Philosophical Papers I* (n 126) 35.

convictions'.[129] Because a self that evaluates is necessary for any evaluation, in an attempt to detach from these deepest evaluative commitments and projects, both components could be lost: the possibility to evaluate and the self.

It is inevitable for reflection to begin with introspection, which implies distinguishing more and less genuine interpretations of one's own identity. The notion of identity does assign introspection some normative weight, as the process consists in a 'struggle of self-interpretations', and includes finding out 'which is the truer, more authentic, more illusion-free interpretation, and which on the other hand involves a distortion of the meanings things have for me'.[130] Because asking which values are absolutely true becomes pointless, we ask which values are truthful to the way we are or the way we want to be: the focus on identity thus helps us exchange the talk of robust mind-independent truth with a more modest talk of authenticity or sincerity. This incorporates the idea that values forming identity are different from just any values we happen to have at that particular moment; it distinguishes those values that we want to be identified *with*, ones that characterize the kind of subject we wish to be recognized *as*. Identity involves, in other words, dimensions of depth and integrity. For example, I may highly value and take pleasure in excessive eating and drinking at one point or the other, but I am quite certain that I do not want this value to define me and I am not at all confident that this is the value I wish to retain. If I reflect, I recognize these desires as trivial and temporary. When I ponder existential and self-definitional commitments, I list those values that make me the person I want to be. The question to be asked then is: upon the loss of which values would I cease to be who I am? Which are the ones that *I* cannot renounce? Where are the limits of the detachment that I am capable of? The core of the values revealed by these questions will form not the timelessly true starting point of reflection, but a sincere and inescapable one. To be confident in them is to retain sanity.

Yet identity—understood as a set of self-definitional values—cannot become the ultimate vantage point for evaluation. It presents a core of certainty that we can be presumptively confident about in the process of reflection, and can also be incrementally re-examined in the course of it. This is because—if values are not mind-independently true—we are freer to detach from them in order to attune our moral sensibilities. Let me mention two mechanisms in particular. First, we may wish to achieve more *coherence* within the practical perspective. In this picture, coherence is not a demand of mind-independent rationality, in a sense that I must bring my beliefs in coherence

[129] Bernard Williams, 'A Critique of Utilitarianism' in JJC Smart and Bernard Williams (eds), *Utilitarianism For and Against* (Cambridge University Press 1973) 116.

[130] Taylor, *Human Agency and Language: Philosophical Papers I* (n 126) 27.

if they are all to be true. Instead, coherence becomes a pressing concern upon the realization that I may not be able to attain all of my ends; some of my values can exclude each other.[131] If all values are taken for granted, we do not always see the analogies, relations, and inconsistencies among them; if we understand values as contingent, the conflict between them becomes more intelligible, as they are not a consequence of a flawless divine plan or timeless truth. Similarly, bringing our values or conflicting courses of action into coherence stops being dependent on finding out which one is universally true, but rather lies in considering the alternatives and settling on the one that makes more sense within our contingent practical outlook. Second, thinking of values as non-eternal opens new venues for creativeness and choice: it allows us to be more *imaginative*. Imagination provides a counterbalance to the conserving tendency of coherence, and helps us develop moral views beyond those already implied by our existing standpoint. In this view, values are not fully determined in advance but can be changed to fit the circumstances of life and evaluative horizons can evolve. We stop seeing past attitudes as always wrong and current as always right: we are allowed to question, abandon, or replace them.

In the process of considering how to live, we build new connections between existing values and form novel emotional reactions. The final outcome of the internal dimension of reflection should be greater self-awareness. The hope is that we will be able to map the web of our evaluative attitudes with some precision, and shall perhaps be capable of indicating different spheres of intuitions, forming radiuses from the core of our identity to its outer boundaries. We should also be able to spot the connections between them and see how the changes in the outer range affect the ones in the core, and the other way round.

The *external* dimension of reflection pertains to the interaction with other practical outlooks. This dimension itself consists of two sets of concerns. First, contact with different evaluative standpoints helps us clarify what exactly we believe in. An important part of reflection consists in being exposed to other forms of life, and pondering whether they could be a real option for us. So the external dimension builds on the internal but also refines it. If we are no longer certain that our values are absolutely true, we are prone to be more *open* and *flexible*. If we settle on a set of values, we can still coherently think that this is not the outlook that is obligatory for others, and the way we look at the world need not be the one others must embrace. This opens up a possibility to realize that others have managed to lead a more fulfilling life, or that they chose their values more courageously and with less self-deception. Interaction with them may lead us to reconsider

[131] Gibbard, *Reconciling Our Aims: In Search of Bases for Ethics* (n 1) 29.

some of the assumptions within our system of values that we did not question, and—given that these assumptions are no longer necessary in a metaphysical but only psychological sense—we may treat them more flexibly. We can also realize that others have chosen badly, and after the encounter we want to hold on even more strongly to our own set of values. The important point is that the experience of interaction can be unsettling, in that our own value system becomes more porous, but that it also can be reaffirming once we realize that there is nothing else for us to think.

Second, the external dimension determines how we treat others. This is a distinct issue, and one that is shaped by the political context and relationships of power. Within the whole reflective exercise one's position in a society will matter a great deal; however, when it comes to the treatment of others it will matter even more, for one could be in a position to change the entitlements of others. Nonetheless, the inability to claim the absolute truth for one's values can point to general sensibilities that seem apposite on both personal and institutional level. Once we cannot immediately refute other practical outlooks by pointing to the absolute truth of our own, we need to engage with them. To engage means first to understand. It is appropriate—if an evaluative standpoint is not in an irresolvable conflict with our own—to make an effort to comprehend the reasons of that other perspective from within. Confidence based on identity is modest enough to realize that there could be more than one way of life worth living, and ought to make us more sensitive and responsive to the different ways in which the fundamental questions of how to live could be answered.

It is sometimes argued that being suspicious of mind-independent ethical truths leads to indifference towards one's own evaluative standpoint and towards others, so that it makes tolerance superfluous. Bernard Williams suggests that 'with indifference and skepticism ... the point will be reached at which nobody is interested enough in the disagreements for there to be anything to put up with, and toleration will not be necessary'.[132] The view assumes that to tolerate also means to think of something as unacceptable, misguided, or wrong, and that 'toleration ... is required only for the intolerable'.[133] This is not implausible, but it does overstate the consequences: doubts about the character of ethical truths need not lead to apathy in which it is impossible to disapprove of something. It does mean, however, that there will be more indifference at the borders of our practical perspective, more tolerance in its middle, and more caution at its core. To lose the trust in truth is not to stop caring, but it does call for more restraint. In addition, it can

[132] Bernard Williams, 'Toleration: An Impossible Virtue?' in David Heyd (ed), *Toleration: An Elusive Virtue* (Princeton University Press 1996) 25.

[133] ibid 18.

actually generate more engaged and empathic attitudes rather than indifference. The contingency and perspective dependence of values reveals—somewhat paradoxically—our common human predicament. The values we hold on to enable us to make sense of and cope with our existence. Awareness of this is one step from feeling empathy and understanding for others who struggle in a similar way.[134] The idea is that a reflective attitude makes it possible to see each other as participants in a common enterprise—even with significant differences in concrete moral attitudes—rather than as foes. The result should be a more careful and considerate approach to those that do not share all the details of our perspective.

This, of course, will not resolve the problem of disagreement. Any mind-dependent conception of value must presuppose a certain amount of agreement, and could thus dissolve in the face of disagreement. Recall that I criticized some emotivist arguments for presupposing agreement without providing a framework within which it could be overcome. In the conception I am proposing, agreement is also presupposed; it is not based on sheer optimism, for it is explained by the shared circumstances of life that lead to a significant overlap between different moral codes. But it also supplies the framework in which disagreement can be resolved and managed. A reflective attitude towards one's own practical perspective implies responsiveness to other perspectives and—given that they are not less true than ours—enables us to accommodate differences without deeply regretting each concession or seeing it as fundamentally wrong. Disagreement could be superficially resolved through authority, and this was possible with the robust mind-independent truth in hand. Upon reflection, we move from authority to persuasion, as we cannot always assert our own position. But the equilibrium achieved through persuasion is more stable and in the long run will prove to be a better foundation for resolving disagreements than authority. Lack of absolute confidence makes us responsive to the specific demands of others and pushes us to find solutions that are sensitive to their perspective; agreement reached on this basis is more likely to achieve a balance of perspectives and interests.

It is an illusion to think that a mere realization that absolute truths are beyond our reach will prevent radical conflicts of evaluative perspectives. However, if such a conflict comes, a reflective attitude may prepare us to ask the right questions. The reaction will depend on where the interaction occurs, and some conflicts will stop being seen as important while others will deserve our confidence and assertiveness. If another evaluative standpoint violates the core of our values, we need to ask: is it justified in this

[134] Samuel Scheffler, *Equality and Tradition: Questions of Value in Moral and Political Theory* (Oxford University Press 2010) 332 and ch 12.

particular case to force others into our own world view, to impose our own identity on them? The answer will depend on how inescapable this particular judgment is for our own practical identity, and how incompatible is the identity of the others. It is perhaps easy to retain confidence when we face the amoralist, but much less so when we face someone whose form of life could be a real option for us. We will then need to inquire whether we are practically able to live with the fact that we may be merely affirming our own views, and understand how that fits with our other ethical convictions. This will be the ultimate test of confidence.

5.5 CONCLUSION

In this chapter, I argued that there is a tension between two perspectives—theoretical and practical—that needs to be resolved. The need stems from the aspiration to have a unified world view in which there would be enough space for both perspectives. The theoretical perspective tells us that we have no reason to trust that the values within the practical perspective correspond to mind-independent facts. I relied on the argument from evolution to show this, but the gist is that any credible causal explanation of values raises doubts about their ability to evince mind-independent truths. To the extent that we do not want to have a schizoid attitude in which we at the same time believe and do not believe that our values are robustly true, we need to adjust either the practical or the theoretical perspective. I opted for adjusting the practical. This is not because—given the results that the theoretical perspective has delivered—any attempt to renounce it would be in vain. Rather, it is because the practical can survive this encounter and, in so doing, become stronger. The assumption that there are mind-independent normative truths undermines confidence in values; it makes values seem unreachable. This ought to be rejected on normative grounds. We have no reason to sustain the belief in robust mind-independence of value, for it makes us seem incompetent to answer the most crucial question of human existence: how should I live? Once this assumption is rejected, we enter a *process* of reaffirming and curtailing our practical *confidence* through *reflection*. It is in this process that values are revealed and shaped.

At the foundation of this approach are evaluative intuitions. We depart from these simple emotional reactions, and then try to understand and situate them within the framework of other attitudes, and further connect them to other experiences through which we make sense of life. On the one hand, evaluation demands introspection, coherence, and imagination, in order to regain confidence through greater self-awareness and with a reference to the most central evaluative attitudes forming our identity. On the other hand—when faced with different evaluative frameworks—it calls for caution, openness, flexibility, tolerance, and persuasion. These normative suggestions are not deduced from absolute moral truths; the only hope is that they would be intuitive enough within our contingent practical perspective.

The next chapter will reconstruct the ways in which ethical arguments in constitutional interpretation fit together, starting from this understanding of value. We will hence look at the ideas of confidence and reflection through the lens of constitutional practice. I shall argue that—taken together—ethical arguments actually used by courts can be adjusted to reflect the process in which moral judgments are and ought to be made. There is an appealing analogy between constitutional and ordinary ethics; however, this analogy needs to be appropriated to the institutional and social context in which the courts operate.

6

Constitutional Ethics, Confidence, and Reflection

6.1 INTRODUCTION

Divergent visions of moral value have surfaced throughout the analysis of ethical arguments. Let me briefly recapitulate. There are three relatively systematic patterns of value-based constitutional reasoning. The argument from constitutional identity relies on a specific conception of *identity* as a source of value. It departs from the identity of a community governed by a constitution to resolve moral problems, both in the abstract (as an identity that arises from having a constitution as such) and concrete sense (as an identity that grows out of the particular constitutional tradition). The argument from common sentiment appeals to the current *emotive intuitions* of a particular community. It refers to the moral feelings of the population as expressed directly or through institutions such as legislatures, juries, and courts. The argument from universal reason uses the language of *reason* and is not community-bound. In particular, the argument holds that normative reasons can be cognized by looking at how other jurisdictions have grappled with the same question.

These arguments are not completely adequate when taken in isolation from each other. First, they are profoundly intertwined: identity cannot be detached from the emotive moral intuitions of citizens, emotive intuitions should in some sense be reasonable, and a plausible conception of reason cannot replace but must build on existing emotive intuitions. Second, their normativity is unclear. Why does identity matter? How are the contingent emotive intuitions of a community normative? What is the authority of reflection? The last chapter provided a conception of value that accommodates these divergent sources and explains their interaction using the notions of confidence and reflection. In this conception, values are complex evaluative attitudes that arise in a process of simultaneous engagement with our emotive intuitions and detachment from our personal point of view through reflection in an attempt to understand and develop our own identity. There is an important similarity between this process and constitutional ethics. When used together in constitutional reasoning, the three apparently divergent ethical arguments come to be supported by a unified conception of value: constitutional ethics may emulate the ordinary moral point of view by departing from contingent emotive intuitions and developing them through reflection, in order to gain confidence and further advance the underlying constitutional identity.

This, however, cannot settle the issue. While such a conception of value is capable of connecting different ethical arguments into a plausible and coherent constitutional ethics, the analogy must be explored further. It needs to be situated in the institutional context of judicial reasoning. The purpose of this chapter is to flesh out in more detail how the theory developed in the last chapter applies to constitutional reasoning and to show how it relates to other normative concerns that we may have in this domain. Rather than bringing new insights, the goal is to connect the arguments that have already been put forward into a coherent framework and—in so doing—resolve some pending issues. The chapter proceeds in three steps. The first part translates and appropriates this theory of value to the context of constitutional reasoning; the purpose is to move the discussion from the abstract level of metaethics to the more concrete and specific level of constitutional ethics. The second part discusses the theory of constitutional ethics in the context of typical dilemmas of constitutional interpretation. The third part concludes.

6.2 FROM METAETHICS TO CONSTITUTIONAL ETHICS

We have seen that many constitutional arguments demonstrate uncertainty about the place of value in the universe. The last chapter provided the theoretical umbrella for thinking about these issues. But it is not sensible to apply ordinary ethical thinking straightforwardly to the constitutional context. The problem is that there is also a multitude of other normative concerns that apply to constitutional reasoning which do not arise in ordinary moral reasoning. A constitutional framework establishes a system of government and authority, and there is a difference in duties that we may impose on ourselves and duties that a public authority may impose on us. To be sure, all these concerns are first-order normative issues that are explained by the devised metaethical framework: they must ultimately be attributable to us as the bearers of evaluative attitudes. There is no escape from this. But these other normative concerns become important precisely by virtue of the metaethics that affords a constitutive role to contingent moral intuitions; the very metaethical framework that explains these intuitions also prioritizes them.[1]

[1] We should—for example—respect these contingent normative intuitions to the extent that they can be reflectively attributed to our identity as persons living in democratic polities at the beginning of the 21st century.

This is why *application* of the metaethical framework is primarily an issue of *translation*. Constitutional ethics needs to be developed by building an analogy with the ordinary moral point of view and not through its direct implementation. And if we look closely at the arguments used in constitutional reasoning we may notice that the translation is already under way. The identity that courts refer to is not personal but constitutional: it is supposed to be attributable to the constitutional community as a whole. Common sentiments are not the private feelings of a judge but the dominant sentiments of the public. Reflection presupposed by the argument from universal reason is directed at a better self-understanding and development of the deep moral commitments of the constitutional system.[2] Yet, the translation of metaethics to the constitutional domain is more complicated: there is the problem of the appropriate *perspective* and suitable *role of courts* in this process. Let me explain.

The first question is how to determine the relevant perspective. The moral point of view is a process of immersion in emotional reactions and reflection upon them in search of deep moral commitments. This provides the framework for making moral decisions, including a moral reading of the constitution. But when we move from the personal to the political domain—even if the general framework stays the same—the key question becomes *who* decides and in *whose name*. This will inevitably demand an adaptation of the framework as the relevant facts have changed: we now do not decide for ourselves but for the political community as a whole. This is one of the primary reasons why ethical arguments in constitutional reasoning differ from ordinary ethical arguments as they evolve in a specific institutional and legal context. It is implicit in the existing ethical arguments—and it also seems apposite as we move from individual to political or legal decision-making—that the self that the courts proceed from becomes the collective self of the community that bestows upon them the power to decide in their name. Identity, emotions, and reason thus all come back to the evaluative attitudes that can be properly attributed to the constitutional community in question.

But there is more than one perspective implicated and thus more than one moving target. There is the perspective of the individual, who is a member of a collective judicial institution, and who decides in the name of the community. None of these perspectives can be silenced in constitutional ethics, nor should they be. There is, however, strong reason for a judge—once she understands the contingency of her moral attitudes—to show a high level of respect for the opinions and identity of the people whose entitlements she

[2] Of course, we cannot exclude a more sceptical view that this is just masking the personal preferences of judges. However, the book has tried to show both *how* we may prevent this and *why* we may want to prevent this.

is empowered to change. Recall that reflection, among other things, entails working out what *we* stands for and what we stand *for*.[3] A judge performing this exercise ought to realize that she is delivering a decision *for the people*, and *what people stand for* is what actually matters: the constitutional community is thus the unit which determines the relevant perspective.

This default perspective is unstable and can only serve as a starting point. On the one hand, a judge will have a set of evaluative attitudes which form part of her identity. While the role of a judge in a society ought to affect the confidence with which she asserts her own personal views, this does not mean that she can renounce them completely. Her identity, however, ought to incorporate the identity of being a judge which presupposes certain virtues that should make her cautious in deciding against public opinion. Furthermore, the contingency of value should remind her that she is justified in doing so only when public emotions are insufficiently reflective and diverge from the profound moral values embedded in constitutional identity.

On the other hand, there need not be an easily discernible core of evaluative attitudes in modern political communities, or—more precisely—it is more difficult to find such attitudes in controversial constitutional cases. There is often a multitude of competing identities and opinions and it would be naïve to presuppose a unified community of value as a justificatory foundation for moral decisions; such an assumption about a coherent and cohesive set of values would not even be warranted in the case of a single individual, let alone a complex constitutional community.[4] Courts must be aware of the fact that there is more than one site at which the converging evaluative attitudes are formed. The metaethical theory developed in the last chapter elucidates the perspective of the individual as she makes ethical choices and assumes that some of these choices are made in the context of overlapping common attitudes that arise on different levels: local, national, supranational, or global. Courts need to manage these various sites of normativity in a way that both finds common ground between them and corrects their excessive confidence.

The second question identified above pertains to the appropriate role of courts in this process. The bottom line is that constitutional ethics must derive its confidence from the deep evaluative commitments of the constitutional community as a whole and that courts ought to correct this confidence through increased reflection. Instead of imposing their own evaluative attitudes, the courts need to be the guardians of reflectiveness. We have thus come to the issue of democracy and the legitimacy of judicial review

[3] See ch 5.

[4] Bernard Williams, *Moral Luck: Philosophical Papers, 1973–1980* (Cambridge University Press 1981) 72–73.

through a detour that enables us to explain why the courts ought to respect public opinion under the circumstances of discretion.[5] Democratic concerns feed into the theory of constitutional ethics on at least three levels: first, respect for the democratic will follows from the realization that there are no universal and timeless answers, which undercuts the confidence of the courts in claiming the truth for their own views; second, much of our contingent intuitions about the way in which moral problems ought to be resolved in modern political communities point to democratic representation as the most appropriate institutional venue; third, democratic representation better echoes common intuitions and identity, while it might secure even more reflection than judicial review.[6]

The theory hence accommodates and vindicates democratic sensibilities but simultaneously accounts for the intuition that the majority ought not to prevail all the time. The democratic process can fail to be representative and reflective. We should not forget that many moral changes that we are proud of are a consequence of judicial oversight of common sentiments, and that they included reflection upon our own deep commitments. The theory of constitutional ethics grants the courts a critical edge over communal sentiments in two principal ways: by explaining the authority of reflection, and by differentiating between the normativity of superficial emotive reactions and inescapable moral attitudes that are constitutive of identity. It gives the courts reason to defer to more representative branches of government—or perhaps foster their reflectiveness through carefully crafted decisions—but also to step in if the process is not reflective enough or suffers from an unwarranted confidence which makes one perspective silence the others.[7]

[5] But instead of arguing from moral disagreement to democracy, which—as we have seen—makes the argument open to the very same disagreement challenge and does not explain why agreement matters, we now have an answer to both of these puzzles. See the earlier discussion of Jeremy Waldron, 'The Core of the Case against Judicial Review' (2006) 115 Yale Law Journal 1346 and Richard Posner, 'Foreword: A Political Court' (2005) 119 Harvard Law Review 32.

[6] This is an empirical question that we need not resolve here. Recall that the book is not asking should there be written constitutions, should we have judicial review, or should judges generally prefer justified authority to moral value. It is inevitable that under the current system some choices will need to be made by judges instead of the political process. This is not to say that we should prefer judicial review; in fact, we would have reasons to prefer the political process capable of both reflecting common moral attitudes and reflection upon them. Or perhaps a process that includes a weak form of judicial review. A more general institutional theory could be based on this metaethics, but the focus of the book is narrower: it attempts to make sense of judicial ethical arguments under currently dominant systems of judicial review.

[7] In its outcomes, this is intentionally reminiscent of Ely's famous democratic theory of judicial review, although the underlying foundation is different. See John Hart Ely, *Democracy and Distrust: A Theory of Judicial Review* (Harvard University Press 1980).

6.2.1 *Identity*

With this scheme in mind we can proceed to see how constitutional ethics so understood could be applied. Values are complex evaluative attitudes pertaining to a set of similar moral problems. They include particular moral judgments and the principles that explain them, and arise in a dynamic and continuous process of immersion into and reflection upon our contingent attitudes. Values are in other words partly *constructed* in this process. The process is best understood as an everlasting quest for *self-understanding* by a constitutional and political community. At its centre is the evolving *identity* reaffirmed by reflection upon our contingent attitudes. Identity thus denotes the deepest evaluative commitments that persist through reflection.

Constitutional identity—akin to personal identity in everyday ethical decisions—plays a crucial role in constitutional ethics. It is, however, important to underline that there is nothing valuable about identity as such; rather, the normative significance of identity arises from the inescapability of occupying an evaluative standpoint with some core ethical commitments in order to make *any* normative judgment. This affects how we ought to treat it: we cannot fully overcome it but we ought not to assert it in an overly confident manner. Identity—on this understanding—becomes different from mere tradition or an unreflective celebration of national specificities.[8] It is an ever-changing and dynamic category, a process rather than an endpoint. It is a source of confidence but is also consistently challenged by critical reflection through which we rethink and reimagine it.

The argument from constitutional identity is on the borderline between legal-proper and ethical-legal arguments, and only its fluid character and the idea that it will lead to apposite moral answers put it in the latter group.[9] It derives its normative force from its proximity to the constitution and constitutional practices, to the extent that they can be understood as the embodiment of the deepest evaluative commitments of a community. As other

[8] For a helpful distinction along these lines see Daniel Augenstein, 'The Contested Polity: Europe's Constitutional Identity between Religious and Secular Values' [2009/3] University of Edinburgh School of Law Working Paper Series, 1–2.

[9] It has been outside the scope of this book to discuss the relative importance of ethical arguments over more traditional legal arguments such as textual or doctrinal; on the one hand, it would have taken us too far afield in answering whether there is a duty to obey the law in general, and on the other, ethical arguments appear in a niche of cases in which ethical concepts from the constitution are interpreted under the circumstances of discretion. But the distinction between legal and ethical arguments—I also insisted—is not clear-cut in the sense that ethical arguments gain legal force over time and become legally accepted ways in which ethical concerns enter judicial reasoning. This means that their acceptability will (partly) depend on the general normative force of the law itself. In whichever way we think of grounds of legal duties—in terms of stability, ability of law to coordinate human behaviour, accumulated wisdom of previous generations, or simply in terms of the contingent belief of people that law creates genuine moral duties—we cannot neglect that constitutions carry certain normative force as long as they respect our central normative concerns and stay within the boundaries of our wider evaluative frameworks.

ethical arguments, it can be traced back to the moral attitudes of the people living under the constitution, but in this case such attitudes emerge in virtue of having a constitution. This gives it an additional weight for—arguably—constitutions can often be understood as being expressive of settled and authentic values in contrast to more fluctuating common sentiments.[10]

The content of constitutional identity can, however, be thin under modern circumstances. First, the ability to discern some moral answers from constitutional practice as a whole—but not from any authoritative decision in particular—will depend on the richness of ethical, legal, and political processes that the system has gone through during its evolution. It will give more substantial answers when there are layers of meaning that have been ascribed to constitutional practices through an organic development of constitutional community (as is the case in mature constitutional systems such as the US), but also when new constitutional regimes establish themselves in an attempt to transform or simply give effect to existing deep evaluative commitments (as is the case in South Africa). In most systems there is an idea about the general principles that the constitutional framework embodies; however, it can take a great deal of time for these rudimentary normative tendencies to develop and become accepted as a part of the identity of the constitutional community.

Second, individual and cultural differences are rife in modern political communities, and constitutional identity is often different from more substantial and concrete identities, and from the world views they entail. We have seen that this identity is not tangible and is subject to persistent reimagination and disagreement over its content.[11] The most controversial issues in constitutional adjudication arise precisely in virtue of disputed interpretations of the constitutional authority of the state, and because of divergent visions of identity embedded in the constitution.

It is for this reason that the theories discussed in Chapter 2 fail to legitimize judicial review with reference to constitutional identity.[12] They wish to kill two birds with one stone: constitutional identity ought to tie the moral judgment of the court to the constitution and reduce discretion at the same time. While they fail to deliver this—both because deep moral attitudes cannot be far from the democratic will of the citizens and because they are often too thin to render concrete results—their general intuition is right: if there are evaluative attitudes that can be properly ascribed to the identity of the constitutional community as a whole they should present the focal point of

[10] This of course will not always be the case, but part of the very notion of identity is that it will be contested and developed over time. For a 'disharmonic' conception of constitutional identity see Gary J Jacobsohn, *Constitutional Identity* (Harvard University Press 2010).

[11] See ibid ch 6.

[12] See the discussion of Bobbitt's and Waluchow's work in ch 2.

judicial moral inquiry. As I have argued, this is because attitudes forming the constitutional identity are a subset of our general moral attitudes that enable us to conduct our lives together in modern political communities, and because there is nothing that transcends these practices that we could rely on instead.

Although constitutional identity may not be thick enough to, by itself, legitimize robust judicial review of legislation by legally reducing judicial discretion, it is not completely without bite. Constitutional identity derives its force from general reasons to have a constitution and specific reasons to have a particular constitution; in both instances reasons are understood as shared evaluative attitudes that people have towards the legal framework that establishes the system of government and rights in the constitution. It would of course be an illusion to think that all citizens at all times share the evaluative commitments that arise in the inherently elite-driven processes of constitution-making and constitutional interpretation; however, constitutions are typically part of the common evaluative experience of a political community and express the terms in which it establishes itself *qua* political community.[13] It is then not implausible to assume that the continuous acceptance of this constitutional framework establishes two tendencies that carry normative weight and that constitutional ethics needs to account for.

The first is the general strand of constitutional identity, which assumes that the constitution establishes a safeguard for the protection of minorities and demands an additional level of reflective scrutiny over state action. We can also understand this requirement in terms of the dialectic between confidence and reflection: it places a burden on constitutional authority to reflect on its moral judgment and take the perspective of minorities into account as much as possible. As we have seen, this general demand can support—together with other arguments—an array of specific judgments: from the establishment of judicial review of legislation (US), to banning the display of crucifixes in classrooms (Germany), and allowing gay marriage (South Africa).[14] More importantly, it provides an additional reason to balance different points of view and serves as a reminder that we commonly commit to securing the conditions for the flourishing of a plurality of perspectives, even against our initial emotional reactions. This general constitutional identity is embedded in the very notion of having a constitution; it is a contingent—but

[13] As Walker puts it, constitutions are 'joined by a claim collective *self-authorisation*'. Neil Walker, 'Taking Constitutionalism Beyond the State' (2008) 56 Political Studies 519, 530. As such they 'may provide a resilient but flexible structure for political-ethical debate, an anchor for a continuing conversation about the meaning of political community that operates in a Janus-faced manner to strengthen that political community'. See ibid 532.

[14] See the discussion of constitutional identity in ch 2.

nearly universal—feature of modern political systems and a specific way in which *our* political communities resolve the problem of political authority.

The second strand is the particular constitutional identity that pertains to the values arising in the constitutional practice of one constitutional system that may not be shared by other systems. This strand of identity is capable of delivering more substantive results as it contains more precise evaluative commitments: for example, it shows that the understanding of equality is formal in the United States and substantive in South Africa, or that the specific conception of dignity plays a prominent role in Germany. A constitutional ethics that is divorced from the search for universal, mind-independent, and timeless moral truths relieves these types of arguments from a constant struggle to demonstrate their normative import. If the source of moral obligations are non-contingent moral truths then we cannot explain different traditions as normative: there is a sense that we are inferring normative conclusions from descriptive premises, and that—given the variety of identities even among the liberal democratic constitutional systems—we are somehow desperately off-track in our moral judgments. If political morality is premised upon the simple model of universal values applied to specific facts, we can justify the variety of evaluative commitments arising from different constitutional identities only as a consequence of the application of values to these facts and not—much more plausibly—as simply different but nonetheless genuinely normative requirements.

Such metaethics allows us to see that a constitutional system may be justified—upon reflection and, importantly, from its own practical point of view—in retaining these specific values even in spite of consensus in the world. For example, we have seen that the particular identity of the US constitutional system has sometimes been upheld despite global trends, while South African constitutional identity has set these global standards as aspirational. In the model of constitutional ethics based on confidence and reflection, there need not be anything inherently wrong with these different choices. They must only be—again *on reflection*—true *of* constitutional community. Analogously, this model does not prevent us from criticizing such choices from our own practical perspective; nothing precludes us from persuading others that there are different solutions that better conform to their needs, interests, and values.[15] Finally, while the attitudes forming identity are central, they are not static; as I have argued, they evolve and acquire further content—for example—through interaction with other systems.

[15] To underline, this conclusion will follow from a specific practical point of view. Our judgment about other systems will—conversely—follow from our point of view, so it means that even if we accept that there is divergence we can criticize it from our own framework of values.

Most constitutional dilemmas cannot, however, be resolved by a straightforward inference from constitutional identity.[16] A theory that aims to make sense of ethical choices under the circumstances of legal indeterminacy should be careful not to recreate the problem by suggesting a similarly indeterminate solution. For example, if constitutional identity includes a notion of substantive equality, this does not tell us if gay marriages are permitted or required, and it does not say much about the kinds of affirmative action measures policy-makers can employ; it provides only tendencies and sensibilities that ought to be incorporated in thinking about these issues which at times may not be specific enough. This does not mean that weighing different ethical concerns can be presented in a precise formula,[17] but it is to say that there are other ethical arguments that bear on the explication of ethical concepts and need to figure in a sound conception of constitutional ethics.

6.2.2 *Sentiment*

To gain additional content constitutional ethics must turn to less deep but more concrete emotive intuitions of the members of the constitutional community present in the argument from common sentiment. It may seem that the book supports an ambivalent position towards this argument. While I have rejected the idea that our emotive attitudes can be the exclusive basis of constitutional ethics, I have also argued that there is nothing beyond such responses taken together that can provide its metaphysical foundation. This is not yet another incarnation of a 'schizoid attitude': seeing the world in both causal and normative terms while being unable to resolve the tension. Instead, I have maintained that the role of common sentiments ought to be subtler. They are essential, but corrigible through reflection.

Contingent moral agreement matters to the extent to which it is reflective. The argument from common sentiment often assumes the inability to reason about values;[18] however, while it is true that there will be a point where we will have to say that there is nothing more to go by except our moral intuitions, this point will come much later than it is envisaged by the argument from common sentiment. It will not necessarily occur in the moment we realize that there is an agreement in the community. Through reflection

[16] As Gary Jacobsohn aptly observes, 'constitutional identity will be fashioned—and refashioned—through the struggle *over* constitutional identity'. Jacobsohn, *Constitutional Identity* (n 10) 135.

[17] This is for example the main inadequacy of Alexy's balancing formula. See eg Robert Alexy, *A Theory of Constitutional Rights* (Oxford University Press 2002).

[18] See eg the discussion of Scalia's opinion in *Lawrence v Texas* 539 US 558 (2003), Marshall's in *Furman v Georgia* 408 US 238 (1972), Powell's in *McCleskey v Kemp* 481 US 279 (1987), La Forest's opinion in *United States v Allard* [1987] 1 SCR 564, Swiss Court's in *Müller v Switzerland* (10737/84) [1988] ECHR 5 (24 May 1988), all in ch 3.

we have the means to inquire about the depth and quality of such agreement even if there is nothing outside of our psychology to tell us where things might have gone wrong. The argument from common sentiment attempts to couch its normativity in the vocabulary of *objectivity*,[19] while it can only be properly understood in terms of *inescapability*. The difference is in the way we treat our converging emotive reactions: the latter understanding demands that we accept them but with a dose of scepticism, and with a critical and open mind.

It is important to notice many connections between the argument from common sentiment and constitutional identity. Common sentiments will supply constitutional identity with much of its content. In an attempt to establish what people truly think and want, one cannot neglect their opinions and wishes. It is a false assumption that identity can give courts a fully detached Archimedean point from which they can assess moral opinions of the day, for these opinions must feed into the conception of identity. But identity in turn demands a certain depth of opinions before they gain normative force.

An example of how this interaction could be managed is the Canadian 'shocks the conscience' doctrine discussed in Chapter 3. Recall that through this doctrine the court tied its moral judgment to the prevailing emotive reaction of Canadians. The court did so in order to understand the concept of 'fundamental justice' from the constitution and—in light of this concept—evaluate penal practices of another country and allow or deny extradition. But the justices did not fully surrender their judgment to the majority's emotive reactions. They accepted the fact that moral opinions are at the bottom a matter of emotional intuitions that cannot be fully explained, systematized, and rationalized. However—moving away from the pure version of the argument from common sentiment in the early case law—they focused on intuitions that are strong, immutable, irreversible, deep, and central: they described giving up on these intuitions as 'unimaginable' and 'inconceivable'.[20] This is not to say, in the Kantian spirit, that these emotive moral reactions suffer from a contradiction that makes them inconceivable; rather, they are unimaginable for Canadians at a given point in time.

The link between common sentiments and identity is thus fundamental: there is no identity without common sentiments but not all sentiments are important enough to survive reflection. The last chapter has shown that identity involves the dimensions of depth and integrity, which can help us decide which values are more authentic and truthful to the way we are

[19] See the discussion in ch 3.

[20] See the discussion of *Kindler v Canada (Minister of Justice)* [1991] 2 SCR 779 and *United States v Burns* [2001] 1 SCR 283 in ch 3.

or—even more importantly—the way we want to be. For example, Chapter 3 has discussed some trends in American constitutional jurisprudence that neglect this and instead search for unconstrained sentiments,[21] relieve them from the burden of reasoning,[22] or even celebrate their illogical character.[23] They appear to understand the contingent foundations of moral judgments, but in fact they fail to see that our practical confidence cannot be unrestricted. The courts have a role in managing practical confidence and correcting it for a lack of reflection and authenticity.

There is more than one way in which this can be done but it is important that—in an effort to correct the excessive confidence of common sentiments—the courts should not simply assert confidence in their own sentiments. For instance, the argument from common sentiment could be acceptable to the extent that the process behind it *reflects* common sentiments and at the same time *reflects upon* them. By taking this approach, the courts could focus on the quality of the process from which they learn about common sentiments instead of trying to conduct it themselves. This may transform the argument in practice: the question would not then be which institution or public opinion poll better represents emotive intuitions, but which one does it without making the intuitions overly confident. The choice whether to defer to legislatures, juries, or referendums can thus also be based on the assessment of the ability of these processes to induce reflection, and not only of their capacity to accurately represent common sentiments.

This may seem as a complete renouncement of common sentiments as an acceptable basis of ethical arguments. But this is not so. Common sentiments are the essential ingredient of constitutional ethics even if they are transformed in this way. Let me explain. It is often the case that the understanding of ethical concepts from the constitution—such as equality and dignity—evolves over time. The typical question in this context is when it is appropriate for courts to give effect to moral changes that amend previously established doctrines.[24] In the approach taken here we ought to ask whether these new sentiments can be ascribed to the community as a whole and—if so—whether they are a consequence of a thoughtful process that did not succumb to initial and pre-reflective emotive reactions without thinking them through in an open and flexible process. To the extent that sentiments

[21] See the discussion of Stevens' opinion in *Spaziano v Florida* 468 US 447 (1984) in ch 3.

[22] See the discussion of Marshall's opinion in *Furman v Georgia* (n 18) in ch 3.

[23] See the discussion of Scalia's opinion in *Lawrence v Texas* (n 18) in ch 3.

[24] See eg Joseph Raz, 'On the Authority and Interpretation of Constitutions: Some Preliminaries' in *Between Authority and Interpretation: On the Theory of Law and Practical Reason* (Oxford University Press 2009).

have these qualities we should prefer the new settlement based on the novel understanding of these concepts.

There will of course be a need for a fine balance between the rigidity of constitutional amendment procedure (that ought to guarantee the fundamental character of the moral change) and the legitimate scope of judicial freedom to decide such issues. Much will also depend on the difference between, on the one hand, the interpretive leeway left by elusive constitutional concepts and, on the other, moral judgments that transgress the boundaries of these concepts. Notice, however, the inescapability of sentiments: they are both the point of departure and the ultimate result of the exercise. When we find the new equilibrium, it will be constituted by common sentiments.[25]

Not only are common sentiments central to an understanding of our own constitutional ethics, the realization that there is nothing beyond these contingent sentiments also affects the way we approach other moral equilibriums. The example is the margin of appreciation doctrine of the European Court of Human Rights (ECtHR). Recall that this doctrine roughly means that under the circumstances of discretion the ECtHR will not interfere with national approaches to some moral problem in the case there is no emerging consensus in Europe on the same issue. The court has often been criticized for taking the relativist approach: if there are right moral answers independent of our sentiments, it is probably a mistake to defer to different sites at which consensuses are formed.[26] As we have seen, the issue cannot be understood as merely institutional for even institutional choice must follow from a conception of what is better or worse. But if we understand the problem in terms of confidence and reflection, we can see why the margin of appreciation and deference to parochial sentiments could be justified.

This approach explains why the convergence in moral feelings is normatively important. If there is for example no agreement that can be ascribed to the identity arising under the framework of the European Convention,

[25] This of course intentionally alludes to John Rawls' work. Much of contemporary moral theory is inspired by his work, this book included. But—as I hope has become obvious—there are clear metaethical differences that I do not suppose, while he eventually does: on my account there is no such thing as an 'unreasonable' ethical outlook in a robust sense and thus I follow a different path of trying to get to the core of our own outlook through identity to understand this 'unreasonableness'. See in particular his *Political Liberalism* (Columbia University Press 1993). Even though he can be credited for initiating many of the discussions which I touch upon in the book, Rawls tries to steer away from metaethics with his political conception of objectivity (see John Rawls, 'Kantian Constructivism in Moral Theory' in Samuel Richard Freeman (ed), *Collected Papers* (Harvard University Press 1999)), while I believe that metaethics is indispensable. Finally, his inspiration is Kantian and mine Humean. However, the conclusions I reach are in many ways reminiscent of his, and I acknowledge his work as an immense source of inspiration.

[26] George Letsas, 'Two Concepts of the Margin of Appreciation' (2006) 26 Oxford Journal of Legal Studies 705. However, we could for example have reason to respect the autonomy of those that formed moral agreement hence it could be a mistake to defer to national compacts even on the realist approach.

then the confidence of the court to impose moral answers ought to be undermined. If there is a core of values that cannot be renounced without the Convention ceasing to be what it is, then the court ought to interfere. Furthermore, the respect granted to moral agreements depends on their quality: on the one hand, if national moral agreements are not reflective enough this should make the court more willing to step in; on the other, if the consensus arising in Europe is not reflective and sensitive to different perspectives then it ought to be treated with less esteem.

The foundational role of moral sentiments perhaps makes constitutional ethics less stable or predictable, but is able to account for some of the intuitions about the restricted role of courts under the circumstances of a plurality of moral frameworks without at the same time completely abandoning judicial oversight. It does so by explaining why local specificities matter, and also why they may be inadequate. For example, we sometimes feel that the court paid more respect to some national measure than it should have done: but this feeling arises from the view that the court failed to see important parts of European moral identity—and our commitments that arise from it—and not from the fact that it failed to grasp universal moral answers. It thus does not leave the courts without leverage to assess national measures, but makes them aware of the underpinnings of this leverage and thus more careful about its use. They must be confident; nonetheless their confidence can only come through reflection.

6.2.3 Reason

Pursuing the analogy between ordinary and constitutional ethics, we may understand the arguments from constitutional identity and common sentiment as parts of *constitutional confidence*. Although I have reinterpreted both of these arguments to include the idea of reflectiveness, they are always a more or less accurate representation of the existing commitments of the constitutional community. However—as the last chapter showed—we can only achieve practical confidence through relentless reflection. This provides a counterbalance to the possible undue confidence of judgments stemming from identity and prevailing moral intuitions. The notion of constitutional ethics that I defend neither embraces identity for its own sake nor celebrates common sentiments as such: their force arises from their unavoidability and not from their intrinsic worth. We thus ought to be critical of both of these sources of evaluative intuitions while at the same time we have nothing but these intuitions to provide us with the necessary critical perspective. The conception of *constitutional reason* is hence limited but essential: reflection is repairing the ship of constitutional ethics while at sea, but the ship must constantly be repaired to be able to sail.

The goal of reflection is to understand the ethos of a constitutional community and settle on a judgment in the particular case that would be apposite from the perspective of such an ethos. This is anything but an easy task. The identity of a community often entails a struggle between different self-interpretations, sometimes even to the extent that the struggle itself becomes a part of the identity.[27] As Walker puts it, constitutionalism could be conceived of as 'an ethical discourse under a constant process of re-imagining and reconstruction'.[28] It is then better to think of identity as a set of self-defining but evolving moral attitudes, which are not simply discovered in the process of reflection and contestation but also arise from it. The goal of reflection is greater self-awareness but also the imaginative development of the (collective and political) self.[29]

I have argued that one of the best ways to achieve this is to engage with other constitutional systems. Constitutionalism aims to restrain the exercise of public authority by legal means: this central idea is interpreted in uncountable different ways but many of the questions the courts need to answer are similar. While this does not entail that there are right answers to these questions, a comparison can be useful. The analogy with individual ethical judgments can be pursued here as well. Although we may have different goals, hopes, and dreams, we eventually face the same questions. Through engagement we can realize which of our commitments are more central and which we can sacrifice. We can for example see that because of a mere habit we accepted things we do not really want, or that some of our goals do not fit our moral outlook anymore.

It is not all that different with constitutional systems. Through a careful comparison it is possible to grasp the range of available options and choose the one that is truer to the central commitments of the constitutional system. I expressed this intuition in the vocabulary of virtues of reflective judgment: information, flexibility, coherence, imagination, maturity, openness, sensibility, and clarity. In Chapter 4 I also detailed the ability of the use of foreign law to foster each of these virtues. There is no need to repeat these arguments here: it is clear from the discussion why such reflective virtues are compatible with arguments from common sentiment and constitutional identity. The problem is that this approach will not enable us to see true reasons, but only reasons that are true of us. We fall short of reaching objective

[27] See eg the discussion on two different limbs of Israeli constitutional identity—'Jewish' and 'democratic' in ch 4. See also Jacobsohn, *Constitutional Identity* (n 10) ch 6 and Ran Hirschl, *Comparative Matters: The Renaissance of Comparative Constitutional Law* (Oxford University Press 2014) ch 1.

[28] Walker, 'Taking Constitutionalism Beyond the State' (n 13) 525.

[29] See more on the analogy between individual and collective identity and on the consequences on moral reflection in Jürgen Habermas, *Between Facts and Norms: Contributions to a Discourse Theory of Law and Democracy* (MIT Press 1996) 94–99.

mind-independent values and fall back on contingent social facts about our (often parochial) moral attitudes. The last chapter went to great lengths to show that this is inevitable and that we ought not to be concerned about it: all we can do in the end is work out how we want to live together.

In the course of answering this question, judicial practice often recognizes this interconnectedness of arguments from sentiment, identity, and reason. Let me illustrate this with an example. Acknowledging the meta-ethical tensions behind his moral reading of the constitution, Justice Sachs in *Makwanyane* dedicates a whole part of his opinion to the question of 'the source of values'.[30] As he explains, 'the function given to this court by the Constitution is to articulate the fundamental sense of justice and right shared by the whole nation as expressed in the text of the Constitution'.[31] In Sachs's view, the task of the constitutional court is to pronounce the moral sensibilities of the entire community as articulated in the constitution. The starting point for interpretation is thus constitutional identity and the assumption that the constitution does express the fundamental moral commitments of the population: the idea is that 'the Constitution speaks for the whole society'.[32] But this is not enough, for the text is often not clear and the consequences of constitutional values are underdetermined.

On the one hand, an important dimension of the process of interpretation includes a keen appreciation for 'traditions, beliefs and values of all sectors of South African society'[33] and for the 'evolution of core values in all sections of the community'.[34] This part of the inquiry connects constitutional ethics to deeper layers of common evaluative experience; it extends the search for value from the particular strand of constitutional ethics to common sentiments. For example, clues and values are to be found in 'traditional African jurisprudence'.[35] On the other hand, a counterbalance to this is the general strand of constitutional identity, because 'one of the functions of the Constitution is to protect unpopular minorities from abuse'.[36] This is why the court does not 'automatically invoke each and every aspect of traditional law as a source of values'.[37] Furthermore, the general component of constitutional identity paves the way for reflection, as the court rejects 'spontaneous and irrational form[s] of crowd behaviour',[38] searches instead for 'the rational and humane adjudicatory approach',[39] and—in particular—pursues 'openness, accommodation and tolerance' in 'free discourse and rational debate'.[40] Justice Sachs' outline of the sources of evaluative judgment nicely illustrates how the particular limb of constitutional identity finds additional foothold in societal traditions and common sentiments, and how the general

30 *S v Makwanyane and Another* 1995 (3) SA 391 paras 358–91 (Sachs). 31 ibid para 362.
32 ibid. 33 ibid para 361. 34 ibid para 373. 35 ibid. 36 ibid para 369.
37 ibid para 383. 38 ibid para 381. 39 ibid para 382. 40 ibid para 391.

limb of constitutional identity demands further reflection upon this foundation. Together they feed back into a conception of constitutional identity that is then both *reasonable* and *ours*.

The book has attempted to reveal the deeper philosophical foundations of this approach, and to demonstrate why it would make sense as an answer to the question about the source of value. But there are additional complications to this picture in the context of public authority and I must be careful not to stretch the analogy beyond its limits. We must investigate what reflection ought to entail when the unity of the reflective subject dissipates in the political context and the court still must decide in the name of all. This by no means implies that the overall approach can be different: the nature of normative judgment is the same regardless of the context. There are, however, some concerns that might play out differently when a judge is deciding how *we* ought to live in contrast to when a judge is deciding how *she* ought to live.

I have explained before why the default perspective of constitutional ethics ought to be the perspective of the constitutional community as a whole. Perhaps the best way to think about the problem of the appropriate perspective is to understand constitutional decision-making as a point of intersection of a multitude of evaluative frameworks. The concentration of public authority at the constitutional level makes a constitutional community's perspective relevant: because constitutional systems remain the central bearers of authority—and conversely, because we tend to think that any accumulation of public authority is to be justified in constitutional terms—interactions between different evaluative frameworks are particularly salient in constitutional interpretation.[41] Constitutional interpretation is therefore a point of introspection where these frameworks come to meet and where they need to be accommodated. Constitutional identity becomes important in this process because it consists of a set of deep evaluative commitments that define our collective thinking about justified political authority and about ways to resolve conflicts that arise in the course of exercising such authority. But because normativity is generated on different levels—individual, cultural, national, transnational, and international—the friction along their borderlines is inevitable.

I should not even pretend that an account of constitutional ethics could solve all of these issues. There is no blueprint for easy constitutional

[41] This claim holds partly as a matter of definition of constitutionalism: if supra-national legal constructs such as the EU are considered constitutional, this vocabulary expresses the fact that they become the main locus of power and authority and we thus want to subject them to at least some of the principles that justify such authority on the domestic level. On taking constitutional ideas beyond the frame of the nation-state see: Neil Walker, 'The Idea of Constitutional Pluralism' 65 Modern Law Review 317 and Mattias Kumm, 'The Cosmopolitan Turn in Constitutionalism: On the Relationship between Constitutionalism in and beyond the State' in Jeffrey L Dunoff and Joel P Trachtman (eds), *Ruling the World? Constitutionalism, International Law, and Global Governance* (Cambridge University Press 2009).

solutions. The theory instead aims to illuminate the complex relationship between divergent sources of value in constitutional interpretation, provide the vocabulary to express different concerns that ought to bear on these problems, and—finally—organize some of the normative intuitions pertaining to complicated constitutional problems. Moreover, we must also remember that the alternative is doubtful without having any obvious advantages: assuming mind-independent moral values will not make these problems go away; if anything, it makes them seem extraordinary. Having in mind these caveats, let us see how the modest idea of reason together with the arguments from identity and sentiment copes with quintessential constitutional dilemmas.

6.3 CONSTITUTIONAL ETHICS AND CONSTITUTIONAL DILEMMAS

It is useful to distinguish between two different dimensions of the problem of changing or divergent moral attitudes: we can tentatively call them *diachronic* and *synchronic*. The first concerns the evolution of moral attitudes in a community and their proper effect on constitutional interpretation; the second concerns the horizontal tensions that exist at a certain point in time internally (within the constitutional system) and externally (between constitutional systems). If the theory of ethical arguments based on constitutional confidence and reflection pertains to situations in which moral concepts are applied, it needs to tell us something more about these problems. While on the level of *ethics* of personal choices we may assume the unity of the self that reflects—and hence downplay the importance of the evolution of attitudes over time or internal moral conflicts and dilemmas—this problem is considered to be the principal problem of *political philosophy*.[42] We can nonetheless approach this issue from the viewpoint of ethics and extend the analogy to some fruitful conclusions.

6.3.1 *Diachronic changes*

Let us start from the less challenging problem: *diachronic* differences in moral attitudes. This problem could be understood in terms of a choice between two different sources of legitimacy. On the one hand, there is the legal form

[42] This is for example the motivating concern behind Rawls, *Political Liberalism* (n 25). As I explained in the Introduction, I do not make the distinction between ethics and morality or ethics and political morality as many authors—sometimes for quite different reasons—do. See eg Bernard Williams, *Ethics and the Limits of Philosophy* (2nd edn, Routledge 2006) ch 10, and Habermas, *Between Facts and Norms: Contributions to a Discourse Theory of Law and Democracy* (n 29) 94–99. Deciding how to live—individually or collectively—is the same question as far as the conception of value is concerned. Morality in a pejorative sense is also of no help for this project either: I did not aim to differentiate between right or wrong 'moralities'.

of legitimation according to which the constitution derives its authority from its law-maker, and on the other there is the popular or democratic form of legitimation encapsulated in the idea that people should govern themselves. There are many interconnections between these two sources and they often work together: the central idea of modern constitutionalism is that the will of the people ought to stay within the boundaries of law, but also that the law ought to reflect the will of the people.[43] Clashes between these two sources of legitimation cause some perplexing paradoxes of constitutional theory: for example, the possibility of an unconstitutional amendment to the constitution, or the ability of people to limit and retain their sovereignty at the same time.[44] In the domain of constitutional adjudication this tension is most visible when there is a new moral equilibrium that contradicts the attitudes that were dominant at the time of constitution-making. For example: how can the death penalty be unconstitutional if it was constitutional when the constitution was adopted? It seems that options are exclusionary: we either comply with the authority of the constitution-maker or defer to contemporary opinions.

There are roughly two ways to deal with this problem. One is to suppose that there is an overarching common-denominator source of legitimacy that allows us to compare these options: for instance, we could situate the source of constitutional legitimacy in the will of the people, so if the will has changed then we ought to follow it even against the constitution that is (or should be) a mere expression of this will.[45] The other is to assume that the constitution itself commands that new moral attitudes ought to affect its interpretation: for example, the constitution may entrench an abstract notion of equality and leave it to future generations to specify the concrete details of its application.[46]

The problem is that if we take the first approach then any converging attitude will justify constitutional change, while the very idea behind a

[43] Constitutional theory has struggled with this question of the relationship between collective agency and autonomy at least since Rousseau. See Jean-Jacques Rousseau, *The Social Contract and Other Later Political Writings* (Victor Gourevitch (ed), Cambridge University Press 1997).

[44] For an exploration of these themes see Martin Loughlin and Neil Walker, *The Paradox of Constitutionalism: Constituent Power and Constitutional Form* (Oxford University Press 2007).

[45] Of course, this entails that for the will to be expressed it first has to be organized, which is a problem that may lead to some unfortunate theoretical solutions. For a paradigmatic example see Schmitt's concept of the political that—in his view—must predate the state and be based on a 'friend-enemy' distinction. According to Schmitt: '[t]he concept of the state presupposes the concept of the political', while '[t]he specific political distinction to which political actions and motives can be reduced is that between friend and enemy'. Carl Schmitt, *The Concept of the Political* (George Schwab (tr), expanded edn, University of Chicago Press 2007) 19 and 26.

[46] See eg Ronald Dworkin, *Freedom's Law: The Moral Reading of the American Constitution* (Harvard University Press 1996).

constitution is that it is a more stable framework that does not give way to any popular mood or fashion; the concept of the constitution cannot be thus simply replaced by popular will but it has to stay intrinsically connected to it. The second approach supposes that the constitution delegates the decision to the people but this neither tells us what kind of change in attitudes justifies a change in the meaning of constitutional concepts, nor does it explain the cases in which the assumption that this was the will of constitution-makers does not hold; we thus need to inquire into the quality of attitudes that legitimate the change in constitutional interpretation.

Constitutional ethics as explained here can further specify these two lines of argument: it considers both sources of legitimacy as parts of a single narrative of moral identity evolving in relation to the constitution, and this determines the amount of respect that ought to be given to conserving and innovative elements of interpretation. As I have already argued, the courts ought to give effect to deep and reflective transformations in moral attitudes that are not excessively confident. On this approach, there is no mystery in the fact that moral attitudes both evolve and remain genuinely normative. Their normativity does not arise from their proximity to universal moral truths but from our inability to renounce them. This also means that not every popular opinion ought to be equally respected: the model gives us an argument why only widely and reflectively accepted attitudes matter.

At the same time, the process of constitution-making or constitutional amendment is the most appropriate venue for expressing a change in the moral identity of the community. If a polity wishes to renounce a discredited ethical concept, or a particular understanding of an ethical concept, the best way to do that is to change the constitution. However, as these concepts are typically underdetermined and there are further political obstacles to constitutional change, the courts may give effect to novel ethical attitudes through their interpretation. They have the justification to do so to the extent that a new equilibrium has been reached through a reflective and inclusive process.[47]

It will of course not be easy to tell whether moral change is deep enough to justify a change in constitutional interpretation. There is a significant leeway left for the courts to decide this and they must be reflective and ready to challenge their own assumptions. A clear sign that the change is deep enough is that it is not possible to imagine that a different conclusion could be justified; some attitudes become so obvious over time to the extent that other

[47] Although it is not in focus here, we may even get a sense of the relationship between other legal arguments and ethical arguments in this example. Ethical arguments gain force from new moral understandings that are reflectively adopted even if not effectuated through the political process that might be clogged; however, other legal arguments have force until it is clear that there is such a new prevalent attitude. All this holds, of course, under the assumption that the political and legal system is generally legitimate.

possibilities seem plainly 'wrong'. As Justice Kennedy put it in *Lawrence* v *Texas*: 'times can blind us to certain *truths* and later generations can see that laws once thought necessary and proper in fact serve only to oppress'.[48]

But Kennedy's opinion in *Lawrence* is an example of a reflective judicial approach that transforms such obvious 'truths'. Kennedy admits that 'for centuries there have been powerful voices to condemn homosexual conduct as immoral' and that 'for many persons these are not trivial concerns but profound and deep convictions accepted as ethical and moral principles to which they aspire and which thus determine the course of their lives'.[49] The power of his challenge to such ethical practice comes from the reflective point of view, which demands a more detached perspective and changes the relevant question. In Kennedy's view, '[t]he issue is whether the majority may use the power of the State to enforce these views on the whole society'.[50] The challenge to this approach comes then from a different direction. The problems arise when there is an emerging agreement that is not fully accepted but it is quite probable that it will be accepted at some point. Most practical problems I dealt with in previous chapters are of this kind. Should capital punishment be abolished or gay marriage be recognized? There is every possibility that people will come to think at some point that they should, and that they will consider some of our current practices to be deeply unjust.

The most difficult task for the court is to settle these kinds of issues. The temptation is to push the decision in the direction that becomes obvious to those that had the time and resources to reflect enough about it: courts may be in a privileged position of both being immersed in communal values and facing persistent challenges to these values in the legal process. While there cannot be steadfast rules for these situations, the interaction between constitutional confidence and reflection could give us some guidance. The question to ask is whether the new consensus that is emerging is more reflective than the previous one. If the new consensus is reflective and conforms better to all other values that we hold important, it means that its confidence is in better shape and the courts could therefore embrace it. It is not uncommon for the courts to help us to overcome our own illusions and give effect to new moral attitudes that better fit with our moral framework. We have also seen that convergence in foreign law could provide significant clues in this regard: in *Roper* the court 'confirmed' the developing domestic consensus by looking at foreign law.[51] Because we share the same set of questions as humans living in modern constitutional systems, it is possible to glimpse the future developments of our own system by looking at foreign law, without necessarily deducing conclusions directly from it. The court in *Roper* dealt

[48] *Lawrence v Texas* (n 18) 579 (Kennedy) (emphasis added). [49] ibid 571. [50] ibid.

[51] *Roper v Simmons* 543 US 551 (2005).

with an ongoing diachronic change in moral attitudes and prompted a new interpretation even before there was a clear and definitive change in moral sentiments and identity, but it could sense the direction of the emerging constitutional confidence on the basis of foreign law.

This is obviously a thin line and courts must not be excessively confident in their own judgment. The very idea of constitutional identity as a source of normativity demands a cautious approach until the new equilibrium emerges: we should remember how beneficial waiting can be if the new agreement in sentiments proves to be unacceptable later on. The task is delicate and courts often rush into inducing changes they believe are apposite—no one wants to be remembered as being the one who opposed moral progress.[52] But they should also exercise the appropriate amount of modesty as a decision that comes too early affects the formation of a new equilibrium and may polarize the public to the extent that is almost impossible to overcome. People come to identify themselves with one or the other position and refuse to be reflective about it: *Roe v Wade* being a classic example.[53] So, the courts must not preclude reflection with their own confidence even if they are convinced of their own position.

6.3.2 Synchronic differences

This brings us to a more pressing issue of *synchronic* divergence in moral attitudes. It is relatively unproblematic for the court to change the understanding of an ethical concept from the constitution when there is a clear, confident, reflective, and self-aware convergence of moral attitudes in the community. Much more common are horizontal differences and disagreements at the same point in time. The unity of the reflective self is challenged from both directions: by sites of normativity internal and external to the constitutional system.

The former problem is the classic question of the relationship between the majority and minority that liberal democracies have struggled with ever since the rise of modern constitutionalism. Once political authority could no longer be justified by reference to God the question became: what opinions can we impose on others even upon realization that they are just our opinions? The reflective restraint advocated by constitutional ethics is thus already present in the DNA of constitutionalism and the disenchanted political authority it establishes. These themes have also been explored at

[52] It is also too demanding to ask the judges to completely overcome their own moral identity and do what they deem utterly wrong because of their institutional position; instead, we should perhaps choose judges better if we want to avoid this, as their own moral judgment (which is at times necessary) must come from somewhere.

[53] *Roe v Wade* 410 US 113 (1973).

length in political philosophy. We may for example notice the same intuition in Rawls' move towards the 'political, not metaphysical conception of justice' and his reliance on 'overlapping consensus'[54] in an attempt to sidestep the question of moral truth and instead build his political theory on the 'background culture' of liberal democratic societies.[55] The idea is to proceed from the agreement between different moral outlooks and clarify the ways in which it can be advanced through the use of publicly shared values and standards.[56] It is obvious that constitutional ethics—when situated within the context of liberal democratic constitutionalism and its values—shares many affinities with such approaches. But instead of circumventing the metaphysical question, as I have argued, the only honest, stable, and viable solution is to face it directly.[57] What constitutional ethics then needs to do is to say more about how confidence is retained if we fully embrace its non-metaphysical underpinnings, and when 'unreasonable' simply denotes something that we reject from our own standpoint after reflection.

The question is thus whether such *diffidence*—to use Hayek's term to describe this sort of liberal scepticism—leaves constitutional ethics without enough *confidence*.[58] We have seen that constitutional ethics builds its confidence on a convergence in identity and sentiments. But we have also seen in Chapter 3 that the convergence model of ethics may dissolve in the face of disagreement. From there I have been building a case for the unavoidability

[54] John Rawls, 'Justice as Fairness: Political not Metaphysical' (1985) 14 Philosophy and Public Affairs 223, 226.

[55] Rawls, *Political Liberalism* (n 25) 14.

[56] On Rawls' idea of public reason and duty of civility see ibid 212–14.

[57] As I have already argued, any such Kantian/contractarian approach—to the extent to which it aims to answer the metaphysical and not only normative question—must explain the source of the initial normative intuitions and authority of reflection or 'public reason' (or in Habermas' version the normative presuppositions of ideal discourse; see eg *Justification and Application: Remarks on Discourse Ethics* (MIT Press 1993)). To the extent that these are only normative approaches—as in Rawls' restatement of his theory as merely 'political'—they are valuable but are always under threat from a 'schizoid attitude' when the convergence in moral attitudes breaks down.

[58] While the label 'liberal' is used in so many ways that it raises more questions than it provides answers, Hayek's following remarks about liberalism are applicable to much of contemporary liberal democratic and rights-based constitutional systems: 'What I have described as the liberal position shares with conservatism a distrust of reason to the extent that the liberal is very much aware that we do not know all the answers and that he is not sure that the answers he has are certainly the rights ones or even that we can find all the answers. He also does not disdain to seek assistance from whatever non-rational institutions or habits have proved their worth. The liberal differs from the conservative in his willingness to face this ignorance and to admit how little we know, without claiming the authority of supernatural forces of knowledge where his reason fails him. It has to be admitted that in some respects the liberal is fundamentally a skeptic—but it seems to require a certain degree of diffidence to let others seek their happiness in their own fashion and to adhere consistently to that tolerance which is an essential characteristic of liberalism'. See FA Hayek, *The Constitution of Liberty* (Routledge & Kegan Paul 1960) 406–407. In a similar vein, Nagel reports that 'Robert Frost defined a liberal as someone who can't take his own side in an argument'. Thomas Nagel, 'Moral Conflict and Political Legitimacy' (1987) 16 Philosophy and Public Affairs 215.

of reflection, also with a view that it could restore confidence. It is probably an illusion to think that conflicts can be completely avoided or that convergence can be fully rebuilt through reflection. There is no moral endpoint towards which we converge, so we can only hope that reflection itself will give us enough common ground to keep searching for appropriate solutions in an attempt to overcome the differences. But there are reasons to trust that this hope is not idle: first, reflection consists of a set of intuitions on which we do converge after the primary loss of confidence; second, reflection eliminates undue confidence hence allowing us to overcome differences and accommodate the views of others; and third—when disagreement cannot be overcome—this approach prioritizes more reflective views for they have reached the core of moral attitudes that cannot be renounced.

Let me be a bit more specific. Two problems dominate the discussion of internal divergence in moral attitudes: cultural differences and moral disagreements. The approach to these problems follows from the general gist of constitutional ethics. While it is inevitable that some attitudes will prevail over others, they can only achieve this in a manner that is sensitive to the fact that they are not strictly speaking *right*. The result is a need to accommodate as much as possible the views of others that are not infringing upon the core of our identity, but also that this accommodation becomes less of a concession because it is not considered as fundamentally *wrong*. As Taylor argues, the first precondition to reaching 'genuine, unforced consensus' is to accept the possibility that our moral views need not be true and open ourselves to the moral imagination of others.[59] Instead of relying on the authority of moral truth, courts ought to promote persuasion and accommodation.

Courts are, however, in a specific position, for they must sometimes take the perspective of an impartial spectator between two equally entrenched world views: they do not have the privilege of not caring about the solution because they have to decide. In such cases, they ought to build on and further develop constitutional identity in order to accommodate differences within a common framework. This demands fine-tuning of the argument from identity, sentiment, and reason—as described in the first part of this chapter—in order to find a point at which they intersect. But there may well not be such a point: in the case of an intractable conflict, the courts will have to impose the prevailing view to the extent to which it is reflective and self-aware. Sometimes the non-reflective world views will just have to give way. The right question to ask then is whether such moral world views imperil our constitutional identity to the extent that the absence of reaction amounts to the loss of such identity. Being able to live with this reaction is

[59] Charles Taylor, 'Conditions of an Unforced Consensus on Human Rights' in Joanne R Bauer and Daniel Bell (eds), *The East Asian Challenge for Human Rights* (Cambridge University Press 1999).

the only thing that can tell us that the decision was proper. An important part of this process—and a consequence of seeing values as contingent—involves giving up on the idea that there are always neat solutions to moral problems (perhaps as part of a divine plan) which would enable us to avoid *choice* and *judgment*.[60]

A challenge to this view may come from those that think that there is no overlapping consensus or that it is so thin that reliance on it renders the court's position feeble. Moral disagreement is sometimes considered to be *the* problem of constitutional interpretation.[61] I have already explained in Chapter 3 why disagreement might be a nonstarter normative argument: disagreement in any human practice can only exist against the background of prevailing agreement,[62] and such arguments must explain why contingent moral agreement is normative in the first place. The book has primarily been concerned with the latter question. While the problem of disagreement becomes even more obvious in the approach that rejects the mind-independent conception of value, once we understand why agreement matters and which qualities make it important, we might seek creative solutions to enable it. I have argued that the depth and integrity of moral agreement give us practical confidence: such agreement arises in the process of thoughtful endorsement of our moral sentiments and the reflective overcoming of our differences. Constitutional ethics should thus not understand disagreements as a fatal feature of our moribund moral practices, but an important part of establishing how we want to live together through engagement with each other's opinions.

The important institutional consequence of constitutional ethics based on confidence and reflection is that the courts should respect the will of the people to the extent that it can be ascribed to the reflective identity of the constitutional community. It follows that they should also respect the process of consensus-formation to the extent that it contributes to the realization of this goal: they ought to enable an open debate in which an agreement will be reached without excessive confidence in any of the sides involved. This issue is mostly a matter of institutional design and thus outside of the scope of the book that focuses on constitutional interpretation and the interplay between ethical arguments; but it is important to underline that—once we wish to explore how constitutional ethics fits with other pieces of the political and

[60] Bernard Williams is illuminating on this point: 'If there is such a thing as the truth about the subject matter of ethics—the truth, we might say, about the ethical—why is there any expectation that it should be simple? In particular, why should it be conceptually simple, using only one or two ethical concepts, such as *duty* or *good state of affairs*, rather than many? Perhaps we need as many concepts to describe it as we find we need, and no fewer'. Williams, *Ethics and the Limits of Philosophy* (n 42) 17.

[61] See eg Jeremy Waldron, *Law and Disagreement* (Clarendon Press 1999).

[62] See Dennis Patterson, *Law and Truth* (Oxford University Press 1996).

institutional puzzle—we can see that it demands this kind of institutional wisdom and modesty from courts. There will be times where disagreement is instigated by a non-reflective confidence of the parties involved, but at times disagreement shall form a part of reflection, and the courts will need to be sensible to this fact and decide when to interfere accordingly.

Apart from synchronic differences *internal* to a constitutional system, there are also *external* sites of normativity that challenge unwarranted constitutional confidence from the outside. Interactions between different constitutional systems and clashes between their claims of authority are ever more frequent: while it has probably never been plausible to imagine constitutional communities as insular and self-sufficient evaluative frameworks, today it is quite certainly impossible. I have tried to show that one dimension along which the friction between values occurs in constitutional interpretation is between local and global evaluative commitments. The conception of value from the previous chapter makes the possibility of overlap between these commitments less puzzling and constitutional systems even more open to the possibility of external influence: as humans who share a certain historical moment and social context, we also share similar moral attitudes. Even to the extent there is no shared evaluative framework, foreign influences are an almost indispensable part of the reflective exercise that courts ought to undertake in the course of making an appropriate normative judgment.

The question, however, is to what extent local identity and sentiments ought to be protected when they conflict with the larger evaluative frameworks that we participate in. Constitutional discourse always articulates the idea of *self*-government and establishes the principles of political organization of a *community*, but this need not impede the possibility of reimagining the terms on which such community is established and organized.[63] To what extent should polities accommodate the competing claims of other constitutional systems is a question that probably cannot be answered in the abstract. Much depends on the context in which such problems arise and the kind of entity that makes the competing claim.[64] Nonetheless: constitutional ethics should at least point to the questions the courts need to ask when facing such dilemmas.

[63] Walker, 'The Idea of Constitutional Pluralism' (n 41) 340–59.

[64] The question has for example gained much prominence in constitutional theory of the European Union, especially after several constitutional courts started using 'national' or 'constitutional' identity as a concept that affects the competences of the EU or derogation from rules and principles of EU law. For an overview of these developments see Monica Claes, 'National Identity: Trump Card or Up for Negotiation?' in Alejandro Saiz Arnaiz and Carina Alcobero Llivina (eds), *National Constitutional Identity and European Integration* (Intersentia 2013). For an account of constitutional identity in the context of EU federalism see Francois-Xavier Millet, 'The Respect for National Constitutional Identity in the European Legal Space: An Approach to Federalim as Constitutionalism' in Loïc Azoulai (ed), *The Question of Competence in the European Union* (Oxford University Press 2014).

From the perspective of constitutional ethics, interactions between constitutional systems on the post-national level are explicable in terms of the dynamics between constitutional confidence and reflection. One obvious way in which claims of competing authority coming from entities beyond the nation state add to this dynamic is through increased reflection. We have seen that internal sources of disagreement contribute to the common goal of working out how to live together. But it is also clear that significant parts of our constitutional identity remain unchallenged in these disagreements; for instance, because minorities do not have the opportunity to voice their concerns, or because national constitutional communities build on the pre-existing and relatively homogeneous evaluative outlooks embedded in distinct cultural or ethnic backgrounds. Over time our contingent and parochial values become entrenched and begin to be treated as eternal and ahistorical truths. The reflective challenges to the established constitutional confidence then come from the outside: constitutional systems inevitably start to question their world views once they begin to participate in larger structures that acquire constitutional space of their own.[65]

In the language of confidence and reflection, it is possible to see some of the dialogue occurring between constitutional and supra-national courts—especially in the case of the EU—as initiating a healthy existential crisis on the part of national constitutional identity and as the reflective shaping of an emerging supranational constitutional identity. As I have already explained, the German Constitutional Court has—in a series of judgments since the 1970s—challenged the supremacy claims of the Court of Justice of the European Union (CJEU)[66] and asserted its authority to review EU law on the basis of fundamental rights,[67] distribution of competences,[68] and principles and state functions central to German constitutional identity.[69] Without doubt, the German court has at times been too confident about the ethical core of German constitutional identity and has thus failed to articulate it in a coherent way.[70] But—notwithstanding these shortcomings—we may also notice that the very fact that the court has been forced to spell out the evaluative commitments of the constitutional system that cannot be renounced has generated a great deal of reflection.

[65] I assume here a rather non-controversial claim that certain constitution-like features can be shared on a post-national level. See more in Walker, 'The Idea of Constitutional Pluralism' (n 41).

[66] Before the Lisbon Treaty of 2009: the European Court of Justice.

[67] *Internationale Handelsgesellschaft von Einfuhr- und Vorratsstelle für Getreide und Futtermittel* (1974) 37 BVerfGE 27, [1974] CMLR 540, and *Re Wünsche Handelsgesellschaft* (1986) 73 BVerfGE 339, [1987] CMLR 225.

[68] *Brunner v European Union Treaty* (1993) 89 BVerfGE 155, [1994] CMLR 57.

[69] *Lisbon Judgment* (2009) 2 BvE 2/08.

[70] See eg Daniel Halberstam and Christoph Möllers, 'The German Constitutional Court Says "Ja zu Deutschland!"' (2009) 10 German Law Journal 1241.

The German Constitutional Court has attempted to express the 'inalienable essential features'[71] and 'identity'[72] of the constitutional system: in other words, to find the vital self-defining attitudes without which the system loses the foundation that enables it to make any evaluative judgment. The fact that the court has gone through quite a bit of adjustment in its position—alternating between harder and softer approaches to EU law—testifies that these evaluative commitments of the system are rebuilt and reshaped in the process rather than discovered.[73] We should therefore not expect that confidence could be established once and for all on the basis of an argument detecting the conceptually indispensable features of the state (as the court perhaps attempted to do in its *Lisbon* judgment);[74] instead, the process of rethinking these features will allow us to settle on a judgment that seems apposite in the particular historical moment from the standpoint of the reflective commitments of the particular political community.

On the other side, the interaction has forced the CJEU to take into account concerns about the justification of its own authority. As a response to these challenges, the CJEU developed the EU constitutional framework to better fit expectations about the appropriate normative underpinnings of its supremacy claims.[75] In so doing, it had to accommodate the specific constitutional traditions of member states,[76] but also asserted its authority when it considered such accommodation impossible or inappropriate.[77]

There is still much truth in Weiler's account of the interaction between *national*, which satisfies the need for communal and emotional attachment, and *supranational*, which remedies the excessive irrationality of the national.[78]

[71] See *Internationale Handelsgesellschaft von Einfuhr- und Vorratsstelle für Getreide und Futtermittel* (n 67), in the context of fundamental rights.

[72] *Lisbon Judgment* (n 69) inter alia paras 240–52.

[73] For example, a less confrontational judgment in *Honeywell* (2010) 2 BvR 2661/06 came out one year after the Lisbon decision, claiming that it would apply ultra vires control of EU law, thus retreating to the position from the Maastricht judgment (*Brunner v European Union Treaty* (n 68)).

[74] See more on this in Halberstam and Möllers, 'The German Constitutional Court Says "Ja zu Deutschland!"' (n 70).

[75] Most importantly, it included fundamental rights as the basis of review and this has eventually led to the adoption of the Charter of Fundamental Rights. See more in Gráinne de Búrca, 'The Evolution of EU Human Rights Law' in Paul Craig and Gráinne de Búrca (eds), *The Evolution of EU Law* (2nd edn, Oxford University Press 2011).

[76] See eg in the context of the already mentioned specifically German conception of dignity: Case C-36/02 *Omega Spielhallen- und Automatenaufstellungs-GmbH v Oberbürgermeisterin der Bundesstadt Bonn* [2004] ECR I-9609.

[77] At times, it also demonstrated excessive confidence in the fundamental freedoms of the EU and thus failed to see opportunities for accommodation. This has perhaps been the case in the context of the right to strike in Case C-438/05 *International Transport Workers' Federation v Viking* [2007] ECR I-10779 and Case C-341/05 *Laval un Partneri Ltd v Svenska Byggnadsarbetareförbundet* [2007] ECR I-11767.

[78] JHH Weiler, *The Constitution of Europe: 'Do the New Clothes Have an Emperor?' and Other Essays on European Integration* (Cambridge University Press 1999) ch 10, esp 347.

Although constitutional ethics starts from very different premises, the intuition it explores is similar: normative judgment arises from the interaction both along the local-universal and emotion-reason dimensions of our ethical experience. However, the supranational can no longer be merely seen as the embodiment of reason, or as a collective *super-ego* that remedies the excesses of the national, instinctive, and emotional id. We ought to treat both national and supranational as sites that generate evaluative attitudes, acquire constitutional identity of their own,[79] and gain confidence through accommodation of each other's claims.

The emphasis on a specifically *constitutional* identity could clarify what exactly is at stake. Constitutional identity is not necessarily embedded in previous communal attachments, but also arises from the very act (or practice) of self-constitution. It is thus a particular kind of identity: it presents a set of attitudes that govern our ideas about how common affairs ought to be conducted. Constitutional identity provides a compass for pursuing normative claims in the public domain without promoting deception about the special worth of any particular community: it precisely challenges these kinds of illusions and forces us to confront the contingency of our moral attitudes.[80] It is not surprising that new constitutional identities can evolve in a supranational context and gain normative traction. While they do perhaps lack the excessive confidence of ethno-cultural attachments, they do not lack the emotional and motivational content that directs our normative thinking.[81]

[79] This is most clear in the interaction with systems external to the EU when the specific constitutional identity of the EU is protected. See in particular (stressing the importance of fundamental rights and judicial review, repeating the pattern visible when domestic constitutional identity is asserted): Joined Cases C-402/05 P and C-415/05 P *Kadi and Al-Barakaat International Foundation v Council and Commission* [2008] ECR I-6351; and Joined Cases C-584/10 P, C-593/10 P, and C-595/10 P *European Commission and Others v Yassin Abdullah Kadi* ECLI:EU:C:2013:518.

[80] This distinguishes it from liberal nationalism and communitarianism. I am, however, reluctant to ascribe a label or opinion to a loose intellectual and political project as a whole as many nuances might be lost. For example, communitarianism need not value any particular community as such but just underline that communal heritage crucially influences the way we see the world in normative terms.

[81] The idea here comes close to the concept of constitutional patriotism, although I do find constitutional patriotism puzzling as long as it presupposes universalist normative foundations and wishful thinking about their widespread acceptance in the population. The concept aims to gain normativity from universal values, and motivational force from parochial and communal emotions and thus runs the risk of amounting to a noble dream (but still a dream) that everyone actually accepts universal values. My account is different in two senses: first, I aim to explain the source of value and evaluative attitudes, while constitutional patriotism can only be an attitude and not the source itself; second, I do not presuppose universal values to motivate my account of constitutional identity but only contingent and prevailing attitudes that arise in relation to the constitution. Notwithstanding the differences I do find that constitutional patriotism is possibly an attractive way of thinking about these issues (if successfully clarified). See more on constitutional patriotism in Habermas, *Between Facts and Norms: Contributions to a Discourse Theory of Law and Democracy* (n 29) 490–515, and Jan-Werner Müller, 'A General Theory of Constitutional Patriotism' (2007) 6 International Journal of Constitutional Law 72.

One could then ask: why does a constitutional perspective matter? Why—among all other identities—should we choose constitutional? After all, in the clash between other more deeply embedded identities, the seemingly fragile constitutional identity could easily vanish. Its worth is not intrinsic: the normativity of such an identity does not follow from the fact that it satisfies a human need for social attachment, or from the necessity of such attachment for social cooperation and solidarity. As such, it is also not exclusive: it presents just one possible evaluative system among many.

Part of the answer comes from the already explained perspective of the court that makes the decision in the name of constitutional community and with a constitutional warrant to do so. But a more important reason follows from the empirical and normative resilience of constitutional identity. Empirically, constitutional identity has proved to be more robust than it may appear at first; it arises precisely from the clashes of different identities as the most viable way to resolve the problem of collective action and political organization of a particular society, and has survived many (although certainly not all) such challenges. It is accepted as a point of reference for people who advance normative claims in the public context and as such has more relevance for our common life than we may sometimes think it does. Normatively, its force stems from the fact that the reflective restriction of the instinctive moral impulses is a sensible reaction after their contingent foundation is exposed. Constitutional identity—in the liberal democratic form discussed here—seems as the least self-righteous option that can still guarantee enough confidence for an effective public authority. In other words, constitutional identity sometimes *is* the point of intersection between confidence and reflection: it embodies the optimal level of attachment and detachment that is appropriate for a disenchanted normative perspective.

6.4 CONCLUSION

This chapter has discussed the implications of metaethics on the judicial pursuit of the source of value: it applied the ethics of confidence and reflection to the constitutional context. The important message is that moral judgments arise from the interplay between identity, sentiments, and reason. The ambition of the chapter was to illuminate these distinct sources of value and shed some light on their interaction. But an equally important message is that finding answers to constitutional dilemmas is not easy: the process does not involve discovery, but invention, imagination, and—most importantly—persuasion. The hope is that constitutional ethics can give us the vocabulary to express the concerns that ought to play an important role in this quest.

One might find this answer dissatisfying. It may appear that the theory of constitutional ethics does not have enough practical bite. On the one hand, it leaves many things as they are: the theory only finds a distinct place for ethical arguments that already exist in comparative practice. On the other hand, it abstains from giving fixed answers to concrete moral problems: instead of clear-cut solutions it promotes an abstract process that can lead to quite different results. Let me finish with some observations about these important issues.

First, while the theory of constitutional ethics does not introduce radical changes, it does unsettle the usual ways in which these issues are addressed, and—in so doing—allows us to see some of the disputes about constitutional interpretation in a new light. Recall that in many systems arguments from identity, sentiment, and reason exclude each other and sometimes lead to a standstill between different conceptions of legitimacy. In other systems some of these arguments are used in a very different way or not at all. Constitutional ethics therefore does have an important transformative potential.

Second, to the extent that constitutional ethics does not aim to transform the practice—or resists transformations that are definite and crude—this is consistent with its metaethical foundations. Our moral practice itself is not neat. This fact should probably be celebrated: it allows us to experience *emotional* attachments, *reason* about them, and choose the course of action with our *will*. Devising a formula that should give us exact moral answers would go against the spirit of the book, and against the very idea that there ought to be enough space for different perspectives and for their development over time. Nonetheless, constitutional ethics does try to devise an approach to moral problems that—hopefully—makes sense from our current moral perspective, and—even more hopefully—allows the courts to realize what it takes to make a sound normative judgment.

Third—and perhaps most importantly—there is space for future work within this framework of thinking about constitutional ethics. Apart from the issue of the concrete application of constitutional ethics, there is much to be said about the import of each ethical argument in different contexts, both national and post-national. There is also a lot to be explored in terms of the institutional consequences *of* constitutional ethics, and in terms of the consequences of institutional context *on* constitutional ethics. Possibly, there are also interesting questions for other branches of law. There is—in other words—more *reflection* to be done if we wish to be *confident* in constitutional ethics.

7

Conclusion

The book began with a vignette about Socrates' contestation of Euthyphro's views on the source of moral value. Their dialogue ends with Euthyphro leaving the scene, unwilling to accept further challenges that could undermine his judgment. It is a great victory for Socrates and his philosophical method. And we should probably celebrate it as a triumph of reason over unreflective beliefs. But there is something to be said about Euthyphro. While we may condemn him as a dogmatic theologian, we should also be aware that there is Euthyphro's spirit behind every moral judgment: an inescapable level of confidence in our contingent moral attitudes accompanies each moral choice we make. Metaphorically speaking, moral decisions are made in a process similar to the dialogue between Socrates and Euthyphro, and require finding the internal balance between these two poles of our moral experience.

Difficult questions about the nature of value arise from the tension between the theoretical and practical perspective. The practical perspective aims to answer a theoretical question about the mind-independence of moral values, and in so doing undermines our confidence in such values. We can regain confidence in the practical perspective by rejecting its theoretical claims. But when these theoretical claims are rejected, the redemption of our practical perspective is possible only through reflection that curbs the excessive confidence. Values are then revealed and reshaped in the dynamics between practical *confidence* and *reflection*. Confidence denotes the inescapability of the self and of the contingent evaluative attitudes it entails in making any moral judgment. Reflection denotes the process of challenging and questioning these attitudes. A credible conception of value, one that leaves enough space for both the practical and theoretical perspective, suggests that the appropriate moral judgment emerges from the equilibrium between confidence and reflection. This judgment arises from a disenchanted practical perspective that incorporates reflective virtues—such as self-awareness, maturity, coherence, imagination, sensitivity, openness, and flexibility—in a process that integrates both Euthyphro's and Socrates' point of view.

Two types of conclusions follow for constitutional adjudication: critical and constructive. First, when taken separately, all three regimes of ethical arguments identified in comparative constitutional practice—the argument from constitutional identity, common sentiment, and universal reason—are supported with inadequate conceptions of value and fail as self-standing approaches to moral judgment. The argument from common sentiment does not allow for the reflective endorsement of moral attitudes; the argument from universal reason presupposes a detached practical perspective that would render us incapable of making any moral judgment; the argument from constitutional identity is between these two poles, which makes it both unable to give enough substance to our moral judgments and provide sufficient critical distance towards them. Expressed in the vocabulary of confidence and reflection: the argument from common sentiment is overly confident; the argument from universal reason is implausibly reflective; and the argument from constitutional identity is neither confident nor reflective enough.

Second, when taken together, these arguments have a potential to refashion the moral perspective of a constitutional court so that it conforms to a sound conception of value. On the model proposed in this book, judicial moral inquiry proceeds from the emotive intuitions of a constitutional community present in the argument from common sentiment; these intuitions are then challenged with the argument from universal reason through reflective exposure to different moral perspectives; finally, the goal of this exercise is to contribute to a better understanding and development of constitutional identity. Combining these arguments allows constitutional courts to emulate the moral point of view in a process that is both sensitive to different moral perspectives and attuned to the institutional position of the court in the constitutional system. This framework enables us to perceive some common problems of constitutional adjudication—such as diachronic changes and synchronic differences in moral opinions—in a new light and explore the limits of confidence with which the courts can assert particular moral views. This conception of constitutional ethics contends that courts—when they make moral judgments—ought to respect the moral intuitions of the people that can be reflectively attributed to their constitutional identity. If Euthyphro sat on a constitutional court today, this is the answer he could give to Socrates.

The goal of this book has been to develop a notion of constitutional ethics that would give due regard to both our existing moral attitudes and our ability to change them through reflection. The intention was to leave space for people to choose their constitutional destiny, while being aware that their choices do not occur in a normative vacuum, but in the context of contingently shared moral attitudes. The hope is that this model of constitutional ethics resonates with some of the intuitions we have about our common lives in modern constitutional communities, and that it can assist us in developing them further. But perhaps even more importantly, the book has attempted to show that there are pressing metaethical questions—for example, about the normativity of our contingent evaluative attitudes, accommodation of otherness without collapsing into self-defeating relativism, and authority of reflection—that cannot and should not be neglected when we discuss the place and role of moral judgments in constitutional adjudication. Unless we tackle these questions, we are destined to run around in circles, without a clear idea of where to search for value. Even if we must have some of Euthyphro's confidence to make moral judgments, we can only figure out how to live together if we embrace Socrates' reflection.

Bibliography

Ackerman BA, *We the People: Foundations* (Belknap Press 1991)

Ackermann LWH, 'Constitutional Comparativism in South Africa: A Response to Sir Basil Markesinis and Dr Jörg Tiedke' in Markesinis B and Tiedke J (eds), *Judicial Recourse to Foreign Law: A New Source of Inspiration?* (UCL Press 2006)

Alexy R, *A Theory of Constitutional Rights* (Oxford University Press 2002)

Alford RP, 'In Search of a Theory for Constitutional Comparativism' (2005) 52 UCLA Law Review 639

Alford RP, 'Roper v. Simmons and Our Constitution in International Equipoise' (2005) 53 UCLA Law Review 1

Anscombe GEM, 'Modern Moral Philosophy' (1958) 33 Philosophy 1

Audi R, *The Good in the Right: A Theory of Intuition and Intrinsic Value* (Princeton University Press 2004)

Augenstein D, 'The Contested Polity: Europe's Constitutional Identity between Religious and Secular Values' [2009/3] University of Edinburgh School of Law Working Paper Series

Ayer AJ, *Language, Truth, and Logic* (2nd edn, Victor Gollancz 1946)

Barak A, *Purposive Interpretation in Law* (Princeton University Press 2005)

Barak A, *The Judge in a Democracy* (Princeton University Press 2006)

Bentele U, 'Mining for Gold: The Constitutional Court of South Africa's Experience with Comparative Constitutional Law' (2009) 37 Georgia Journal of International and Comparative Law 219

Bickel AM, *The Least Dangerous Branch: The Supreme Court at the Bar of Politics* (Bobbs-Merrill 1962)

Blackburn S, *Spreading the Word: Groundings in the Philosophy of Language* (Oxford University Press 1984)

Blackburn S, *Ruling Passions: A Theory of Practical Reasoning* (Clarendon Press 1998)

Bobbitt P, *Constitutional Fate: Theory of the Constitution* (Oxford University Press 1982)

Bobbitt P, *Constitutional Interpretation* (Blackwell 1991)

Bowles S, 'Group Competition, Reproductive Leveling, and the Evolution of Human Altruism' (2006) 314 Science 1569

Boyd RN, 'How to Be a Moral Realist' in Sayre-McCord G (ed), *Essays on Moral Realism* (Cornell University Press 1988)

Brink DO, *Moral Realism and the Foundations of Ethics* (Cambridge University Press 1989)

Búrca G de, 'The Evolution of EU Human Rights Law' in Craig P and Búrca G de (eds), *The Evolution of EU Law* (2nd edn, Oxford University Press 2011)

Calabresi SG and Zimdahl SD, 'The Supreme Court and Foreign Sources of Law: Two Hundred Years of Practice and the Juvenile Death Penalty Decision' (2005) 47 William and Mary Law Review 743

Claes M, 'National Identity: Trump Card or Up for Negotiation?' in Saiz Arnaiz A and Alcobero Llivina C (eds), *National Constitutional Identity and European Integration* (Intersentia 2013)

Clarke-Doane J, 'Morality and Mathematics: The Evolutionary Challenge' (2012) 122 Ethics 313

Copp D, *Morality, Normativity, and Society* (Oxford University Press 1995)

Copp D, 'Darwinian Skepticism about Moral Realism' (2008) 18 Philosophical Issues 186

Darwall S, Gibbard A, and Railton P, 'Toward *Fin de siècle* Ethics: Some Trends' in Darwall SL, Gibbard A, and Railton PA (eds), *Moral Discourse and Practice: Some Philosophical Approaches* (Oxford University Press 1997)

Darwin C, *The Descent of Man, and Selection in Relation to Sex* (first published 1871, Bonner JT and May RM (eds), Princeton University Press 1981)

Davis DM, 'Constitutional Borrowing: The Influence of Legal Culture and Local History in the Reconstitution of Comparative Influence: The South African Experience' (2003) 1 International Journal of Constitutional Law 181

Dixon R, 'A Democratic Theory of Constitutional Comparison' (2008) 56 American Journal of Comparative Law 947

Dorsen N, 'The Relevance of Foreign Legal Materials in U.S. Constitutional Cases: A Conversation between Justice Antonin Scalia and Justice Stephen Breyer' (2005) 3 International Journal of Constitutional Law 519

Durkheim E, *Durkheim and the Law* (Lukes S and Scull A (eds), St Martin's Press 1983)

Dworkin R, 'Lord Devlin and the Enforcement of Morals' (1966) 75 Yale Law Journal 986

Dworkin R, *Law's Empire* (Belknap Press 1986)

Dworkin R, *Freedom's Law: The Moral Reading of the American Constitution* (Harvard University Press 1996)

Dworkin R, 'Objectivity and Truth: You'd Better Believe It' (1996) 25 Philosophy and Public Affairs 87

Dworkin R, *Justice for Hedgehogs* (Belknap Press of Harvard University Press 2011)

Dworkin R and others, 'Assisted Suicide: The Philosopher's Brief' *The New York Review of Books* (27 March 1997)

Ely JH, *Democracy and Distrust: A Theory of Judicial Review* (Harvard University Press 1980)

Engle E, 'European Law in American Courts: Foreign Law as Evidence of Domestic Law' (2007) 33 Ohio Northern University Law Review 99

Enoch D, 'The Epistemological Challenge to Metanormative Realism: How Best to Understand It, and How to Cope with It' (2010) 148 Philosophical Studies 413

Fallon RH, 'A Constructivist Coherence Theory of Constitutional Interpretation' (1987) 100 Harvard Law Review 1189

Fallon RH, *Implementing the Constitution* (Harvard University Press 2001)

Foot P, 'Morality as a System of Hypothetical Imperatives' (1972) 81 The Philosophical Review 305

Foot P, 'Does Moral Subjectivism Rest on a Mistake?' (1995) 15 Oxford Journal of Legal Studies 1

Foot P, *Moral Dilemmas and Other Topics in Moral Philosophy* (Oxford University Press 2002)

Foot P, *Virtues and Vices and Other Essays in Moral Philosophy* (first published 1978, Clarendon Press 2002)

Frankfurt HG, 'Freedom of the Will and the Concept of a Person' (1971) 68 Journal of Philosophy 5

Garland D, *Peculiar Institution: America's Death Penalty in an Age of Abolition* (Oxford University Press 2010)

Geach PT, 'Assertion' (1965) 74 Philosophical Review 449

Gensler H, 'Cultural Relativism' in Shafer-Landau R (ed), *Ethical Theory: An Anthology* (2nd edn, Blackwell 2013)

Gibbard A, *Wise Choices, Apt Feelings: A Theory of Normative Judgment* (Clarendon Press 1990)

Gibbard A, *Thinking How to Live* (Harvard University Press 2003)

Gibbard A, *Reconciling Our Aims: In Search of Bases for Ethics* (Oxford University Press 2008)

Goldschmit C, Gross M, and Schachar Y, '100 Leading Precedents of the Supreme Court: A Quantitative Analysis' (2004) 7 Haifa University Law Review 243

Gross M, Haris R, and Schachar Y, 'References Patterns of the Supreme Court in Israel: Quantitative Analysis' (1996) 26 Hebrew University Law Review 115

Guyer P, 'Moral Feelings in the Metaphysics of Morals' in Denis L (ed), *Kant's Metaphysics of Morals: A Critical Guide* (Cambridge University Press 2010)

Habermas J, *Justification and Application: Remarks on Discourse Ethics* (MIT Press 1993)

Habermas J, *Between Facts and Norms: Contributions to a Discourse Theory of Law and Democracy* (MIT Press 1996)

Haidt J, 'The Emotional Dog and its Rational Tail: A Social Intuitionist Approach to Moral Judgment' (2001) 108 Psychological Review 814

Halberstam D and Möllers C, 'The German Constitutional Court Says "Ja zu Deutschland!"' (2009) 10 German Law Journal 1241

Hamilton WD, 'The Genetical Evolution of Social Behaviour. I' (1964) 7 Journal of Theoretical Biology 1

Hamilton WD, 'The Genetical Evolution of Social Behaviour. II' (1964) 7 Journal of Theoretical Biology 17

Hare RM, *The Language of Morals* (Clarendon Press 1952)

Harman G, *The Nature of Morality: An Introduction to Ethics* (Oxford University Press 1977)

Harman G, 'Moral Relativism' in Harman G and Thomson JJ (eds), *Moral Relativism and Moral Objectivity* (Blackwell 1996)

Harman G, *Explaining Value and Other Essays in Moral Philosophy* (Oxford University Press 2000)

Harman G, Mason K, and Sinnott-Armstrong W, 'Moral Reasoning' in Doris JM and Group MPR (eds), *The Moral Psychology Handbook* (Oxford University Press 2010)

Hart HLA, *Law, Liberty and Morality* (Oxford University Press 1962)

Hayek FA, *The Constitution of Liberty* (Routledge & Kegan Paul 1960)

Hirschl R, *Comparative Matters: The Renaissance of Comparative Constitutional Law* (Oxford University Press 2014)

Homiak M, 'Moral Character' in Zalta EN (ed), *The Stanford Encyclopedia of Philosophy* (Spring 2011 edn) <http://plato.stanford.edu/archives/spr2011/entries/moral-character/> (last accessed 16 July 2014)

Horwich P, 'The Frege-Geach Point' (2005) 15 Philosophical Issues 78

Hume D, *Enquires Concerning the Human Understanding and Concerning the Principles of Morals* (first published 1777, Selby-Bigge LA (ed), 2nd edn, Clarendon Press 1902)

Hume D, *A Treatise of Human Nature* (Selby-Bigge LA and Nidditch PH (eds), 2nd edn, Clarendon Press 1978)

Inglehart R, *The Silent Revolution: Changing Values and Political Styles among Western Publics* (Princeton University Press 1977)

Jackson VC, 'Constitutional Comparisons: Convergence, Resistance, Engagement' (2005) 119 Harvard Law Review 109

Jacobsohn GJ, *Constitutional Identity* (Harvard University Press 2010)

Jacobsohn GJ, 'Constitutional Values and Principles' in Rosenfeld M and Sajo A (eds), *The Oxford Handbook of Comparative Constitutional Law* (Oxford University Press 2012)

Joyce R, 'Darwinian Ethics and Error' (2000) 15 Biology and Philosophy 713

Joyce R, *The Evolution of Morality* (MIT Press 2006)

Kant I, *Groundwork for the Metaphysics of Morals* (Wood AW (tr), Yale University Press 2002)

Kitcher P, 'Biology and Ethics' in Copp D (ed), *The Oxford Handbook of Ethical Theory* (Oxford University Press 2006)

Kitcher P, *The Ethical Project* (Harvard University Press 2011)

Koh HH and Treanor WM, 'Keynote Address: A Community of Reason and Rights' (2008) 77 Fordham Law Review 583

Komesar NK, *Imperfect Alternatives: Choosing Institutions in Law, Economics, and Public Policy* (University of Chicago Press 1994)

Komesar NK, *Law's Limits: The Rule of Law and the Supply and Demand of Rights* (Cambridge University Press 2001)

Kommers DP, 'Germany: Balancing Rights and Duties' in Goldsworthy J (ed), *Interpreting Constitutions: A Comparative Study* (Oxford University Press 2007)

Korsgaard CM, *The Sources of Normativity* (Cambridge University Press 1996)

Kramer L, *The People Themselves: Popular Constitutionalism and Judicial Review* (Oxford University Press 2004)

Kumm M, 'The Cosmopolitan Turn in Constitutionalism: On the Relationship between Constitutionalism in and beyond the State' in Dunoff JL and Trachtman JP (eds), *Ruling the World? Constitutionalism, International Law, and Global Governance* (Cambridge University Press 2009)

Larsen JL, 'Importing Constitutional Norms from a "Wider Civilization": *Lawrence* and the Rehnquist Court's Use of Foreign and International Law in Domestic Constitutional Interpretation' (2004) 65 Ohio State Law Journal 1283

Lee Y, 'International Consensus as Persuasive Authority in the Eighth Amendment' (2007) 156 University of Pennsylvania Law Review 63

Leiter B, 'Nietzsche's Metaethics: Against the Privilege Readings' (2000) 8 European Journal of Philosophy 277

Leiter B, 'Moral Facts and Best Explanations' (2001) 18 Social Philosophy & Policy 79

Letsas G, 'Two Concepts of the Margin of Appreciation' (2006) 26 Oxford Journal of Legal Studies 705

Levinson S, 'Looking Abroad When Interpreting the U.S. Constitution: Some Reflections' (2004) 39 Texas International Law Journal 353

Loughlin M and Walker N, *The Paradox of Constitutionalism: Constituent Power and Constitutional Form* (Oxford University Press 2007)

Lyons D, 'Ethical Relativism and the Problem of Incoherence' (1976) 86 Ethics 107

MacCrudden C, 'Human Dignity and Judicial Interpretation of Human Rights' (2008) 19 European Journal of International Law 655

Mackie JL, *Ethics: Inventing Right and Wrong* (2nd edn, Penguin 1990)

Mautner M, *Law and the Culture of Israel* (Oxford University Press 2011)

Mazie SM, *Israel's Higher Law: Religion and Liberal Democracy in the Jewish State* (Lexington Books 2011)

McDowell J, *Mind, Value, and Reality* (Harvard University Press 1998)

Mill JS, 'Hedonism' in Shafer-Landau R (ed), *Ethical Theory: An Anthology* (2nd edn, Blackwell 2013)

Millet F-X, 'The Respect for National Constitutional Identity in the European Legal Space: An Approach to Federalim as Constitutionalism' in Azoulai L (ed), *The Question of Competence in the European Union* (Oxford University Press 2014)

Möller K, 'On Treating Persons as Ends: The German Aviation Security Act, Human Dignity, and the Federal Constitutional Court' [2006] Public Law 457

Moore GE, *Principia Ethica* (first published 1903, Baldwin T (ed), 2 edn, Cambridge University Press 2000)

Moore MS, *Placing Blame: A Theory of the Criminal Law* (Oxford University Press 1997)

Müller J-W, 'A General Theory of Constitutional Patriotism' (2007) 6 International Journal of Constitutional Law 72

Nagel T, *The View from Nowhere* (Oxford University Press 1986)

Nagel T, 'Moral Conflict and Political Legitimacy' (1987) 16 Philosophy and Public Affairs 215

Nagel T, *The Last Word* (Oxford University Press 1997)

Nagel T, *Mind and Cosmos: Why the Materialist Neo-Darwinian Conception of Nature is Almost Certainly False* (Oxford University Press 2012)

Navot S, 'Israel: Creating a Constitution: The Use of Foreign Precedents by the Supreme Court (1994–2010)' in Groppi T and Ponthoreau M-C (eds), *The Use of Foreign Precedents by Constitutional Judges* (Hart Publishing 2013)

Nietzsche F, *The Gay Science; With a Prelude in Rhymes and an Appendix of Songs* (Kaufmann W (tr), Vintage Books 1974)

Nietzsche FW, *On the Genealogy of Morals and Ecce Homo* (Kaufmann W (ed), Kaufmann WA and Hollingdale RJ (trs), 2nd edn, Vintage Books 1989)

Nozick R, *The Nature of Rationality* (Princeton University Press 1993)

Parfit D, *On What Matters: Volume Two* (Oxford University Press 2011)

Patterson D, 'Normativity and Objectivity in Law' (2001) 43 William and Mary Law Review 325

Patterson D, *Law and Truth* (Oxford University Press 1996)

Perju V, 'Cosmopolitanism and Constitutional Self-government' (2010) 8 International Journal of Constitutional Law 326

Plato, *The Collected Dialogues of Plato* (Hamilton E and Cairns H (eds), 14th edn, Princeton University Press 1989)

Porat I, 'The Use of Foreign Law in Israeli Constitutional Adjudication' Paper presented in a Conference on Israeli Constitutional Law (Tel Aviv, May 2010)

Posner R, 'Foreword: A Political Court' (2005) 119 Harvard Law Review 32

Post R and Siegel RB, 'Democratic Constitutionalism' in Balkin JM and Siegel RB (eds), *Constitution in 2020* (Oxford University Press 2009)

Prinz JJ, *The Emotional Construction of Morals* (Oxford University Press 2007)

Putnam H, *Philosophy of Logic* (Harper & Row 1971)

Putnam H, *The Collapse of the Fact/Value Dichotomy and Other Essays* (Harvard University Press 2002)

Putnam H, *Ethics without Ontology* (Harvard University Press 2004)

Quine WVO, 'Two Dogmas of Empiricism' (1951) 60 The Philosophical Review 20

Quine WVO, 'The Scope and Language of Science' in *The Ways of Paradox and Other Essays* (Harvard University Press 1976)

Railton P, 'Darwinian Building Blocks' in Katz LD (ed), *Evolutionary Origins of Morality: Cross-Disciplinary Perspectives* (Imprint Academic 2000)

Railton P, 'Realism and Its Alternatives' in Skorupski J (ed), *The Routledge Companion to Ethics* (Routledge 2010)

Rautenbach C, 'South Africa: Teaching an "Old Dog" New Tricks? An Empirical Study of the Use of Foreign Precedents by the South African Constitutional Court (1995–2010)' in Groppi T and Ponthoreau M-C (eds), *The Use of Foreign Precedents by Constitutional Judges* (Hart Publishing 2013)

Rawls J, 'Justice as Fairness: Political not Metaphysical' (1985) 14 Philosophy and Public Affairs 223

Rawls J, *Political Liberalism* (Columbia University Press 1993)

Rawls J, 'Kantian Constructivism in Moral Theory' in Freeman SR (ed), *Collected Papers* (Harvard University Press 1999)

Rawls J, *A Theory of Justice* (first published 1971, rev edn, Belknap Press 1999)

Raz J, 'On the Authority and Interpretation of Constitutions: Some Preliminaries' in *Between Authority and Interpretation: On the Theory of Law and Practical Reason* (Oxford University Press 2009)

Rorty R, *Philosophy and the Mirror of Nature* (Princeton University Press 1979)

Rorty R, *Contingency, Irony, and Solidarity* (Cambridge University Press 1989)

Rosen A, 'Two Logics of Authority in Modern Law' (2014) 64 University of Toronto Law Journal 669

Rosenfeld M, *The Identity of the Constitutional Subject: Selfhood, Citizenship, Culture, and Community* (Routledge 2010)

Ross WD, *The Right and the Good* (Clarendon Press 1930)

Rousseau J-J, *The Social Contract and Other Later Political Writings* (Gourevitch V (ed), Cambridge University Press 1997)

Ruse M, *Taking Darwin Seriously: A Naturalistic Approach to Philosophy* (Blackwell 1986)

Sapir G, 'Constitutional Revolutions: Israel as a Case-study' (2009) 5 International Journal of Law in Context 355

Scalia A, 'Foreign Legal Authority in the Federal Courts' (2004) 98 Proceedings of the Annual Meeting of the American Society of International Law 305

Scanlon T, 'The Appeal and Limits of Constructivism' in Lenman J and Shemmer Y (eds), *Constructivism in Practical Philosophy* (Oxford University Press 2012)

Scheffler S, *Equality and Tradition: Questions of Value in Moral and Political Theory* (Oxford University Press 2010)

Schmitt C, *The Concept of the Political* (Schwab G (tr), expanded edn, University of Chicago Press 2007)

Schneewind JB, *The Invention of Autonomy: A History of Modern Moral Philosophy* (Cambridge University Press 1998)

Schulz AW, 'Sober & Wilson's Evolutionary Arguments for Psychological Altruism: A Reassessment' (2011) 26 Biology and Philosophy 251

Segal Z, 'The Israeli Constitutional Revolution: The Canadian Impact in the Midst of a Formative Period' (1997) 8 Forum Constitutionnel 53

Shafer-Landau R, *Moral Realism: A Defence* (Oxford University Press 2003)

Shafer-Landau R, 'The Possibility of Metaethics' (2010) 90 Boston University Law Review 479

Shafer-Landau R, 'Evolutionary Debunking, Moral Realism and Moral Knowledge' (2012) 7 Journal of Ethics and Social Philosophy 1

Sidgwick H, *The Methods of Ethics* (first published 1907, 7th edn, McMillan 1962)

Singer P, 'Moral Experts' (1972) 32 Analysis 115

Singer P, 'Ethics and Intuitions' (2005) 9 The Journal of Ethics 331

Singer P, 'Morality, Reason, and the Rights of Animals' in Waal F de (ed), *Primates and Philosophers: How Morality Evolved* (Princeton University Press 2006)

Sinnott-Armstrong W (ed), *Moral Psychology, Volume 1. The Evolution of Morality: Adaptations and Innateness* (MIT Press 2007)

Smith A, *The Theory of Moral Sentiments* (Haakonssen K (ed), Cambridge University Press 2002)

Sober E, *From a Biological Point of View: Essays in Evolutionary Philosophy* (Cambridge University Press 1994)

Sober E and Wilson DS, *Unto Others: The Evolution and Psychology of Unselfish Behavior* (Harvard University Press 1998)

Stevenson CL, *Ethics and Language* (Yale University Press 1944)

Street S, 'A Darwinian Dilemma for Realist Theories of Value' (2006) 127 Philosophical Studies 109

Street S, 'Constructivism about Reasons' in Shafer-Landau R (ed), *Oxford Studies in Metaethics: Volume 3* (Clarendon Press 2008)

Street S, 'Reply to Copp: Naturalism, Normativity, and the Varieties of Realism Worth Worrying About' (2008) 18 Philosophical Issues 207

Street S, 'Objectivity and Truth: You'd Better Rethink It' unpublished draft https://files.nyu.edu/ss194/public/sharonstreet/Writing_files/Paper%2012%20for%20website%20-%20Objectivity%20and%20Truth%20-%20You%27d%20Better%20Rethink%20It.pdf (last accessed 16 July 2014)

Street S, 'What is Constructivism in Ethics and Metaethics?' (2010) 5 Philosophy Compass 363

Street S, 'Coming to Terms with Contingency: Humean Constructivism about Practical Reason' in Lenman J and Shemmer Y (eds), *Constructivism in Practical Philosophy* (Oxford University Press 2012)

Street S, 'Does Anything Really Matter or Did We Just Evolve to Think So?' in Rosen G and others (eds), *The Norton Introduction to Philosophy* (Norton 2015)

Sturgeon NL, 'Harman on Moral Explanations of Natural Facts' (1986) 24 The Southern Journal of Philosophy 69

Sturgeon NL, 'Moral Explanations' in Sayre-McCord G (ed), *Essays on Moral Realism* (Cornell University Press 1988)

Sturgeon NL, 'Relativism' in Skorupski J (ed), *The Routledge Companion to Ethics* (Routledge 2010)

Sunstein CR, *One Case at a Time: Judicial Minimalism on the Supreme Court* (Harvard University Press 1999)

Sunstein CR, *A Constitution of Many Minds: Why the Founding Document Doesn't Mean What It Meant Before* (Princeton University Press 2009)

Taylor C, *Human Agency and Language: Philosophical Papers I* (Cambridge University Press 1985)

Taylor C, 'Conditions of an Unforced Consensus on Human Rights' in Bauer JR and Bell D (eds), *The East Asian Challenge for Human Rights* (Cambridge University Press 1999)

Tripkovic B, 'Judicial Comparativism and Legal Positivism' (2014) 5 Transnational Legal Theory 285

Tushnet MV, 'Referring to Foreign Law in Constitutional Interpretation: An Episode in the Culture Wars' (2006) 35 University of Baltimore Law Review 299

Waldron J, *Law and Disagreement* (Clarendon Press 1999)

Waldron J, 'The Core of the Case Against Judicial Review' (2006) 115 Yale Law Journal 1346

Waldron J, *'Partly Laws Common to All Mankind': Foreign Law in American Courts* (Yale University Press 2012)

Walker N, 'The Idea of Constitutional Pluralism' 65 Modern Law Review 317

Walker N, 'Taking Constitutionalism Beyond the State' (2008) 56 Political Studies 519

Wallace RJ, 'Constructivism about Normativity: Some Pitfalls' in Lenman J and Shemmer Y (eds), *Constructivism in Practical Philosophy* (Oxford University Press 2012)

Waluchow WJ, *A Common Law Theory of Judicial Review: The Living Tree* (Cambridge University Press 2007)

Waluchow WJ, 'Constitutional Morality and the Bills of Rights' in Huscroft G (ed), *Expounding the Constitution: Essays in Constitutional Theory* (Cambridge University Press 2008)

Weber M, *The Protestant Ethic and the Spirit of Capitalism* (Routledge 2001)

Weiler JHH, *The Constitution of Europe: 'Do the New Clothes Have an Emperor?' and Other Essays on European Integration* (Cambridge University Press 1999)

Wielenberg EJ, 'On the Evolutionary Debunking of Morality' (2010) 120 Ethics 441

Wiggins D, *Needs, Values, Truth: Essays in the Philosophy of Value* (Blackwell 1987)

Williams B, *Morality: An Introduction to Ethics* (Harper & Row 1972)

Williams B, 'A Critique of Utilitarianism' in Smart JJC and Williams B (eds), *Utilitarianism For and Against* (Cambridge University Press 1973)

Williams B, *Moral Luck: Philosophical Papers, 1973–1980* (Cambridge University Press 1981)

Williams B, *Making Sense of Humanity* (Cambridge University Press 1995)

Williams B, 'Toleration: An Impossible Virtue?' in Heyd D (ed), *Toleration: An Elusive Virtue* (Princeton University Press 1996)

Williams B, 'Philosophy as a Humanistic Discipline' (2000) 75 Philosophy 477

Williams B, *Ethics and the Limits of Philosophy* (2nd edn, Routledge 2006)

Wolf S, 'Moral Saints' (1982) 79 Journal of Philosophy 419

Wong D, 'Relativism' in Singer P (ed), *A Companion to Ethics* (Blackwell 1991)

Wong D, *Natural Moralities: A Defense of Pluralistic Relativism* (Oxford University Press 2006)

Index